Cognitive Variations

Cognitive Variations

Reflections on the Unity and Diversity of the Human Mind

G. E. R. LLOYD

CLARENDON PRESS · OXFORD

OXFORD

UNIVERSITY PRESS

Great Clarendon Street, Oxford OX2 6DP

Oxford University Press is a department of the University of Oxford.
It furthers the University's objective of excellence in research, scholarship,
and education by publishing worldwide in

Oxford New York

Auckland Cape Town Dar es Salaam Hong Kong Karachi
Kuala Lumpur Madrid Melbourne Mexico City Nairobi
New Delhi Shanghai Taipei Toronto

With offices in

Argentina Austria Brazil Chile Czech Republic France Greece
Guatemala Hungary Italy Japan Poland Portugal Singapore
South Korea Switzerland Thailand Turkey Ukraine Vietnam

Oxford is a registered trade mark of Oxford University Press
in the UK and in certain other countries

Published in the United States
by Oxford University Press Inc., New York

© G. E. R. Lloyd 2007

British Library Cataloguing in Publication Data
Data available

Library of Congress Cataloging in Publication Data
Data available

Typeset by Laserwords Private Limited, Chennai, India
Printed in Great Britain
on acid-free paper by
Biddles Ltd, King's Lynn, Norfolk

978-0-19-921461-7

1 3 5 7 9 10 8 6 4 2

CONTENTS

PREFACE

THIS book derives from the interests that I have had, over many years, in comparing the cognitive capacities displayed and the modes of reasoning used by the members of different societies, ancient and modern. What are the commonalities that link us all as human beings? What is the extent, and what are the limits, to human variability in this domain? Claims for cross-cultural universals have been made, in recent years especially, in such areas as colour perception, animal classification, and the emotions. How robust is the evidence for these? At what points and in what respects do we have to acknowledge that cognition varies as between individuals or collectivities, in response to cultural, linguistic, or even physical factors?

If my starting point on these issues has been how to compare and contrast ancient Greek and Chinese thought, I have found myself drawn into wider and wider aspects of the questions, into the lively discussions in which social anthropologists, psychologists, biologists, and philosophers, as well as historians have participated. They have not always engaged in debate across disciplines. It is my belief, however, that a cross-disciplinary approach is required, one that brings to bear evidence and arguments from many different fields of research, difficult as that is to achieve. This has guided my own methodology here. The end product is a study that owes a very great deal to the conversations I have had with scholars working in many different areas and to the audiences at seminars in which I have presented some of these ideas, at Cambridge and in Paris especially. I must mention here my specific debts of gratitude to Mike Bravo, Rachel Cooper, Elisabeth Hsu, Stephen Hugh Jones, Nick Humphrey, Evelyn Fox Keller, David Konstan, Steve Levinson, Eduardo Viveiros de Castro, and Giselle Walker, while emphasizing the customary disclaimer that they bear no responsibility for the ways in which I have used the advice they have given me. My warm thanks also go to three anonymous readers for their comments on an earlier draft and to

Peter Momtchiloff and his colleagues at Oxford University Press for the exemplary manner in which they have overseen the production of this book.

G.E.R.L.

Introduction

THE concept of the 'psychic' unity of humans, in the sense not of 'spiritual', let alone of 'spiritualistic' unity, but rather of the uniformity of cognitive capacities, has been used by different individuals and groups in many different ways. Already in the ancient world, both Greeks and Chinese had a particular term, *anthropos*, *ren*, that picked out human beings as such. Even though members of both those societies saw plenty of differences that separated 'barbarians' from themselves, and even differences between males and females, they recognized that there are some features in virtue of which human beings are human beings. Both Aristotle and Xunzi located the distinctive humanity of humans not in any physical characteristics, but, in Aristotle's case, in the rational faculty of the human soul, and in Xunzi's in the human capacity for morality.

Once early modern Europe began to be more familiar with those whom they so readily categorized as 'exotic' peoples—after the discovery of America especially—questions to do with the essential characteristics of humans were often framed in terms of where different peoples fitted in to the creation story. The notion of lost tribes of Israel was put to work to supply some sort of answer. Of course the need to save people's immortal souls figured prominently in justifications for the appropriation of their lands and the destruction of their cultures. For Rousseau, however, the chief argument was not theological. In his influential view, all humans share certain emotional characteristics. His 'noble savage' is a creature of spontaneous feeling, and in that respect is held to contrast favourably with Rousseau's own fellow-countrymen, who had to suffer the constraints of living in a regulated 'civilized' society.

Yet the predominant view during the nineteenth and early twentieth centuries was, to be sure, that 'civilized' human beings represent the pinnacle of human progress, while primitive peoples, so-called, were just that—primitive. In the early days of the founding of ethnography as an academic discipline, both Tylor (1871) and Frazer (1890) signed up to a notion of the psychic unity of mankind,[1] though to one that allowed, and even insisted upon, major differences in the abilities of different groups of humans to make the most of the capabilities that they all, nevertheless, potentially shared.

However, a similar belief in the superiority of civilized over primitive peoples led Lévy-Bruhl to a very different conclusion, namely that each was characterized by a distinctive mentality, mystical and pre-logical in the case of primitives, logical and scientific in his case. Towards the end of his life he came to admit that *both* mentalities are exemplified, to different degrees, in all humans, and that may be said to have allowed for a certain uniformity across the human race. Yet he never backtracked on his postulate of distinct 'mentalities', and that continued adherence pointed rather towards cognitive diversity than to cognitive unity.

Both the assertion and the denial of the global thesis continue to play important roles in many fields of enquiry, although ideological considerations, especially accusations or rebuttals of racism, have often drawn attention away from precisely what those who propound either thesis are committed to. Those who have chosen to emphasize what all humans share biologically, psychologically, and socially have insisted that we all think and feel and perceive in the same way. To quote one typical statement (Spiro 1984: 327) 'the processes that characterize the working of the human mind are the same everywhere', though the same writer in the same article and even on the same page used a much weaker formulation, namely that 'the human mind works (*or has the capacity to work*: italics added) the same everywhere.'

Sometimes the psychic unity of humans is an axiomatic assumption guiding research but not itself subject to question or challenge. For other investigators it is a conclusion claimed to be supported by their research, whatever field that is in, whether developmental psychology, linguistics, anthropology, evolutionary biology, or cognitive science. Everyone recognizes the diversity of human cultures, to be

---

[1] So too did Franz Boas (1911/1938), though without the emphasis on the evolutionary models that were such an important preoccupation for both Tylor and Frazer.

sure, but the 'psychic unity of mankind' insists on the transcultural characteristics of a generic human mind (Spiro 1984: 334) as such.

Against the universalists, there are those for whom the diversity of humankind goes all the way down. There are fundamental differences not just in the belief systems, but also in the very way the mind works, that—for them—expose the fallacy of the view that we are all basically the same. Here too this is sometimes an unquestioned axiom, sometimes a hypothesis to be tested, sometimes a conclusion held to follow from empirical investigations. A recent book (Nisbett 2003) had as its subtitle, 'How Asians and Westerners Think Differently . . . and Why'. Another important study by the anthropologist Descola (2005) identifies four quite different ontologies to be found in different societies across the world.

The issues are often stated globally and the repercussions of the two contrasting positions are considerable. When we encounter apparently radically different world-views or values, the reactions of the two schools of thought are very different. The unitarians will argue that these differences can be adjudicated. The relativists will insist that there is no neutral vantage point from which that can be done. Faced with reports of apparently irrational beliefs or practices, the unitarians will of course first agree that the data for such have to be assessed with great care. But they will allow that in the final analysis—after the assessment has been done—the verdict that they are irrational may have to stand. The relativists will equally wish to be careful that there has been no misrepresentation in the reports, but faced with a possible diagnosis of irrationality, will revert to the point that frames of reference, and so what counts as 'rationality', differ fundamentally. It is not just the case that the beliefs and practices in question have to be looked at from the actors' own viewpoint, not from ours, the observers'. Some will further argue that the canons of rationality that are appropriate vary with the culture, like many other features that may be society-specific. The relativist will compare the way in which no one natural language can be judged more adequate to communication than any other. Where the universalist will proceed to an analysis of the deep structures of language in order to secure comparability, some relativists will counter that the trouble with deep structures is that they do not help in assessing the pragmatics of the communicative process. At that level diversity prevails, and that is the level that counts if we are to compare viewpoints.

An immense amount of work has been done, in recent years, on a wide range of problems, all of which have a potential bearing on this set of controversies. There have been studies of the way the human brain works, its neurophysiological and biochemical processes, its limited or possibly massive modularity, of the similarities and differences between humans and other primates, of the stages in the development of children's cognitive processes, of the problems of mutual understanding across cultures, of the great diversity of views that humans have adopted in many domains from ethics to psychology to cosmology, and much else besides. Yet in several cases the results of detailed work have not impinged much beyond the restricted circles of fellow specialists and the possible implications for the wider issues I have outlined have only rarely been directly addressed. It is my ambition, in this book, to engage in a cross-disciplinary analysis of those problems.

My own interest in these questions stems, in the first instance, from my investigations of two ancient societies, Greece and China, both of which share a number of features that invite reflection. Both proposed views—indeed a variety of them—on such questions as the emotions, the self, and causation. That immediately poses the question of the circumstances in which such pluralism is possible. Both offer opportunities to study the changes that occurred in key concepts and beliefs over time and that too raises analogous issues: how did that happen and why? Although we cannot conduct empirical investigations, of course, on ancient subjects, both societies provide precious prima-facie evidence for the plasticity and the adaptability of the human mind, though that still leaves the twin problems (1) of the extent of that adaptability, and (2) of how individuals or groups can come to challenge the deep-seated assumptions of the society in which they have been brought up.

It goes without saying that human cognitive equipment has been well adapted enough to ensure our survival as a species. But within what limits does it exhibit variation? Do the apparent differences we discern in belief systems, for example, merely reflect differences in the contents of thought? Or do they correspond to differences in the ways in which we think? And if the latter, what precisely do we mean by a 'way' in which we think? Are such ways constrained by who we are, by our social persona, by our upbringing, by our values, by the societies we belong to, or the language we speak—or by some combination of those factors? Again are such constraints determining factors or merely influential ones, from which it is possible to break free?

I mentioned that the problems of psychic unity versus psychic diversity have often been discussed in global terms as if the two points of view expressed represent mutually exclusive and exhaustive alternatives. My tactics throughout this book will be to resist global theses and perspectives. I shall tackle specific issues in order to evaluate the various contributions of the factors in play in each. I shall argue that the weight to be given to different factors varies across these issues and accordingly that what we conclude on the controversy between unity and diversity, or between the universalists and the cultural relativists more generally, should vary too. The truth does not all lie with one party or with the other. But to be able to go beyond that bland observation, we need to be able to specify how far the commonalities extend, and which they are, and again precisely where diversity kicks in. What we may hope to gain from a survey of the problems is not the endorsement of one position against the other, but rather a clarification of what exactly is at stake in each of the complex issues in question. The claims to overall victory in the debate that have so often been made all look distinctly flawed.

The three main types of factors that have to be weighed against each other comprise first biological, neurophysiological, and biochemical processes that there is no reason to think are not common to all humans, even though they may exhibit some variation as between different individuals and populations. Some indeed do in important and relevant ways, as I shall illustrate. What is common, and what subject to variability across human populations, in this domain can certainly not be settled by a priori assumptions, but can be elucidated by painstaking empirical investigations, not that the results of such researches all tend to lead to the same general conclusion. As we shall see, the relevance of neurophysiology and biochemistry to the study of the emotions takes a different form from that in play in spatial cognition, and different again from those we need to take into account in colour perception.

Second, there are cultural, social, political, and ideological factors that influence belief systems and that are particularly relevant where evaluative judgements are at stake. How far do the different natural languages spoken across the globe govern or at least influence what can be, or is, expressed in them? The theses of Sapir and Whorf and their followers, and the objections of their critics, will be a recurrent theme. Cultural factors, including linguistic ones, are not immune to change and so a further problem, relevant in some cases, is the extent to which, or the circumstances in which, existing or traditional assumptions may be subject to revision or modification—an issue of special interest where ancient societies are concerned. History provides crucial evidence for the possibility of differences and variation, on fundamental issues, within a single culture.

Third, there are considerations from the side of what belief systems are beliefs about. I do not, of course, suppose that we can have immediate access to the raw physical data that are the target. For all accounts of such will be mediated by more or less theory-laden language. But where we are dealing with representations of physical phenomena (colour, for instance, or animal kinds) there will be input of some kind from the side of what is represented, though I shall be concerned to point out where its diversity is relevant to our adjudicating between diverging views. I shall call this the multidimensionality of the phenomena[2] and link that to different possible modes or styles of enquiry.[3] Those representations will never be the product solely

---

[2] The notion of the multidimensionality of the phenomena allows for different accounts to be given of different aspects or dimensions of a single domain of investiganda. Thus in the case of colour, such accounts may focus either on hues or on intensity or on saturation, or of course on some combination of these (cf. Ch. 1). In the case of spatial cognition, the frame of reference may be intrinsic, absolute, or relative (cf. Ch. 2). This notion should thus be contrasted with the far stronger claims that have sometimes been made for multiple *global* world-views by those who, in the wake of Goodman (1978) especially, have sought thereby to reconcile scientific, religious, aesthetic, and everyday perspectives, for example, whether or not such world-views are thought to be compatible with the assumption that there is a single world that underlies them all, and whether or not those world-views are held to be intertranslatable and so in that sense commensurable. Compare Tambiah's discussion of what he calls 'multiple orderings of reality' (again a matter of global world-views) (Tambiah 1990: ch. 5). My own use should also be distinguished from that of a writer such as Siegel (2005), who in a recent study of European ideas of the self since the seventeenth century speaks of material, relational, and reflective dimensions. This is described by Siegel himself as a heuristic device, whereas the cases of multidimensionality I shall be concerned with reflect objective features of the investiganda that may be the focus of attention of different modes of enquiry.

[3] I here borrow and adapt an expression from Crombie (1994) and Hacking (1992b). They were concerned primarily with scientific styles of reasoning. Hacking in particular defined styles first in terms of their bringing new objects into existence, and secondly by their self-authenticating character. They create the criteria of truth and falsehood that are appropriate to an investigation. My own use of styles is both looser and more general. I use it to draw attention to the different possible foci of attention of enquiries within a single domain and to the corresponding differences in the manner in which the enquiry will be conducted. My use has in common with Hacking's that different styles incorporate

of the free play of the imagination, however much imagination may indeed be at work.

The topics I have selected for analysis include several on which entrenched positions have already been staked out, where my aim will be to show what qualifications have to be entered when a more thorough cross-disciplinary analysis is undertaken. The limits and constraints on psychic unity, and the range of psychic diversity, differ in different cases, as I hope to show.

I shall discuss colour perception, spatial cognition, animal and plant taxonomy, the emotions, health and well-being, the self, agency, and causation. I shall then move on to the more general questions of how far our distinction between nature and culture is applicable cross-culturally, and whether or to what extent we should suppose that different cultural groups operate with radically different ontologies. To the extent that they do, the issues we must confront include (1) how they can be said to be mutually intelligible and (2) how any change is possible. Cultures have sometimes been imagined to be the prisoners of their ideologies, or of their natural languages: how far are they the prisoners of deep-seated ontological assumptions? My penultimate study will tackle reason itself. What sense, if any, does it make to say that different human beings reason differently? Should that be put down to skills in logic, or to the availability or application of formal logical analyses, for instance, or of informal rules of procedure? How far do such differences merely reflect the different attitudes and values of the reasoners? It is evidently crucial to disambiguate 'how people think' and to distinguish differences that stem from the contents of thought from those that relate to the form the reasoning takes. My concluding discussion will undertake not so much to resolve the questions in the terms in which they have generally been posed, as to clarify the issues and suggest the basis on which further discussion may make progress.

different criteria by which an investigation is to be judged. Those criteria may indeed sometimes be incommensurable with one another, but that does not imply any mutual unintelligibility between the enquiries, which will rather be complementary to one another in so far as they relate to different aspects of the phenomena in question.

1

Colour Perception

EVER since Berlin and Kay (1969), colour perception has been cited as one of the prime examples where, despite great surface diversity, robust cross-cultural universals can be found. Berlin and Kay organized extensive investigations of the colour terminologies that are expressed in different natural languages in different cultures across the world. Sometimes this involved new research by investigators dispatched into the field for the purpose, equipped with standard questionnaires that would enable the data collected to be analysed and compared; sometimes Berlin and Kay drew on already existing ethnographic reports.

Their findings were sensational. Even though colour terminologies appear to differ so widely, they exhibit—so the claim was—certain patterns and even obey certain general laws. Thus languages that have only three basic colour terms always have black, white, and red. Those with four add yellow or green. Those with five have both yellow and green. Other colours are added in a regular sequence up to a total of eleven basic terms. 'Basic' terms were distinguished from others principally by means of four criteria (Berlin and Kay 1969: 6). (1) They must be 'monolexemic', that is their meaning should not be predictable from the meaning of their parts (that would rule out 'blue-green' for instance); (2) they should not be defined in terms of another colour (that would rule out 'crimson', which is a 'kind of red'); (3) their application must not be restricted to a narrow class of objects (thus 'chestnut' used of horses would be ruled out); and (4) they must be psychologically salient for informants. It is conceded that languages differ appreciably in their non-basic terms. But the basic ones are the same everywhere and there are, so it was claimed, at most just eleven of these.

This work had profound repercussions. It seemed to be a triumphant vindication of the psychic unity of humans. Differences in perception, and in the linguistic expression of what is perceived, were merely superficial phenomena. Just as Chomsky had shown to many people's satisfaction that a universal deep structure underlies all natural languages, so Berlin and Kay were held to have demonstrated cross-cultural universals in the seemingly unlikely case of colour perception. Their work stimulated similar investigations in a number of other fields. Berlin himself collaborated with two other scholars, Breedlove and Raven, to study folk-biological classification and nomenclature and—as I shall be reviewing in Chapter 3—came up with very similar results. Although there may seem to be a bewildering variety in the kinds of animals and plants picked out in different natural languages, a regular sequence can be found in the acquisition of the fundamental categories, just as Berlin and Kay had discovered in colour termin-ology. Atran and his associates went further and claimed that the same broad similarities and differences within the animal kingdom are recognized the world over, in a universal implicit 'common-sense' classification. Similar studies of the emotions have been undertaken in order to pinpoint, in that case too, the underlying universals (cf. Ch. 4). The results that Berlin and Kay presented on colour have been thought to be so robust that their schema can be used to suggest the best English translation of some colour term in another language. When dealing with the fourth and the fifth basic term in a language, it can be assumed that one will be 'yellow', the other 'green'. Thus Shweder (1984: 34) wrote that 'translation of color terms between languages is greatly facilitated by the discovery' (namely of the Berlin and Kay sequence).

However, doubts and criticisms were also expressed, not least by proponents of the extreme opposite culturally relativist view, devel-oping from the linguistic determinism of Sapir and Whorf. Yet the problems, I shall suggest, are more complex than either side has gen-erally appreciated.[1] My aim in this chapter is to explain why I think this is so, even though this will mean going over some familiar points in the arguments on either side. In my view, however, to arrive at a considered verdict on this question, we have no less than five different

---

[1] Those working on the World Color Survey have tended to adopt a modified Berlin and Kay approach. That applies to most of the contributors to the recent collective volume Hardin and Maffi 1997, and especially to Maffi herself. Yet there are important exceptions, notably Lucy (1992: ch. 5; 1997) who has criticized the fundamental notion of a basic colour term as unduly influenced by the English language.

kinds of factor to take into consideration, not just (1) the diversity of natural languages, (2) the richness of the ethnographic reports, and (3) the complexity of the historical data, but also (4) the physiology of vision (where recent studies by Mollon and his colleagues have suggested important new findings), as well, of course, as (5) the physics of light.[2]

Three basic philosophical points (though they are no more than common sense) will form my starting-point, after which some methodological remarks about the studies by Berlin and Kay, and some reflections on what Sapir and Whorf had to say about the influence of language on thought, will take us to the heart of the problem. Mollon's work can be used to clarify what physiology and evolutionary biology can now tell us about the differences between different humans' capacities for colour discrimination, before I turn in conclusion to take stock of the implications of my discussion for the issue of the psychic unity or diversity of humans.

First, it is obvious that our ability to discriminate colours goes far beyond the linguistic resources at our command, the terms that are given by any particular natural language, or even by all of them collectively. We do not need separate names in order to be able to tell one hue from another, although we will need a vocabulary to be able to say any more than (just) that they differ.

Second, all three of the modes of differentiation of colour perception, namely hue, intensity of luminosity, and degree of saturation, form continua. The situation is thus very different from that which obtains in areas of cognition where what is there to be cognized consists of discrete entities—substances as Aristotle would say—as is the case in the animal kingdom, for example, where the familiar animals of ordinary experience (at least) are such entities and are perceived by us as discrete. True, many aspects of human colour categorization remain controversial (Hardin and Maffi 1997). Thus there are studies that suggest that some hues at a certain distance (as measured on the objective, continuous scale, that is by wavelengths) may be perceived

---

[2] Lucy (1992: 127) has observed that while social anthropologists are alert to cultural differences, psychologists often avoid intercultural comparisons and assume too readily that the subjects they use in their experiments allow inferences to human perception as a whole. As a historian, I would add that questions to do with the early history of theories of colour and with their influences on colour vocabulary, including in the shifts in the denotations of terms for hues, have also tended to be neglected.

as more different from one another than other hues of the same distance, and I shall be returning later to the further complicating factor of the differences between individuals' colour discriminations. But what is there to be perceived, both in the case of variations in luminosity and in that of the spectrum of hues, are indeed continua.

Third, while the phenomena to be described do not present distinct boundaries, language inevitably imposes them, especially where the spectrum of hues is concerned. We have, conventionally, seven names for the colours of the rainbow, following Newton, though Aristotle saw the rainbow as made up of three colours, with a fourth as a mere 'appearance' in between two of them (*Meteorologica* 371^{b}33, 375^{a}1, 5 ff.).[3] But however many we name, those names do not correspond to well-marked species.[4] Blue does not have a clear boundary with indigo, nor indigo with violet.

I have mentioned hues and luminosities, that is, variations in the brightness or the intensity of light. But the differences between these two are important. Much of the research done by Berlin and Kay focused on hues. Indigenous peoples were tested using colour charts or Munsell chips under controlled conditions of lighting. Munsell chips consist of rectangular arrays, where luminosities are graded on the vertical axis, hues on the horizontal one. Subjects were invited to point to the box that best matched each of their colour terms and to the region of boxes to which the term could be applied. Differences in luminosity were thus catered for, though they were given less weight when the survey results were evaluated. As I have already noted, the claimed outcome of the investigation was a clear ordering of basic colour terms where those correspond mainly to hues, rather than to distinctions in luminosity or to degrees of saturation.[5]

Standard colour charts and Munsell chips were, of course, used in the research to order to ensure comparability and to discount local differences in the colours encountered in the natural environment. But

[3] He says that the fourth colour (*xanthon*, roughly 'yellow') sometimes appears between those that correspond to 'red' and 'green', but explains this as a mere appearance, due to the juxtaposition between those two.

[4] Mollon 1995: 144, notes that for most people, four hues appear phenomenally pure or unmixed, namely red, yellow, green, and blue, though he adds (ibid. 146) that why this is so is 'perhaps the chief unsolved mystery of colour science'.

[5] Apart from the achromatic black, white, and grey, six of the basic terms are chromatic (red, yellow, green, blue, purple, orange). Brown and pink are the two exceptions, for in their case luminosity, and degree of saturation, respectively, enter into their definitions (Lyons 1995: 204).

their use carried major risks, chiefly that of circularity. The protocols of the enquiry presupposed the differences that were supposed to be under investigation and to that extent and in that regard the investigators just got out what they had put in. That is to say, the researchers presented their interviewees with materials that already incorporated the differentiations the researchers themselves were interested in. Asked to identify, name, or group different items, the respondents' replies were inevitably matched against those differentiations. Of course the terms in which the replies were made—in the natural languages the respondents used—must have borne *some* relation to the differences perceived, otherwise they would not have been used in replying to the questions (assuming, as we surely may, that the questions were taken seriously and that the respondents were doing their honest best). But it was assumed that what the respondents were using in their replies were essentially *colour* terminologies, distinguishing hues, and that assumption was unfounded in general, and in certain cases can be shown to be incorrect.

It was unfounded in general because there are plenty of natural languages in which the basic discrimination relates not to hues, but to luminosities. Ancient Greek is one possible example. Greek colour classifications are rich and varied and were, as we shall see, a matter of dispute among the Greeks themselves. They were certainly capable of drawing distinctions between hues. I have already given one example. When Aristotle analyses the rainbow, where it is clearly hue that separates one end of the spectrum from the other, he identifies three colours using terms that correspond, roughly, to 'red' 'green', and 'blue', with a fourth, corresponding to 'yellow', which he treats (as noted) as a mere 'appearance' between 'red' and 'green'. But the primary contrariety that figures in ancient Greek (including in Aristotle) is between *leukon* and *melan*, which usually relate not to hues, so much as to luminosity. *Leukos*, for instance, is used of the sun and of water, where it is clearly not the case that they share, or were thought to share, the same hue. So the more correct translation of that pair is often 'bright' or 'light' and 'dark', rather than 'white' and 'black'.[6]

---

[6] Berlin and Kay (1969: 70) recognized the range of application of *leukon*, yet still glossed the term as 'white'. Even more strangely they interpreted *glaukon* as 'black'. That term is particularly context-dependent, but when Aristotle (*On the Generation of Animals* 779^{a}26, ^{b}34 ff.) tells us that the eyes of babies are *glaukon*, that corresponds to 'blue'

So one possible source of error in the Berlin and Kay methodology was the privileging of hue over luminosity. But that still does not get to the bottom of the problem, which is that in certain cases the respondents were answering in terms whose primary connotations were not colours at all. The Hanunoo had been studied before Berlin and Kay in a pioneering article by Conklin (1955), and Lyons (1995; 1999) has recently reopened the discussion of this material.[7] First Conklin observed that the Hanunoo have no word for colour as such. But (as noted) that does not mean, of course, that they are incapable of discriminating between different hues or luminosities. To do so they use four terms, *mabiru, malagti, marara*, and *malatuy*, which may be thought to correspond, roughly, to 'black', 'white', 'red', and 'green'. Hanunoo was then classified as a stage 3 language, in Berlin and Kay's taxonomy, one that discriminates between four basic colour terms, indeed those very four.

Yet, according to Conklin, chromatic variation was not the *primary* basis for differentiation of those four terms at all. Rather the two principal dimensions of variation are (1) lightness versus darkness, and (2) wetness versus dryness, or freshness (succulence) versus desiccation. A third differentiating factor is indelibility versus fadedness, referring to permanence or impermanence, rather than to hue as such.

Berlin and Kay only got to their cross-cultural universals by ignoring (they may even sometimes have been unaware of) the primary connotations of the vocabulary in which the respondents expressed their answers to the questions put to them. That is not to say, of course, that the members of the societies concerned are incapable of distinguishing colours whether as hues or as luminosities. That would be to make the mistake that my first philosophical observation was designed to forestall. You do not need colour terms to register colour differences. Indeed Berlin and Kay never encountered—certainly they never reported—a society where the respondents simply had *nothing* to say when questioned about how their terms related to what they saw on the Munsell chips. But the methodology was flawed in so far as it was assumed that the replies given always gave access to a

where *melan*, the usual term for 'black' or rather 'dark', is represented as its antonym, rather than as its synonym, as Berlin and Kay would need it to be.

7 Cf. also Lucy 1992: ch. 5, who similarly criticizes taking purportedly colour terms out of context.

classification of colour, when sometimes *colours* were not the primary connotations of the vocabulary used at all.[8]

What then, we may next ask, is to be said for a view that goes, in a way, to the opposite extreme to that of Berlin and Kay, a view that denies cross-cultural universals and relativizes colour perception to the perceivers themselves? There would be two ways of taking such a line of argument. In one the perceivers are individuals in all their individuality: I shall have a little to say about the privateness of colour vision later. But in the other, colour perceptions are relativized to groups, that is to those sharing the same natural language. In stark opposition to the universalism of Berlin and Kay, Sapir and Whorf suggested that in this field, as in general, cognition is influenced—or in a stronger version of their theory actually determined—by language. Colour perceptions, on this account, will be as diverse as the languages in which they are expressed.

There is plenty of evidence to suggest that discriminations that are marked linguistically, that is either lexically or grammatically, in a particular natural language may contribute to making the differences in question more salient to the speakers of that language. The availability of terms such as 'maroon' or 'magenta' in the colour lexicon helps the identification of a certain range of phenomena to which those terms can be applied. The associations that certain terms have in a particular language may well affect their use. In Spanish the antonym of *verde* ('green') is on occasion *seco* ('dry'), where *verde* is associated with the living, *seco* with the dead, not that there is any reason to suppose there is any systematic confusion between the different components of the semantic range of either term. Conversely, to answer to particular needs, for example to distinguish the particular markings of cattle, as is reported for the Nuer, a vocabulary may expand accordingly, although the supposed great richness of Inuit terms for snow seems to have been based on some overinterpretation of the data.[9]

---

[8] A further complication in the assessment of colour terminology may arise, as it does in the English language, from the ambiguity of the same word used referentially, and attributively or descriptively (cf. Lyons 1995: 206). 'That's brown', for instance, may be paraphrasable first as 'that colour is brown' (referential), or secondly as 'that object is brown' (attributive).

[9] See Dorais 1996: 145 for a careful analysis of the different shades of meaning of different individual terms and of clusters of cognates, used in Inuit to describe different types, or states, of snow.

But as Berlin and Kay erred in their generalizations in one direction, the strong version of the Sapir and Whorf thesis may do so in the other. Some of their prime examples to show the dependence of thought on language were indeed easily refuted. Whorf (1967: 57–8) claimed, for example, that the Hopi recognized no time distinctions, and that Hopi language contains no reference to 'time' either explicit or implicit. But Malotki (1983: 622 ff., cf. Wardy 2000: 14–15) showed conclusively—on the basis of evidence available to Whorf indeed—that the Hopi had no difficulty in making distinctions between past, present, and future.

But where, in the case of colour terminology, a weak Sapir–Whorf thesis, of the influence of language on colour identification, is, as I have just noted, unexceptionable, the strongest version of linguistic determinism faces insurmountable objections. We can go back to ancient Greek to show this. Most Greeks accepted that the primary contrariety, in the visible, is that between *leukon* and *melan*, which (I said) generally correspond to bright or light and dark rather than to white and black. But beyond that, there was very considerable diversity, both as to the numbers of primary colours and as to which they were. Thus some held that there are four basic ones, which were sometimes correlated with theories of the four elements or simple bodies, earth, water, air, and fire, as they were, for instance, by Empedocles and Plato. But others maintained that there are seven primary colours, which, in Aristotle's case, were correlated with seven primary flavours (*On the Senses* 442^{a}12 ff.).

However, the idea that there is an indefinite or infinite number of colours (though not of primary ones) was also expressed. The evidence for Democritus is intriguing though obscure. Some sources ascribe to him a theory of four basic colours. But he is also reported to have held that both colours and flavours are limitless. Colours are certainly not properties of the atoms. His explanation of their variety would be partly in terms of the different interactions or mixtures between percipient and percept, partly on the percept side in terms of different combinations of basic colours, and partly in terms of the variety of atomic shapes that primary or compound colours possess. Thus *leukon* and *melan* were correlated with smooth and rough. For Democritus himself the shapes of the atoms are infinitely varied, though when Plato came to adapt this theory in his account of the atomic structure of the four simple bodies he insisted that their shapes are limited to combinations of two primary types of triangle (namely the right-angled isosceles and the half equilateral). The underlying issue here is what elements of order or determinacy must be postulated in the sensibilia. Against those who were prepared to represent them as continua, as infinitely divisible indeed, Aristotle was one who insisted that they formed determinate species. In a further demonstration of his predilection for determinacy, he explains beautiful colours as constituted by mixtures in determinate proportions, influenced no doubt by the analogy of the simple concords, expressible in terms of ratios of 2 : 1, 3 : 2, and 4 : 3.[10]

Yet among those Greeks who postulated a limited number of basic colours there was no general agreement as to which they were. After *leukon* and *melan*, the four-colour theorists usually included *eruthron* ('red') although Aristotle did not recognize that in his seven-colour theory.[11] But as to the fourth basic colour, several candidates were in the field, *ochron* ('pale', Empedocles), *lampron* ('shining', Plato), and *chloron* (Democritus). That last term is often translated 'green', though the primary connotation of the term (reminiscent of Hanunoo terminology) was rather what is fresh or full of sap.

I need not go into further detail to make the fundamental point. Different individuals within the same culture, and using the same natural language, evidently, in this case, entertained quite different views on the classification of colours. Some of this variation may be put down to differences in the focus of attention or in the mode of investigation attempted. Some theorists, such as Empedocles (Fr. 23) were concerned with the mixing of pigments, while others, such as Aristotle, when discussing the rainbow, focused on the spectrum of light. But that does not provide the whole explanation of that variability. In particular it is striking that while both Xenophanes and Aristotle, for instance, discuss the rainbow, the colours they identify in it, with the

---

[10] Aristotle, *On the Senses* 439^{b}25 ff., 31 ff., 442^{a}12 ff.

[11] Aristotle has some difficulty, at *On the Senses* 442^{a}21 ff., in getting to his seven 'colours', remarking that to do so either *phaion* (grey) has to be treated as a kind of dark/black (*melan ti*), or *xanthon* (yellow) belongs to bright/white (*tou leukou*). He notes, also, that the appearances of coloured objects may be modified by juxtaposition, or by being viewed in artificial light (*Meteorology* 375^a 22 ff., 26 ff.), though he rejects both the theory that colours are formed by superposition and the idea that they are emanations (*On the Senses* 440^{a}6 ff., 15 ff.). But while he recognizes many difficulties, and engages in an analysis of competing views, he remains convinced that there is a determinate number of species of colour.

exception of 'red', *phoinikoun*, differ: Aristotle talks of *prasinon* and *halourgon*, where Xenophanes (Fr. 32) sees *chloron* and *porphuroun*.

These discrepancies were certainly an embarrassment for Berlin and Kay who had to elide all the variety to get to *the* ancient Greek view: but it also represents a difficulty for Sapir and Whorf, in that ancient Greek, the language, in no way constrained its speakers to a single uniform classification. True, these were philosophers arguing with one another, but not even Greek philosophers would, in this context, give analyses of colour phenomena that were totally counterintuitive to their fellow Greeks.

Neither of the general theses so far reviewed captures the full complexity of the issues. Indeed recent work in physiology by Mollon and his associates compounds the problems and introduces both explananda and modes of explanation that are certainly relevant to colour perception but that were generally ignored in both the social anthropological and the linguistic investigations I have so far concentrated on. The phenomenon popularly known as 'colour-blindness' has long been associated with the contrast between dichromatic and trichromatic vision. In dichromatic subjects there are two basic types of cones, sensitive to different parts of the spectrum: in trichromatic there are three.[12] Dichromatic vision is found in many non-primate mammals, in male New World monkeys, and in about 2 per cent of human males (Mollon 1995: fig. 2a). Trichromacy is normally found in Old World monkeys, in apes, and in most humans.

This contrast can be related to evolutionary factors. Mollon points out that trichromacy carried an evolutionary advantage, and not just for certain animals. Trichromacy, the claim is (ibid. 133–4), co-evolved with a class of tropical trees characterized by fruits that are too large to be taken by birds and that are yellow or orange in colour when ripe. 'The tree offers a signal that is salient only to agents with trichromatic vision. This hypothesis of co-evolution of the tree's signal and the monkey's vision can be traced back to nineteenth-century naturalists, but it takes on new plausibility in the light of recent ecological evidence that there are many species of tropical trees that are dispersed exclusively by monkeys . . . In short, monkeys are to coloured fruit what bees are to flowers.'

---

[12] Mollon 1995: 129 further distinguishes anomalous from normal trichromacy, the former associated with only limited discrimination in the red–green range.

But if dichromatic humans thus bear traces of the stages through which the evolution of the eye has passed, that is far from the end of the story. Two further important points have emerged from recent work and these show that variability in human colour perception is greater than has generally been appreciated. First some human females may, in fact, be tetrachromatic, introducing a hitherto unsuspected further element of variation in the structure of the human eye (Jordan and Mollon 1993). Moreover, more generally, we are now in a position to trace certain discrepancies in vision to their genetic origins. Work reported by Baylor (1995) analyses the structure of the protein molecules on which all our vision depends. By collating the genes and the photopigments of New World monkeys, it has been possible to identify the small number of amino acid residues that make the difference between long- and middle-wave pigments (Mollon 1995: 138). A single nucleotide in the DNA changes the protein that is coded for: that alters the spectral sensitivity of the resulting photopigment and that in turn alters neural signals in the visual pathway. Mollon, commenting on this work, speculated that many other differences in our cognitive and emotional worlds would, in time, be found to be traceable to analogous genetic variations, and I shall indeed be reviewing where advances in biological research of different types have had an impact on our understanding of the different subject areas I discuss in later chapters.

Thus what we call 'colour-blindness' is a matter of a relative deficiency in colour discrimination compared with some norm and is only just the most obvious example of such variability. Yet just what should be considered 'normal' has proved increasingly difficult to pin down, even though most of us are, as noted, trichromatic.[13] It is evidently the case that each person's colour perception is, in an important sense, private to that person. But the actual range of variety among those whose colour vision exhibits no obvious deficiency is far greater than we may be led to expect from the apparently generally adequate way in which we communicate our impressions to one another, in whatever natural language we use.

---

[13] Lindsey and Brown (2002), reviewing 203 languages across the world, have recently suggested that some differences in the colour vocabularies found may correlate with variable exposure to ultra-violet B sunlight, though they concede that the ability to make distinctions such as those between 'blue' and 'green' may remain with certain individuals or societies where that contrast is generally lost. This work is controversial, but it is clear that much further research is needed to confirm or qualify how important a factor this is.

There are, to be sure, aspects of the sensibilia, including of colours, that are in the public domain and as such not at the mercy of an individual's subjective responses. Different hues correspond to different wavelengths of light. Physics provides concrete evidence for the correlations between wavelengths and different points on the spectrum of colour. 'Red' can be defined—some prefer to define it—as what corresponds to a band between an upper and lower limit, that is between 650 and 700 nanometres, and there is no great difficulty in arriving at similar values for infrared and ultraviolet light, even though they remain invisible to us. But while objective data are certainly obtainable in the form of measurements of wavelengths, that information has always to be translated into *some* colour vocabulary—which takes us back to our fundamental problem.

What, then, I may now ask, does this admittedly rapid survey of the problem of colour perception suggest? To do justice to the whole range of issues I have identified requires more than an appeal to the global solutions proposed by either Berlin and Kay or Sapir and Whorf, though some elements of both theories can be retained. The phenomena are multidimensional—a point to which I shall be returning on several other occasions in this book—and an adequate account has to be appropriately complex.

Let me elaborate both the critical and the constructive points I have made in conclusion. First, so far as the two main general hypotheses of cross-cultural universals, and linguistic determinism, are concerned, the vocabularies that different natural languages use show more variation than was allowed for by Berlin and Kay when, focusing on hues, they extracted their claimed cross-cultural universals. Yet there are fewer degrees of freedom than extreme linguistic determinism, with its relativistic consequences, would imply. We have seen that there is nothing to dictate that a natural language will have a vocabulary of terms whose primary connotations are colours, and within those where that is the case, sometimes the focus is on luminosities rather than on hues. Our perceptions of differences and similarities in this domain, as in others, will be influenced—how could they fail to be?—by the discriminations encoded in the natural language we use, but they will not be limited to them. Several 'colour' terms appear to group together items that do not obviously have either hue or luminosity in common. One example noticed by Lyons (1995: 207) was the French term *blond,* used of certain types of hair, of beer, and of tobacco—where no English equivalent with a similar range exists. Yet no colour vocabulary, whether of hues or intensities, will consist purely of arbitrary groupings of similarities and differences. Indeed not even when the groups are peculiar to one particular language will they be *arbitrary.*

What is there to be discriminated, by individuals or by groups, using one natural language or comparing several, is not a single field constituting one well-defined set of explananda. There is no single correct way to divide the phenomena up, to classify and order them. But that does not mean that any division will do. The factors that have to be accounted for include physics, physiology, language in general, and the different characteristics of different natural languages as they reflect the interests of the cultures that use them. But when we weigh them up, we can see that neither global hypothesis—the one that maintains an unqualified relativism and the other that insists on cross-cultural universals—is satisfactory. The pressures to opt for one or other of them stem from their appearing as mutually exclusive and exhaustive alternatives. But that appearance is, as I hope to have shown, deceptive. Those pressures should be resisted by allowing for the complexity of the explananda in the ways I have indicated, and indeed for the variety in modes of explanation that different styles of enquiry bring into play.

At the same time we should not lose sight of obvious commonalities. All human eyes share the same basic anatomical structure. A further important feature that we may assume to be shared across the animal kingdom is that eyes are not just passive receptors of data, but active interpreters of the information they receive. The human eye is, as Richard Gregory put it, intelligent, though also, and even by the same token, liable to be deceived. One example of this is the phenomenon of colour constancy discussed by Mollon (1995: 148–9). This is the process that allows us—sometimes—to perceive the permanent surface colours of objects independently of the colour of the illumination. 'A piece of white paper stubbornly looks white, whether we examine it in the yellowish light of indoor tungsten or in the bluish cast of northern daylight.' So much for some of the common factors at work, to which we can add the physical components of the visual inputs, the wavelengths, and variations of intensity, of light.

Yet we also have to acknowledge that variations between different individuals are far greater than are allowed for by a simple distinction between (for example) those who are, and those who are not, 'colour-blind'. Those variations go far beyond what different natural languages make salient to their users in this domain, though there too variety is considerable. Though, as just noted, the input to the eye shares certain common features, the output, in terms of how we individually or as members of collectivities report our colour experience, or what in experimental conditions we can be found to be able to discriminate, exhibits great differences. Some of those correspond to cultural, that is mainly linguistic, factors, others to genetic or physiological ones. It is only by painstakingly building up a picture that takes into account the findings of several different disciplines, from social anthropology, from linguistics, from anatomy, physiology, and physics, that we can begin to do justice to the problems that this area of cognition poses.

2
Spatial Cognition

INTENSIVE studies have been carried out on spatial cognition in recent years by scholars working in a wide variety of fields: cognitive development, linguistics, social anthropology, psychology: not to mention animal behaviourists who have investigated similar questions in the animal kingdom, including the amazing navigational skills of bees, ants, rats, homing pigeons, arctic terns, and other species (see e.g. Schöne 1984; Waterman 1989; Gallistel 1990; Collett and Zeil 1998). Piaget and Inhelder (1948/1956) opened up one line of inquiry in a highly influential book on the child's conception of space. As was typical of Piaget's work, the claim was that a child's notion of space develops through a series of well-defined stages. At first the child grasps topological notions only, then progresses to notions of metric distance and angle, and finally to an understanding of projective geometrical concepts. Those early studies have been criticized on a number of scores. More recent work argues that Piaget underestimated babies' capabilities, though Levinson (2003: 334 n. 5) points out that Piaget himself was generally careful to distinguish their perceptual ability from their cognitive or representational faculties. But then a second methodological criticism, articulated by Levinson himself (ibid. 72), is that the work was done on subjects who were overwhelmingly Western and the results may well have been biased by features of the European languages that they were acquiring.

The question of the robustness of any claim with regard to the uniformity of spatial cognition in all humans is at the centre of Levinson's recent study (2003), a summary of his group's work over the last ten years or so. This stands out for its cross-cultural methodology. The investigations were based on experiments conducted on subjects in many different societies across the world and on assessment of the spatial terminology in more than fifty different languages. From that point of view, this research resembled that of Berlin and Kay on colour terms—yet with almost diametrically opposite results, since what emerged was not uniformity, but diversity. The upshot of these inquiries was to show first that there are three distinct frames of reference (or more strictly families of them) used to locate objects in space, which Levinson dubbed the intrinsic, the relative, and the absolute (see Fig. 2.1)[1] second, that while these can be combined, one is normally dominant in any one natural language, and third, and most importantly from our point of view, that the acquisition of one or other frame of reference is strongly influenced by culture in general and by language in particular.

Thus the intrinsic system involves an object-centred coordinate system, where the coordinates are determined by the 'inherent features', sidedness or facets of the object to be used as the ground or relatum. In English the inherent features correspond largely to functional aspects of the object: the *front* of the TV is the side we attend to and another object can be located 'in front of the TV' in relation to that side. But the inherent features used are not always functional in that sense, for in some languages they are more clearly directly based on shape, where human or animal body-parts provide prototypes, as when we talk of the feet of a table.

The second, relative, frame of reference presupposes a viewpoint (given by the location of a perceiver) and a figure and ground distinct from that. When we say that the boy (the figure) is to the left of the house, that is from a particular viewpoint and in relation to a particular ground (the house).

Then, third, there is the absolute frame of reference, as when we say that a person is north of the house.

Levinson and his collaborators have supported their claims for the fundamental cognitive differences between these three frames of reference by experiments that did not depend on any particular spatial terminology. These show that the differences are indeed cognitive, and not just linguistic. In one set of tests subjects were presented with an array of objects, then rotated round 180°, and then asked to arrange an identical set of objects in the same way. Those using

---

[1] Levinson (2003: 8, 26 ff.) observed that his own use of 'absolute' in connection with a frame of reference, dependent, for example, on cardinal directions, relates to, but is not identical with, the notion of absolute space.

G = Ground
F = Figure
X = Origin of coordinate system
V = Viewpoint of observer

INTRINSIC

'He's in front of the house.'

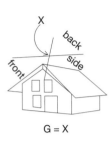

G = X

RELATIVE

'He's to the left of the house.'

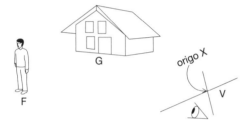

ABSOLUTE

'He's north of the house.'

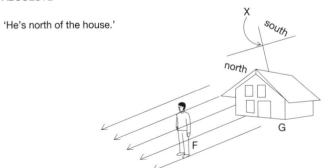

Figure 2.1. Spatial frames of reference. *Source*: S. C. Levinson, *Space in Language and Cognition* (Cambridge: Cambridge University Press, 2003), 40, fig. 2.2.

the absolute frame of reference maintained the north/south cardinal directions of the objects. When they arranged their sets, the objects that had been on their right in the first array were on their left in the second. Right/left distinctions were thus ignored in preference for cardinal north/south ones. On the other hand, those using the relative frame kept the objects that had been on their right in the same relative position to themselves.[2]

Among the surprising and important findings is that some languages do not employ a relative frame of reference at all (Levinson 2003: 46) and thus have no way of expressing notions such as 'to the left of the house' as determined by the location of a viewer or a speaker. 'The boy is to the left of the house' is simply untranslatable into such languages although 'functional equivalents with different logical and spatial properties can be found' (ibid. 15).[3] This and other results will, as Levinson notes, come as a bit of a shock to psychologists who have asserted such propositions as: (1) there will always be terms for left and right in all languages; (2) human spatial thinking is always relative in character, not absolute; (3) it is purely egocentric in character; and (4) it is basically anthropomorphic in the specific sense that our spatial coordinates are derived from planes through our body (cf. Clark 1973: 28; Miller and Johnson-Laird 1976: 394–5; Lyons 1977: ii. 690–1).

---

[2] These results have been challenged by Li and Gleitman (2002) in particular. They claim that the differences Levinson reported as between Dutch speakers adopting a relative frame of reference, and Tenejapans with an absolute one, are an artefact of the experimental situation, and that when they administered similar tests to American subjects out of doors, that induced replies that suggest an absolute frame of reference, the result of the subjects responding to landmark cues. In his reply, Levinson 2003 (cf. Levinson *et al.* 2002) first points out not only that Li and Gleitman made certain erroneous assumptions about his original investigations (for example some speakers using an absolute frame of reference were, in fact, tested indoors by Levinson and his team, when on the hypothesis proposed by Li and Gleitman that should have induced them to adopt a relative frame) but also that they simplified the 180° rotation test by reducing the number of items to be rearranged. More importantly he reports that his team has been unable to replicate some of the findings claimed by Li and Gleitman on Dutch subjects tested out of doors, who persisted in adopting a relative frame of reference even in the presence of prominent landscape cues, and he points out that such cues by themselves do not necessarily imply an absolute or intrinsic frame as opposed to a relative one. Further tests, where the rotation of the tables was 90° rather than 180°, have tended to confirm the differences originally postulated between those with predominantly absolute, intrinsic, and relative frameworks. At this point in the controversy, it would appear that Levinson has had the better of the arguments.

[3] That important observation means that what is at stake in these issues is not just the presence or absence of terms for right and left, but how certain relationships are construed: cf. Lucy (1992).

The absolute frame of reference, by cardinal points for instance, which has so often been left out of account, can be found in many different parts of the world, ranging from Mesoamerica, to New Guinea, to Australia, to Nepal, and is not restricted to societies who live in any one particular geophysical environment: some of those in question inhabit wide open deserts, others closed jungle terrain (Levinson 2003: 48). It is particularly striking that those who use it often exhibit remarkable navigational skills. In one set of experiments members of three different 'absolute' communities (one in Australia, one in South Africa, one in Mesoamerica) were taken up to 100 kilometres away from 'base camp' by truck or on foot or by a combination of both means of locomotion, generally to a spot they had never been to before.[4] They were then asked to point to 'home' and to other invisible locations from where they were, and were able to do so with extraordinary accuracy (ibid. 228 ff.)—certainly far more accurately than Dutch and English subjects on whom similar tests were conducted.

Quite how they achieve this remains rather a mystery, and Levinson himself admits to bafflement, complaining (ibid. 217) that 'in many ways we know much less about navigation in our own species than amongst birds, bees and ants', where the use of the direction of polarized light or the earth's magnetic field has been studied (e.g. Hughes 1999).[5] But Levinson offers some observations on the relative advantages and costs of the absolute versus relative frames of reference. Using absolute coordinates does facilitate mental map-making, but at the cost of a 'significant cognitive overhead', namely that the orientation and dead-reckoning systems must constantly be updated: they 'tick in the background and never go on holiday' (Levinson 2003: 273). Conversely the relative frame frees one of any such need, but leads to impoverished dead-reckoning skills. Those of us who use such a frame (as we all do in English) have 'lost our mental compass', as he puts it (ibid. 316 ff., 324).

It is clear that the work of Levinson's group has overturned many traditional assumptions about spatial cognition. It turns out that there

---

[4] That condition had to be modified in the case of the Mesoamerican group from Tenejapa since their whole terrain is relatively small and finding a completely unfamiliar location was difficult.

[5] Whether human beings are also subliminally able to use those methods to orient themselves is disputed. See Baker (1989).

is far greater diversity across human populations than had generally been assumed by those who worked predominantly or exclusively with Western subjects. In this area unqualified assertions as to the psychic unity of all humans look unwarranted and in many cases conflict with robust evidence to the contrary. In particular if frames of reference were innately given, you would expect them to be 'universal, equally accessible, acquired at the same ages, and acquired young' (ibid. 322), whereas the data concerning acquisition 'do not remotely support those predictions'. In particular the early acquisition of the absolute frame of reference by Tzeltal-speaking children is in stark contrast to what Piaget claimed his studies revealed, for their mastery of the geometry of orthogonal axes and quadrants and other aspects of 'Euclidean thinking' happens far sooner than he suggested. Tzeltal children 'begin to learn the linguistic expressions associated with the absolute frame of reference soon after two years old, with productive uses outside frozen expressions by age two and a half, with the most complex inflected forms by three and a half' (ibid. 309 citing Brown and Levinson 2000).

Thus far I have concentrated on the diversities in human spatial cognition that Levinson's work has brought to light. But that does not mean, of course, that there are no commonalities in this domain of thought. First, there are those that relate to the physical substrate of our cognitive apparatus, the brain, though even here qualifications need to be entered. Human brains everywhere have the same general anatomical structure, and follow the same genetic development patterns, whatever the ethnic, climatic, and environmental conditions (Changeux 1985: 202). Yet there are quite a few variations between different individuals including, for example, in the weight of the brain in relation to the body as a whole (ibid. 172 ff. and cf. 212 on phenotypic variability). Some of these differences are unlikely to impinge on spatial cognition. But we still have much to learn about the precise roles of the hippocampus, and the parietal and frontal lobes (Kolb and Whishaw 2003). Nor can we take it for granted that their functioning is perfectly uniform across all human beings, that is, we should not deny, a priori, the possibility of differential development in different groups or individuals. Indeed there is some empirical evidence that that is the case (Maguire et al. 2000 on taxi-drivers).

Levinson's own favoured hypothesis to help account for the facts that he has uncovered is what he calls co-evolution, that is the interaction of biological and cultural, especially linguistic, factors. That still leaves him with many commonalities, including a number of universals that apply in this domain, no less than fourteen of them, as he sets them out (Levinson 2003: 314, Table 7.1). Yet these universals are not generally of the type that those who argue for a strong thesis of the psychic unity of humankind will find support their view. They include, for instance, that 'all languages use at least one frame of reference' (no. 3) and that 'no language uses more than three frames of reference' (no. 4).

It is of course in particular in the input from language, in the acquisition of a frame of reference, that Levinson's explanatory hypothesis offers the sharpest challenge to the psychic unity position. Acknowledging that the views of Sapir and Whorf were sometimes open to criticism on the grounds of overstatement, Levinson proposes nevertheless a version of what he calls neo-Whorfianism. If we seek to explain the differences in the spatial cognition of different peoples, as they have now been revealed, then the languages that they acquire (including the gestures they use in communication) must be one factor.

It is at this point that some observations from the very different perspective of a study of ancient societies may be pertinent. Let me take some time first to illustrate a point that is analogous to one that I have already made in connection with colour perception, namely that there was no uniformity among the ancient Greeks on several problems concerning space, place, and the void, and on the relations between them, including on the question of whether it makes sense to talk of up and down, right and left, with regard to the cosmos as a whole. This already suggests that on those questions, at least, the Greek language, used by all the participants in those debates, certainly did not dictate determinate solutions to the problems.

One of the first questions to be raised was one that is admittedly remote from Levinson's concerns. This was whether there is such a thing as a void. An apparently empty bag is not really empty, since it contains air, the substantiality of which was shown by simple tests, attributed to the fifth-century BCE Presocratic philosophers Empedocles and Anaxagoras. Wineskins were inflated and the resistance to collapse of the air held inside them was remarked. The clepsydra, a vessel used to transfer wine, was used to make a similar observation. These vessels had a perforated base and a narrow top that could be closed by covering it with the hand. When immersed in the wine with the top stopped up, the air within the clepsydra prevented the wine entering—until the top was opened.

But the denial of the void was sometimes claimed to follow not so much from empirical evidence as from philosophical arguments. Parmenides held that what is is one and continuous, while what is not is inconceivable. From the impossibility of what is not he inferred that what is is a plenum, and his follower Melissus explicitly concluded to the impossibility of the void on those grounds. Some have assumed that the problem here was the ambiguity of the expression for 'what is not' in Greek (not-being being equated with the void). But that does not allow for the fact that the denial of the void was the conclusion of an argument, not just the repetition of its premise.

Parmenides also denied motion and plurality, and it was the acceptance of these two principles that led the fifth-century atomists Leucippus and Democritus to the opposite conclusion, namely that it is necessary to assume the existence of void to ensure both the plurality of things (one thing being separate from another) and to allow for movement—this last being construed as the transfer of substances (atoms in their case) through gaps between them. Facing their Eleatic opponents (Parmenides and his followers), the atomists were prepared to say not only that what is exists (the atoms) but what is not (the void) also does.

But does motion imply void? The atomists thought it did, but others countered that fish, for instance, swim in water without, it seems, moving through gaps in that water. The alternative view of motion that was eventually developed by the Stoics in the Hellenistic period was that it was the transmission of a disturbance in an elastic medium, rather than the transport of substances through gaps between them. By the first century CE Hero of Alexandria attempted further tests to show, among other things, that a partial vacuum could be produced artificially. The trouble about those experiments was that they were inconclusive against his opponents, since the continuum theorists could explain the results in terms of their opposite assumption of the elasticity of air.

One controversy thus centred on whether the void existed and that led some to distinguish void (as unoccupied space) from space itself (which may be either occupied or not), though others, the Epicureans, were accused of ignoring that distinction. However, according to some reports (Sextus in Long and Sedley 1987: i. 28), they coined the name 'intangible substance' as a generic term to cover three modalities. The same substance when empty of all being is called 'void', when occupied by a body is named 'place', and when bodies roam through it becomes 'room'. 'But generically it is called "intangible substance" in Epicurus' school, since it lacks resistant touch.' Effectively, then, it was space in the broadest sense, not void in the sense of space that happens to be unoccupied, that is the second fundamental principle (along with the atoms) in Epicurus' version of atomism. We may remark how an initially quite rich Greek vocabulary of words for place and the void facilitated philosophical debate on the issues—which in turn led to new coinages, indeed new concepts.

But a second controversy concerns whether the world is or is not spatially infinite. Already the Pythagorean philosopher Archytas (a contemporary of Plato) is reported (by Eudemus, according to Simplicius) to have posed the dilemma for any who assumed that the universe is finite. On that assumption, if I am imagined as standing on the outer boundary of the universe, could I or could I not stretch out my hand? It would be absurd to think you could not do so. But that means that there will be either body or place outside the supposed extremity—an argument that can be repeated for whatever extreme point is postulated.

On this topic both major Hellenistic schools accepted a certain notion of infinity, but interpreted that very differently. The Epicureans (like the earlier atomists) assumed an infinite number of worlds separated in time or in space (the void itself was infinite). There is no more reason, a pupil of Democritus, one Metrodorus, had said, for there to be just one world in the infinite void than there would be for there to be just one ear of corn in a vast plain. But for the Stoics the cosmos is finite and continuous—but surrounded by an infinite void. So 'void' for them applies only outside the cosmos: place, being that which body actually occupies, exists within this finite, continuous world.

This Stoic view was maintained despite the arguments against any such assumption of an infinite, external void that Aristotle had mounted. His view was that if there was infinite void, then there could be no centre to the cosmos. Yet in the world as we experience it there are (he held) just three types of natural motion, and all three presuppose some such centre. Heavy objects move towards that centre (which coincides with the centre of the spherical earth) light ones move away from it, and the third type of motion, that of the heavenly bodies, is in a circle *around* the earth. Among the perceived strengths of Aristotle's views were first that he could offer both empirical and abstract arguments to show the sphericity of the earth. Second, those views appeared to do justice to the phenomenon of gravity, as we call it, around the earth. Third, the movements of the heavenly bodies, being eternal, had to take place in a medium that offered no resistance and so quite different from the sublunary elements. Although the introduction of a division between a celestial and a terrestrial region has regularly been attacked as a disaster, his account of the motions that take place in his fifth element, aither, is the point at which Aristotelian dynamics is closest to Newtonian. On the other hand, among the chief weaknesses was the indeterminacy concerning the interface between the sublunary region around the earth, and the higher region composed of aither. How did the region where natural motion was up and down, from or to the centre of the earth, give way to one where natural motion was circular?

There was a further problem in squaring Aristotle's cosmology with his mathematics. Aristotle was already familiar with problems to do with parallels, where some definitions that were given were circular. Later, Euclid's famous parallel postulate specifies that non-parallel straight lines meet if extended. One would have supposed space had to be infinite to meet that condition, but Aristotle argued, rather lamely, that all that the geometers need is the potentiality of infinite extendibility, not an actual infinite extension. However, Aristotle was clear that movement did not require the void. The place of things is determined in relation to other bodies. The cosmos as a whole is a continuum, with both time and space, like geometrical extension, all infinitely divisible.

Then a third and final controversy relates to the applicability of the three dimensions, up/down, right/left, and front/back to the cosmos as a whole, an issue that takes us back to the question of rival frames of reference for spatial coordinates. Plato, arguing for a spherical cosmos in the *Timaeus* 62c–63e, thought it incoherent to talk of above and below in relation to the universe as a whole. Indeed up and down, and heavy and light, are to be relativized to the particular element and place in question. He does allow, however, that the two main heavenly motions (that of the fixed stars, the circle of the Same, and that of the planets, sun and moon, the circle of the Other) can be said to be, the one 'to the right' (that is westwards), the other 'to the left' (eastwards) (*Timaeus* 36c, contrast *Epinomis* 987b).

But Aristotle associated each of the three dimensions with a natural principle, thereby showing a strong penchant for what Levinson called an intrinsic frame of reference. Right is the source or origin of locomotion, up of growth, and front of perception. Humans evidently provide the model and Aristotle is prepared to say that in humans alone 'the natural parts are in their "natural" positions', for our upper part (the part by which we take in food) is directed towards that which is upper in the universe (*On the Parts of Animals* 656[a]10 ff.). This means that in quadrupeds their 'upper part' (where there mouth is) is at the front of their body. Aristotle's idea, based on humans, is quite the opposite of that reported in some modern societies,[6] where it is precisely quadrupeds that are used to determine which is 'upper' (namely their backs) and which is 'lower' (their bellies). On Aristotle's view, plants are 'upside down', since their 'upper', the parts by which they take in food, in other words their roots, are below the rest of the plant (*On the Progression of Animals* 705[a]32–3).

Yet Aristotle gets into further difficulties when applying these ideas to the cosmos as a whole, construed as like a living creature and certainly endowed with a natural motion. Since right is the natural source of movement, the motion of the heavens must start from the right, and indeed be 'rightwards'. This leads to the conclusion that east is right and west left, from which Aristotle infers that the northern hemisphere, the one in which we live, is the lower of the two hemispheres (*On the Heavens* 285[b]22 ff.). That appears to be in flagrant contradiction to what Aristotle had claimed about humans having their upper parts directed towards what is upper in the heavens. Moreover, Aristotle is here deliberately going against what some of the early Pythagoreans had claimed, namely that we are in the right and upper part of the world (285[b]25 ff.). If all of this strikes one as arbitrary, it is only fair to add that with regard to such questions as why the heavens move in one direction rather than in another, Aristotle expressly acknowledges that any answer must be conjectural.

These Greek disputes reflect, as usual for them, one might say, a combination of speculation and polemic. Moreover, it is clear that ideological issues are deeply entwined with what we might have

---

[6] See Levinson (2003: 331 n. 34), reporting Svorou (1994: 75 ff.) and Heine (1997: 40 ff.).

supposed were merely abstract problems. In the atomist view, there is nothing providential about the world we happen to live in—the result of mechanical or physical interactions in which no gods, no immanent craftsmanlike force, has any role. The world we inhabit is, as we have seen, one of an infinite number scattered through space. But the continuum theorists were generally teleologists, arguing that the single cosmos is indeed the product of design, not of chance. Design and providentiality are, they would claim, everywhere to be seen, in the parts of animals and in their overall functional organization. For them it was absurd to say that the eye came to be merely as the outcome of physical interactions: it is there for the good of the animal, and in certain expressions of the teleological view (as in Aristotle) other animals are in some sense 'for the sake of' humans, even though we are not the supreme living beings: the gods are.

It would be an exaggeration to say that such ideological considerations drive the *whole* argument concerning cosmology, including those relating to the spatial representations of the universe, but they are certainly an important and pervasive factor. As in many other cultures,[7] indeed, value judgements were built into common Greek beliefs and practices involving the spatial dimensions, with right superior to left, and up and front to down and back. Right and left figure in the Pythagorean Table of Opposites, which can be seen as in part a systematization of such beliefs, and Aristotle, as we have seen, goes further and gives a theoretical justification, of a sort, for treating one of each of those pairs as a principle. Yet Plato was one who challenged one aspect of such beliefs, as reflected in what may have been a common Greek practice. Although in his view too right is superior to left, he thought that the way in which infants were swaddled to encourage them to use their right hands rather than their left was absurd. In the *Laws* (794de) he writes: 'Through the folly of nurses and mothers we have all become lame, so to speak, in our hands.'

However, my main interest in rehearsing these arguments is to exemplify the diversity of ideas that were put forward on one or other

---

[7] In China, however, the usual preference for right over left is (at least in certain circumstances) reversed. Left is *yang* and therefore superior, and right is *yin* and inferior. Yet the attitude towards this pair is complex, since in the sphere of what is itself inferior, right in some sense has precedence over left. The right hand is used for eating, for example, and the right is the appropriate side for women.

problem that reflections on space and place prompted. The important point is that these divergent views were proposed by different thinkers who (mostly)[8] shared the same language and the same general culture. Of course, as I said, several of the ideas I have reviewed do not directly relate to Levinson's concern with frames of reference. On that score, Greeks and Romans count as (primarily) relativists, though there is a strong admixture of appeals to intrinsic properties, as we have just seen in Aristotle.

Yet the evidence we have reviewed introduces a new element that we have to take into account in any comprehensive analysis of the concepts of space that have been entertained across the world. The further issues that emerge concern the plasticity of human thought, in particular the room for manoeuvre that the participants in these debates enjoyed to develop their own views on matters of considerable importance, how far they were able to challenge assumptions and practices that were deeply rooted in the culture they all shared, and why they did so. One example was Plato rejecting one practice that stemmed from the symbolic values attached to right and left. But on a whole range of issues competing lines of argument were drawn up, on whether the earth is, as it seems, flat, on whether right and left, up and down, front and back can be applied to the heavens and the cosmos as a whole, on whether we should assume that we live in a unique world, the one and only one, or whether there are infinite worlds separated from ours in time or space or both.

What was at stake was the basic place of humans in the scheme of things—and whether there is a scheme of things for humans to take their place in. The continuum theorists confidently presupposed providentiality, but that was equally vigorously denied by the atomists. It was not that all the arguments (when there were arguments) on either side were equally cogent—nor did they seem so to the ancient Greeks themselves. Disputes with moral and metaphysical implications such as these were not going to be—and were not—resolved by knock-down arguments, whether empirical or abstract.

From our perspective the important point is that the differences expressed cannot be put down either to the cognitive equipment or to the general cultural background of the debaters. This phenomenon

---

[8] Of course some of the later exponents of Epicurean and Stoic views wrote in Latin, rather than in Greek.

cannot simply be associated with some distinctive feature of Greek culture, let alone with some aspect of the Greek language. It may be conceded that the particular polemical tone of certain exchanges is peculiarly Greek. But the Chinese too debated the shape of the cosmos, as Cullen (1996) has discussed in relation to the evidence in the early cosmological classic, the *Zhoubi suanjing* (the 'Arithmetic Classic of the Zhou Gnomon'), for example.[9] Reflections on the problems posed by understanding the spatial features of the world we live in were not confined to the Greeks or to Westerners. Rather in all such cases we should allow for that room for manoeuvre, and for the ingenuity of the human imagination, not least when individuals see, or believe they see, ways of impressing their fellows and gaining prestige for superior knowledge and indeed just such ingenuity. I shall be returning to that question in later studies.

So what conclusions does this examination of spatial cognition suggest and how do they compare with our earlier study of colour? Once again the phenomena to be explained are complex, or as I would say multidimensional. To account for the data revealed by psychology and social anthropology—as well as by my ancient historical observations—we need to invoke a combination of factors. In the colour cognition case we noted that while the human eye has the same general anatomical structure, there are significant differences between individuals, not just as between trichromatic and dichromatic vision, but along a whole range of degrees of sensitivity. Now in the spatial cognition case we can similarly agree that the anatomy of the parts of the human brain that are responsible, the hippocampus, the parietal and so on, is generically similar across the species. Yet there are also marked differences—which we are not yet in any position fully to explain—in, for example, navigational abilities and dead reckoning. While some of these reflect the preferred cultural frame of reference, others are likely to be associated with the differential development of particular parts of the brain or the acquisition of particular neurological sensitivities. That remains to be either confirmed or modified in detail in future experimental work. But the fundamental point is that while we all possess the

---

[9] In the *gai tian* (蓋 天, 'canopy heaven') view the heavens are a circular canopy set over a central, square earth. The *hun tian* (渾 天, 'enveloping heaven') view agreed that the earth is square, but maintained that the heavens are a complete sphere, one half of which is invisible below the earth.

same physical organ, as a learning device the ways in which it can and does develop in different individuals in response to experience exhibit considerable variation. I shall be returning to this point in Chapter 4.

So on the first score, the physiological and neurological input, there are both commonalities, and some differences, between different human subjects. As to what there is to cognize, second, the universal elements in the colour cognition case include the physics of the wavelengths of light and in the spatial cognition one, the directionality of gravitational forces—on earth at least—and aspects of the physics and geometry of volumes and shapes.

When we come, third, to culture and language, we can see that differences in both colour and spatial cognition are not confined just to differences between individuals, but relate also and more especially to groups, indeed whole communities. The influences at work are, once again, in both cases, certainly not uniform. In the colour case, some languages concentrate on encoding differences in hue, others those in intensity, while yet others do not have a special vocabulary of terms for use in this area whose primary connotations are colours as such at all. In the first two cases, the terminology available in the language has distinct effects on what its users easily or readily discriminate—not that they are incapable of discrimination beyond the limits of their colour vocabulary. That is obvious from the third type of language I mentioned, not all of whose speakers are totally colour blind! The effect of the spatial frame of reference that dominates in a language seems, if anything, even more pervasive. Yet here too it would be an exaggeration to say that those frames *determine* all aspects of the understanding of space.

As a fourth factor, in the spatial cognition case too, we have to add in that there may be significant differences, as between individuals or groups sharing the same culture and language, in the way in which, once space becomes a topic of explicit reflection, the problems it is thought to pose are resolved. I illustrated this especially with materials from ancient Greece, though noting that parallels exist in other societies. Thus some Greek theorists challenged and rejected the applicability of directionality to the universe as a whole. They raised issues to do with the absolute or relative nature of space that were to reverberate down the centuries, notably in the debates that divided Newton and Kant on the one side from Leibniz on the other. While the ancient Greeks, and those early moderns, all spoke natural languages that incorporated, or even privileged, a relative frame of reference, that did not inhibit some from postulating a view according to which space is absolute. Nor of course did natural language impose constraints on the further development of relativistic concepts of space-time in the twentieth century, even though there remain tensions (to say the least) between, on the one hand, what modern physics demands, and on the other, the concepts we need to live by.

I resisted the suggestion that ideological factors are the sole determinants in the particular views that were adopted. On the other hand, we certainly have to acknowledge that values play an important role, especially on the issues between the teleologists and their opponents. To answer questions to do with space is so often to answer, directly or indirectly, questions as to what it is to be a human being. Yet using space thus as a way of recommending values would never have been possible had there not been a certain room for manoeuvre in reflection on the problems, where an individual's use of their cognitive equipment and of their cultural and linguistic legacy is not totally determined by either factor or by the combination of both. It is particularly the individuality of these responses that dictates reservations and modifications both to the unqualified universalist thesis and to that of the extreme cultural relativist.

3

The Natural Kinds of Animals and Plants

LET me begin with a summary of my argument in this chapter, which will develop from positions I have proposed in earlier studies (Lloyd 2004).

The natural kinds of animals and plants are important to all human societies both as foodstuffs and as models of classification itself, providing what are imagined to be robust paradigms for the notions of species, genera, classes, families, and so on. The actual zoological and botanical classifications recorded from different societies across the world exhibit enormous diversity, and that at first sight seems to scupper any suggestion of some convergence between folk and scientific taxonomies. Yet detailed ethnographic studies of their patterns and implicit assumptions have been carried out in the wake of, and generally modelled on, those of Berlin and Kay on colours that I reviewed in Ch. 1, and these studies have, here too, often given rise to similar claims for robust cross-cultural universals, for example that the same 'common-sense' relationships of similarity and difference are recognized everywhere.[1] Analogous work by developmental psychologists has been undertaken to suggest that as young children grow up, they show an increasing mastery of many of the same universals.

Yet recent and indeed some not so recent work by biologists has shown, first, how problematic the very notion of species is and, second,

---

[1] Atran (1990: 1–2) had this to say about common sense. 'Common sense is used here with systematic ambiguity to refer both to the results and processes of certain special kinds of ordinary thinking: to what in all societies is considered, and is cognitively responsible for the consideration of, manifestly perceivable fact—like the fact that grass is green (when it really is perceived to be green) . . . Common-sense beliefs are beyond dispute not because they happen to accurately describe the facts, but because that is just the way humans are constitutionally disposed to think about things. Of course, this does not define the term "common sense" precisely . . . But . . . cognitive psychology and anthropology can illustrate common sense, for instance plain thinking about the world in terms of universal color schemata, rigid bodies, biological taxa and so forth.'

how difficult it is to propose anything like a definitive taxonomy for either animals or plants. Most of the more familiar kinds seem to fall, to be sure, within well-ordered groups, but the further down the animal or plant kingdom one moves, the more problematic the ordering becomes. Different criteria can be invoked, but the classifications arrived at frequently depend on prior decisions as to which criteria to privilege and how to weight different ones when they appear to give divergent results. Such issues as these may even raise doubts as to whether there *are* natural kinds of animals and plants, that is ones that exist independently of our own needs and interests. Few would go so far as to claim that the distinctions that modern research reveals are *just* the products of that research, but that leaves open whether or how far the results of modern studies are compatible with the original Linnaean dream of a single *natural* classification or even with any of its latter-day avatars.

First, then, there are conflicts between the 'common-sense' taxonomy advanced by some universalists and the findings of science as represented by the most recent studies in biology. But, second, animal and plant classification is not just a problem for us: it has been a matter of recurrent debate and disagreement in the past, including in ancient societies. The historical record, moreover, does *not* suggest that, once the idea of evaluating and criticizing the taxonomy implicit in a given natural language occurred to people, the *same* solution was put forward, let alone one that obviously converges on the postulated universal common-sense taxonomy. In part the divergences (which continue) may be put down to the tensions between different interest groups and sometimes indeed to fairly blatant ideological factors, when animal and plant classifications have been used to justify not just a particular view of the place of humans in the scheme of things, but also specific notions of hierarchy. But while some of the variety reflects extra-scientific influences, and some indeed just differences in different natural languages, the fact remains that—despite claims to the contrary that I shall be considering—no single definitive classification is available by which all others are to be judged.[2]

---

[2] Taxonomists on the whole are in agreement on what would count as robust evidence for decisions to be taken on the groupings of the main eukaryote kingdoms, for example: but as I shall be noting, in many cases that evidence does not yet exist.

In this case—unlike what we found with the differences in di-, tri-, and possibly tetra-chromatic subjects in colour perception—there is no reason to think that the cognitive equipment humans, as humans, possess to classify animals and plants varies in any significant way. That is not to deny that the ways we process what we perceive, and indeed what we perceive, are affected by who we are, whether or not we have experience as hunters, fishermen, farmers, or whatever, and whether or not we belong to literate cultures where canons of encyclopaedic knowledge are handed on from generation to generation. Nor of course is it to deny that molecular biology can now call on remarkable techniques and aids to investigation, many of which do not go back more than a few years. Nor is there any reason to suppose that we, or any human society, are the prisoners of the cultural assumptions that have undoubtedly influenced the actual taxonomies that have been adopted, let alone prisoners of any particular natural language used to express them. There is indeed good evidence, in this area, for the possibility of revision and in that sense of the plasticity of the human mind. But there is also striking evidence of how even today the need to find order sometimes overrides a sense of the complexity of the data, of how expectations of neatness and simplicity can blind us to the actual multidimensionality of the phenomena.[3]

Let me now give substance to that programmatic sketch. Every human society relies on animals and plants for food and so for its very survival. The extent of the dependence on the local fauna and flora in the immediate vicinity may vary greatly, since trade enables many societies to have access to the resources of more or less distant regions. In modern industrialized societies, large sections of the population may have no direct experience of agriculture. They may have little or no idea of where the food products on their supermarket shelves come from, or how they were produced.[4] But in most societies in human history considerable knowledge has been needed, and has

---

[3] This is a recurrent theme (though not in precisely those terms) in Dawkins (2004). How to incorporate lateral gene transfer into the picture is just one of the most striking examples of the problem.

[4] The impoverishment of knowledge about animals and plants among urbanized Westerners has been remarked on in recent studies (Ross 2002; Ross, Medin, Coley, and Atran 2003; Atran, Medin, and Ross 2004). Asked by an interviewer to identify all the trees she knew, an honours student at a major American research university came up with under ten kinds. When asked about plants, she said she could not think of any plants that were not trees. She claimed to know a lot about angiosperms, gymnosperms, and so on, but

been acquired, about which plants are edible, which poisonous, which can be cultivated and how, about how to catch fish, how to hunt, and kill wild animals, about which can be domesticated and the like. Humans share many of those skills with wild animals, who similarly need to know about their foodstuffs, about what and how to hunt, and how to escape those animals that prey on them. Some of that animal knowledge is instinctive, some derived from the animal's own experience, some transmitted to them by other members of their species. Different groups of primates may devise different solutions to how to 'fish' for ants or termites, using sticks as tools to do so (cf. Boesch 1996; Hulme and Matsuzawa 2002). But humans, with speech and then with writing, have, of course, far more efficient means of preserving acquired knowledge and communicating it to other humans.

The need for knowledge of kinds of animals and plants is, then, obvious, and on the side of what there is to be known, those kinds generally seem at first sight eminently well-ordered and classifiable. Wild asparagus can be recognized as the *same* species of plant wherever on the mountainside it grows, though in some spots or conditions it flourishes more than in others. Not only are male and female wild boar easily recognizable, but they normally give birth to young male and female wild boar, thereby providing seemingly unassailable support for the supposition that they form a well-defined natural kind.

The idea, then, that there are well-defined natural kinds in the animal and plant kingdoms can be supported by swathes of evidence, and it has had momentous consequences well beyond its immediate field of application. Within that field, first, it provides the key structuring device for the transmission of essential knowledge. Minor and some not so minor difficulties do arise. Sports and monsters constitute exceptions, and so too, in a different way, do hybrids, whether they occur naturally or as a result of human intervention. Then there is the difficulty of deciding when two distinct items or sets of them represent different species, when just varieties of the same species. But such problems—which are often of little *practical* consequence—can be easily dismissed, given the apparently overwhelming evidence that normally species reproduce true to type.

that was just 'biology': 'it was not really about plants and trees' (Atran, Medin, and Ross 2004: 395).

The power of the idea that animals, especially, fall into well-defined species and genera is such that it has repeatedly served as a model for classification in other fields as well. The most obvious directly analogous examples relate to human groups and characters.[5] There are no clear-cut natural boundaries, most would say, between pride, arrogance, stubbornness, courage, foolhardiness, cowardice, and the like (cf. Ch. 4 below). But it can be made to seem that there are, by associating those qualities with different animals and then using them to suggest natural divisions between types of human being. This is what the Greek poet Semonides notoriously did in his characterization of different types of woman, using a series of animals to convey extremely unflattering images of the various kinds of females whom males were likely to encounter. The sow, bitch, vixen are all painted in highly negative terms: not even the female bee, a model of industriousness, is all good by any means, for immediately after describing her Semonides points the general moral, that women are a bane for men. What different species of animals stereotypically stand for differs from one society to another: for some Chinese the pig represents wealth, not filth. But their use as such stereotypes is very widespread.

Indeed where many continua are concerned, the tendency to see them not as spectra but as made up of discrete entities—a tendency that is, of course, encouraged by the vocabulary of discrete terms available in natural languages—is given a considerable boost thanks to the apparent self-evidence of distinct genera and species in the case of animals and plants. Where humans find *order* in a domain, that is often expressed in terms of the taxonomic structure of genera and species exemplified paradigmatically in the world of living things. For those purposes it does not matter unduly how much detailed knowledge of different natural kinds is available to underpin the classification. Plants and more especially animals may be recognized, as they often are, by what are represented as their stereotypical characteristics, as the tiger by its possessing stripes, being furry, having four legs and so on. An account may be built up by accumulating such features without any commitment to which may be essential, which merely accidental, though the problems that then arise, of specifying the necessary and

---

[5] Gil-White (2001) even suggested that treating diverse human groups as different species is adaptive, though that invoked an incredulous reaction from Ingold (2001).

sufficient conditions for correctly identifying even three-legged tigers as tigers, like those of distinguishing gold from other yellow metals ('fool's gold'), are ones that have much exercised philosophers such as Putnam (1975: chs. 8, 12) and Kripke (1980: 116 ff.).

If we grant first that the recognition of biological kinds has been essential for survival, and second that normal reproductive processes apparently provide overwhelming support for such an assumption, one might have thought it possible or even likely that all humans everywhere would classify animals and plants in more or less the same way. Where local variations occur, they could be ascribed mainly to local differences in the flora and fauna encountered. Just such claims for robust cross-cultural universals in this area have indeed been made. To evaluate these, we need to consider no less than four types of evidence. That comprises first, the ethnographic reports; second, the findings of developmental psychologists; and third, recent work in biology—which is relevant not so much to what is commonly believed, but to how understanding of forms of life has been transformed in the wake of the development of microbiology and molecular biology. Finally, following my usual procedures, I shall review the historical record from ancient societies, to see what light this may throw on the issues.

As I noted before, not long after Berlin and Kay's work on colour classification, Berlin teamed up with Breedlove and Raven (1973) to undertake a similar extensive cross-cultural investigation into folk-biological taxonomies. On the surface these present very considerable variety. In some societies, animals are classified by habitat (as air, water, land animals) or by mode of movement (fliers, swimmers, walkers, crawlers) or by whether they are edible or not, or domesticable or not, or by some combination of such criteria. Again classifications in which animals are grouped according to their assumed natures, as 'hot', 'cold', 'wet', 'dry', and so on, are also common across the world.

The principal finding that Berlin, Breedlove, and Raven proposed, however, was that there are five or six general, if not universal, ethnobiological categories that underpin and are present in such taxonomies worldwide. These categories form a hierarchy, in a descending order of generality, from what is called the Unique Beginner, through Life Form, Generic, and Specific, down to Varietal. What is more or less universally recognized, so the argument is, is this hierarchy. The different taxonomic levels are not all necessarily labelled in any given language (there may, for instance, be no word for the most inclusive taxon, 'animal' or 'plant', as such), but the concepts are nevertheless implicit in the classifications used. Again the natural species and genera that are picked out by a given human population may differ to some extent (where local ecological variations have their part to play), but species will always be subsumed under genera which in turn fall under life form. More and less complex classifications will have more or less taxa, the development of which follows certain patterns that mirror, in a different domain, the argument about the gradual, but determinate, acquisition of more and more complex colour vocabularies that we reviewed in Chapter 1.

Two comments may be made at this stage. First, these findings appear to correspond up to a point with what some developmental psychologists report about the stages through which a child's grasp of living creatures passes. Second, in places, the methodology Berlin and his associates used in this work is open to similar objections to those I mentioned in relation to the work on colour.

Let me deal with the second point first. The objection to the study of colour classifications that I made was that in some cases at least the questions that were put to native informants presupposed the very categories that were supposed to be being tested. The protocols used meant that the investigators got out what they put in. There is a similar risk of circularity in the study of folk biological taxonomy in so far as the animal and plant types and taxa *we* use figure in the questions used to probe the indigenous people's own understanding of the relations in question. I shall come back to this point shortly in relation to Atran.

Then as to the findings of developmental psychology, they do not offer the unequivocal support for Berlin's thesis that may at first be imagined, and this is not just because there is no consensus on whether 'folk biology' is an innate, or an acquired, domain. The essentialists hold that it is innate,[6] but work done by Carey (1985; cf. Carey and Spelke 1994), among others (to which I shall be returning in Ch. 6)

---

[6] Those who claim that essentialism is a universal human trait have usually, though not always, been careful to distinguish between, on the one hand, the ways in which essences figure in humans' representations of the world ('psychological essentialism' in the vocabulary of Medin and Ortony 1989) and, on the other, the question of whether essences actually exist in any given domain. Where animals are concerned, essences have, of course, been generally repudiated by evolutionary taxonomy. Gelman (2003) gives a sophisticated analysis both of what 'essentialism' has been made to cover and of what drives it in its various forms.

was taken to suggest that young children do not initially have a core domain that corresponds to Living Kind, though they later acquire one. To start with, they work with a notion of Animate Being, which includes both humans and animals, but is organized on the basis of a naive psychology. Quite when the transition between these two stages occurs is a matter on which Carey (1995) herself has modified her earlier views though against her critics (for example Keil 1994; 1995; Atran 1994) she continues to maintain that a transition does occur. Yet although that might look promising from the point of view of the analogies with Berlin's proposals, the difficulty of using this evidence as support for claims about what human beings all hold *as adults* is that it simply does not address *that* question. Moreover, the transition does not just involve the elaboration of existing categories (which might be imagined to tally with Berlin's proposals about the different degrees of complexity found in different ethnobiological taxonomies). The child abandons, or at least severely modifies, its assumptions, as it acquires increasing mastery of the domain.

Moreover, a further problem both with Carey's position and with that of her essentialist opponents is that the vast majority of the studies undertaken have been done on North American children. Some limited comparative studies, notably those of Hatano et al. (1993), have brought to light certain differences in the ways in which inanimate objects, plants, and animals are perceived by Israeli, by Japanese, and by American children. The Japanese showed a tendency to attribute living properties to inanimate things, while the Israelis conversely tended not to ascribe living properties to plants—investigations that cast doubt on the confident claims that have often been made that the perception of the kingdoms of 'animals' and 'plants' shows no diversity across the world among all human populations.

By far the most sustained and sophisticated set of studies in support of cross-cultural zoological universals has been carried out by Scott Atran and his associates (1990; 1994; 1995; 1998; Atran, Medin, and Ross 2004), who have undertaken extensive fieldwork both in Mesoamerica—on the Itza' Maya—and on North American college students. This research led Atran to claim that an underlying 'common-sense' classification of animals is to be found across the world, although in his more recent studies he has qualified this: it is the ranks, not taxa, that are 'apparently universal' (Atran, Medin, and Ross 2004: 397). Surface classifications are acknowledged to differ.

Indeed, when Atran and his team first cross-questioned their Itza' Maya subjects about their ideas on the groups and sub-groups of animals, their answers conformed to patterns frequently found elsewhere: they classified animals according to their habitat, edibility, domesticability, and the like, using obviously culturally relative criteria.

However, Atran then proceeded to reformulate his inquiry,[7] to ask which animals are companions, '*uy-et'ok*', to which, or which belonged to the same lineage, *u-ch'ib'al*. When he did so, that yielded results that were claimed to tally, with a few exceptions, with those elicited when his American college students were asked analogous questions about the similarities and differences between different kinds of animals.[8]

There are two main problems with these studies, one minor concerning the artificiality of the protocols, the other major relating to what precisely the findings amount to and how the supposed universal classification squares, or does not square, with what science is held to reveal to be the case. Since I have rehearsed some of these difficulties in an earlier critique (Lloyd 2004), I can summarize the main points briefly here.

The Itza' Maya, to start with, had to be trained to use the name-cards that were presented to them. They had, in some cases, to be taught the correct names. They were then tested to see whether they understood, and those who did not were subsequently discarded from the study. Moreover, they were questioned on how they ranked, for 'companionship', a variety of animals and other objects that they had never seen—and that immediately raises the problem of whether, or to what extent, the results were predetermined by the information that they had previously been given. Roy Ellen (1993), among others, has underlined how unfamiliar situations, such as interviews and questionnaires, may sometimes produce distorting effects in the views elicited from native informants—and Luria's work certainly graphically illustrates the problem (as we shall be considering below, Ch. 6). Since the source of all the information concerning the species they had never encountered before was the

---

[7] In Atran, Medin, and Ross (2004: 416–17 n. 2), there is explicit acknowledgement that different elicitation procedures are likely to yield different results.

[8] Yet, as already observed (n. 4), Atran has latterly come to recognize the impoverished knowledge of plants and animals that urbanized North American college students can command. That would seem to be relevant to the question I go on to raise concerning the extent to which the information provided by the researchers influenced the results they obtained.

investigators themselves, the dangers of circularity in such cases are obvious. The informants would have had to use their ingenuity to answer the questions in terms of, that is by applying, their own usual assumptions: and yet it was just those assumptions that the investigators were hoping to be able to access.

My second and more fundamental difficulty concerns how the supposed cross-cultural universal taxonomy relates to the findings of science, and this will take me to my third group of evidence, from modern biology, and eventually to my fourth, the history of the subject. Atran's position on this fundamental question was always rather guarded and it has become more so in his recent contributions to the debate. On the whole what he calls 'common sense' is claimed to match science pretty well.[9] The exceptions where the two conflict are said to be not numerous. Whales and bats are, from some points of view, anomalies. But such instances are rare though in his latest studies they have received greater attention.[10] In general, however, he continues to maintain that science tends to confirm not, of course, the explicit zoological classifications reported in all their diversity from across the world, but the underlying common-sense folk taxonomy present, in his view, in all cultures.[11]

Yet first it would seem strange, if 'common sense' yields true cross-cultural universals, that it should ever be in disagreement with

---

[9] Berlin, Breedlove, and Raven (1973: 219) already claimed, for instance, that with certain exceptions Tzeltal understanding of the boundaries of the domain of plants corresponded almost perfectly with the standard plant division of Western systematic botany.

[10] Thus in Atran (1998: 566) he remarked that tree, bird, sparrow, and worm are not valid taxa from the scientist's point of view, and he (ibid. 558 ff.) pointed to other mismatches between Itza' taxonomy and science with respect to canines and felines and to the Itza' notion of a group of tree-living creatures that include monkeys, raccoons, and squirrels. He (ibid. 567) even put it that 'from a scientific stand-point, folk-biological concepts such as the generic species are woefully inadequate for capturing the evolutionary relationships of species over vast dimensions of time and space—dimensions that human minds were not directly designed (naturally selected) to comprehend'. Similarly he (1999: 161) noted that Itza' classification of snakes into deadly versus non-deadly violates evolutionary classification. Most recently Atran, Medin, and Ross (2004: 397) note a similar shortcoming in folk-biological treatment of organisms distant from human beings such as insects and bryophytes.

[11] Consider Atran (1998: 547): 'Folk biology, which is present in all cultures, and the science of biology, whose origins are particular to Western cultural tradition, have corresponding notions of living kinds.' In Atran (1999: 120) he put it that 'humans everywhere classify animals and plants into species-like groupings that are as obvious to a modern scientist as to a Maya Indian', and compare Atran, Medin, and Ross 2004: 398: 'When people are asked to sort biological kinds into groups, they show strong agreement, both within and across cultures, that also corresponds fairly well with scientific taxonomy.'

science. When that happens, how is the matter to be adjudicated? Atran sometimes writes as if, in a conflict between how things appear to common sense and what science takes to be the case, the appearances win out.[12] But on that story, if common sense is the arbiter, it is difficult to see how any scientist could come to disconfirm what he or she knows directly merely by using his or her innate cognitive equipment.

The shape of Atran's general argument bears, of course, a striking similarity to that of Chomsky on the deep structure of language, which can be used to explain how it is that we have a capacity to form correct sentences in a natural language even though we cannot say how we do it. There is, however, this crucial difference. The plausibility of Chomsky's theory depends in large part on the solutions offered as to how we, as investigators, can get to the surface structure of a language from the deep one and vice versa. We have protocols for the translation procedures involved. But it is just those that are missing in the account that Atran offers in the zoological taxonomy case.

When we go further into zoological and botanical taxonomy, and especially into recent work in microbiology,[13] what I have been referring to as the findings of science turn out to be far more complex and problematic than has emerged so far from my critique of Atran. We may begin with what Mayr (1957) called the species problem, on which there is now a vast literature.[14] There may be reasonable taxonomic evolutionary order in the higher animals, but this soon runs out when we are dealing with lower life forms. To arrive at an orderly taxonomy, as Jardine and Sibson showed long ago (1971), the similarities and differences invoked have to be weighted and that

---

[12] In Atran (1990: 2) he wrote: 'No speculation can possibly confute the grounds for this common-sense view of things because all speculation must start from it.' In Atran (1998: 563, repeated at 1999: 187) he put it that 'for scientific systematics, folkbiology may represent a ladder to be discarded after it has been climbed, or at least set aside while scientists surf the cosmos'. But then picking up his point about the degraded knowledge of nature in some urban communities he continued: 'but those who lack traditional folk knowledge, or implicit appreciation of it, may be left in the crack between science and common sense. For an increasingly urbanized and formally educated people who are often unwittingly ruinous of the environment, no amount of cosmically valid scientific reasoning skill may be able to compensate the local loss of ecological awareness.'

[13] I am indebted to Dr Giselle Walker for information and advice on this question, and to Professor Evelyn Fox Keller for discussions on the issues. Both these scholars should be exonerated, however, from any responsibility for the ways in which I have responded to their counsel.

[14] For a recent critical review of the state of the debate, see Hull (1997). Cf. e.g. Dupré (1993, 2001), Ghiselin (1997).

obviously, once again, risks circularity: you get out what you put in. In that classic paper, they identified no less than six different criteria used to decide which groups of populations should be accorded species rank. They were (1) morphology, (2) differences in ecological range, (3) interfertility, (4) cytology, (5) serology, and (6) the extent of DNA hybridization. Although some of the results of using different criteria converge, that is far from true across the board. In particular morphology and interfertility do not, and yet these were two of the most favoured candidates, at one time, to crack the problem.

Similar, and maybe even more severe, difficulties arise in botanical taxonomy, where they are certainly not confined merely to the species level. The *orders* of plants, above the family level, remain deeply controversial, despite the very considerable efforts that have been made, including by international committees set up for the purpose, to impose standardization. As to the species within each main genus of plants that have been identified, Walters (1961; 1986) suggested that their number correlates closely with the intensity with which the genus in question had been studied. We should not conclude that those species were just an artefact of scholarly attention: but their abundance certainly seems to reflect the degree of that attention.

The problems posed by the classification of the major groups of eukaryotes are particularly suggestive. In a survey of recent work, Simpson and Roger (2004) proposed that there are six major kingdoms, namely Opisthokonta, Amoebozoa, Plantae (or Archaeplastida as they are now known), Chromalveolata, Rhizaria, and Excavata (see Fig. 3.1), which they suggest should replace the earlier 'Whittaker' scheme, according to which, in addition to the prokaryotes (Monera), there are just four eukaryotic kingdoms, Animalia (Metazoa), Plantae, Fungi, and Protista. Simpson and Roger put it that the popularity of that scheme owed more to pedagogical convenience than to biological realism. Protista, especially, is a 'grab-bag' for all the eukaryotes that could not be assigned to the other three kingdoms.

In advocating a six-kingdom view from an evolutionary perspective, Simpson and Roger still repeatedly underline the indeterminacies that have to be recognized. 'The precise highest-level relationships within Opisthokonta are still under investigation' (ibid. 693. 3). 'The exact relationships' amongst the groups that make up the Rhizaria are 'still uncertain' (695. 1). 'Excavata is the most contentious of the major groups of eukaryotes' and the most recent studies are 'equivocal' as to whether the sub-groups within them are specifically related (695. 2).[15] If the six major kingdoms can be considered 'well-known', the possibility of other additional groups cannot be ruled out. The familiar eukaryotes might even represent only a fraction of the high-level diversity in nature, although Simpson and Roger do not think that the available evidence points in that direction (695. 3).

Obviously, enormous advances have been made in molecular phylogenetics, thanks to new research methods, especially the analysis of SSU rRNA (small subunit ribosomal RNA) gene sequences. Yet the relative determinacy of existing groups is in obvious tension with the processes of evolution that governed their emergence. Lateral gene transfer evidently occurred during those evolutionary processes, though no confident answers can yet be given to such questions as how (or when) the major kingdoms of eukaryotes split off from one another. Simpson and Roger offer one speculation about how the 'tree' is organized, with Opisthokonta and Amoebozoa linked and together separated from the other four kingdoms (ibid. 694 fig. 1),[16] but Dawkins (2004: 436–7) develops a second hypothesis, while Giselle Walker has produced a third on the basis of her own most recent research and survey of the status quaestionis.

If and when all the pieces of the evolutionary story have been assembled, that will no doubt find favour with the systematists.[17] But that dream is still a very long way off.[18] Meanwhile investigators have to adopt pragmatic criteria to give working definitions that will serve to identify the species and groups they are interested in. That does

[15] Similarly, but more radically, Walker (in preparation) states that the Chromalveolata are not well supported, that four other kingdoms are all open to some doubt, leaving only the Opisthokonta as unequivocally supported at this stage in research.

[16] Commenting on the Chromalveolata, Simpson and Roger (2004: 694. 3) remark that 'secondary endosymbiosis' has happened more than once in the eukaryotes. This is the process whereby a eukaryote already containing a primary plastid is engulfed by another host eukaryote, and over time is reduced to an organelle. But most groups of secondary algae, they suggest, descend from one particular endosymbiosis involving a red algal symbiont. 'These organisms, plus their many non-photosynthetic relatives, comprise the group Chromalveolata.'

[17] Simpson and Roger (2004: 693. 1) claim that 'most systematists . . . now hold that only monophyletic groups—an ancestor and all of its descendents—should be formally classified as higher taxa'.

[18] The practical difficulties of determining the relationships between the natural groups of eukaryotes are formidable. 'As we look further back in time, most historical signal is lost from present day molecular sequences, so that non-historical (artefactual) signals in the same data can easily obscure the true relationships' (Simpson and Roger 2004: 695. 3). Compare also Walker (in preparation) on the erosion of phylogenetic signal.

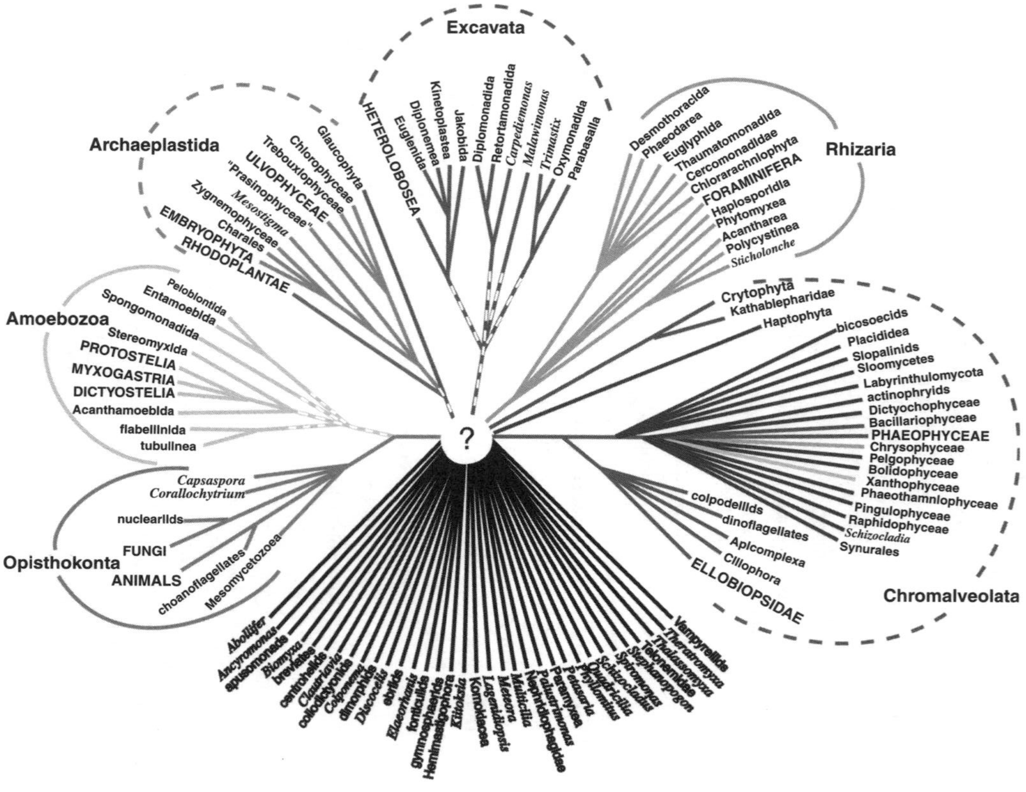

FIGURE 3.1. The main kingdoms of the eukaryotes. By kind permission of Dr Cécile Walter.

not mean criteria that are merely arbitrary. But it does reflect the fact that no single set of them overrides all others in virtue of their being grounded in a single definitive evolutionary taxonomy—since no such is available.

All of this is, no doubt, remote from the ken of ordinary folk and their, our, usual concerns with animal and plant groupings. However one message that modern molecular biology makes loud and clear is indeed the complexity of life forms.[19] One does not need modern biology, to be sure, to have some appreciation of that richness, but certainly modern research has brought to light hitherto unimagined variety. That is surely something that we need to bear in mind when we reflect on the limitations of our own attempts to impose order on the field.

But before attempting to summarize such conclusions as can be suggested in this problematic area, we should consider what can be learnt from our fourth and final source, namely the very early history of attempts at animal and plant taxonomy. Aristotle provides a particularly intriguing case, since the classification of animals he arrived at bears, in certain respects at least, a close resemblance to Atran's common-sense taxonomy. Yet Aristotle's classification did not exist as such before he proposed it. Nor can it be said that he merely systematized what earlier Greek thinkers had believed—explicitly or implicitly—all along. We do not have comprehensive explicit classifications of animals in the extant literature before him, although we do have a detailed account of the differences between them from the perspective of their nutritional qualities in the Hippocratic treatise *On Regimen*. Yet we have every reason to believe that Aristotle's classification is, in important respects, original, not so much in the infimae species he recognized, as in the groups into which he organized them.

First, he introduced the major division between blooded and bloodless animals. Then he subdivided the latter into four main groups, which he named *malakia* ('softies'), *malakostraka* ('soft-shelled'), *ostrakoderma* ('potsherd-skinned'), and *entoma* ('insected')—terms which in some cases he coined himself and in every case defined or redefined. While the first two of these groups correspond roughly to

---

[19] The plasticity of life forms is further suggested by the ability of some creatures to survive in an adapted form even when lesions affect their cell structure. The oblation of a single cell of nematodes, the earth-worm, may lead to the growth of a modified organism.

the cephalopods and crustacea, he used *ostrakoderma* not of what we recognize as the testacea (though that is the conventional translation of the Aristotelian word) but of a variety of shelled invertebrates, including gastropods, lamellibranchs, and some echinoderms (cf. Peck 1937: 23). Moreover, there are some creatures that fall outside the main classes, the sponges for instance. Indeed he sometimes writes that nature moves in a continuous sequence from animals to plants, and again from the living to the inanimate. Although his usual way of demarcating the animals from the plants is in virtue of the faculty of perception (for he denies that plants perceive), he occasionally invokes other criteria, such as movement or the ability to live unattached to a substrate. So he is prepared to treat as animals the jellyfish or holothouria, creatures which he says have no ability to perceive (the evidence is set out and discussed in Lloyd 1996*b*: ch. 3).

Yet remarkably, after Aristotle, no one in pagan Greek antiquity attempted zoological research on such a scale. While anatomical investigations, first by the Alexandrian biologists Herophilus and Erasistratus, then by Galen, certainly made extraordinary discoveries in that field, most post-Aristotelian classifications of animals reverted to simpler schemata focusing on modes of locomotion, or the presumed essential qualities of different groups (hot, cold, wet, dry) without attempting a systematic overview of the problems that Aristotle himself had opened up.

In the analogous situation, in ancient China, we also find different classifications of animals proposed in the *Erya*, the *Huainanzi*, and elsewhere. Both those texts draw, in different ways, on earlier beliefs, but it would be extravagant to claim that all that they were doing was simply to make explicit what was already implicit in earlier Chinese thought. *Huainanzi*, in particular, sets up correlations between modes of reproduction, methods of locomotion, and other factors in a complex polythetic network that goes beyond any earlier attempt at such systematizations (cf. Lloyd 2004: 106). The actual taxonomies of animals found in different texts differ quite appreciably from one another—and differ also from Aristotle's or that of any other Greek. So it is not the case that, once the question of the groups of animals came to be a topic of explicit reflection and comment—in these two societies at least, and maybe in any other—the solution that those who were interested in the subject would come up with would always be the same and would tally with some universal common sense.

It is obvious that, to a greater or less extent, all Greek and Chinese taxonomies underwent interference from cultural, symbolic, even ideological factors. One unsurprising coincidence between Greek and Chinese systematizations is that humans regularly emerge at the top as quite special animals. In Aristotle they serve as the model by which other animals are, in a sense, judged, and compared with which they must all be said to be inferior. Analogously in Chinese fivefold correlations between animals and the five phases, humans are regularly associated with earth and the privileged centre. But while it is certainly true to say that there is an influence from the side of symbolic factors and values, that does not go far enough. The crucial extra point that has to be taken into account is that different factors were evidently at work among different Greek, and again among different Chinese, theorists. There is no uniformity in either Greek or Chinese zoological taxonomy after the first systematizers had begun to tackle the problem, for the solutions proposed reflected different styles of investigation directed to very different agendas. Thus where plants are concerned, there was an ongoing tension, both among Greeks and among Chinese, between those who sought a classification that reflected pharmacological effects, and those whose interests were in how the groups of plants could be fitted into comprehensive cosmological or natural philosophical schemata.[20]

The diachronic historical record suggests a rather more complex picture of the genesis of animal and plant classifications than that which emerges from the synchronic data from ethnography. Among the factors that are evidently in play are the following: first the terms that exist in the natural language (though they may not cover all the distinctions that were recognized: the *Huainanzi* does not have a word for 'animal' as such, and in Chinese the term *yang* (羊) was used for both sheep and goats). Secondly there are more or less traditional, more or less deep-rooted, uses of animals as symbols and stereotypes. Both these factors can be exemplified in large measure in the ethnographic reports. But history also adds documentary evidence concerning the contributions that individual investigators made, suggesting new ways

---

[20] In his two major botanical treatises Theophrastus is repeatedly concerned with whether he is dealing with varieties of a single species or with different species, and in particular whether the characteristics and properties of a species should be judged by investigating its members in the wild, or in their domesticated forms.

of organizing recognized groups and on occasion coining new terms to convey original perceptions reflecting their own enquiries.

The very fact that different taxonomies were proposed both in ancient Greece and in ancient China shows that in neither case were the ideas of those involved determined by their given natural language or by their particular culture. They were attempting, just as modern biologists attempt, to do justice to what research revealed on such questions as the methods of reproduction of different groups, their external morphology and, as time went on, their internal anatomy and so on. We cannot, even now, set out, we said, a definitive taxonomy of what is the case. But humans everywhere, we may believe, are capable of revising their assumptions and those of the society they belong to, even on such a sensitive issue as animal and plant kinds.

Animal and plant taxonomies provide, then, we may say, very good examples where neither the thesis of pure cultural relativism, nor that of cross-cultural universals, will do. The cultural relativist can point to the enormous actual diversity in such taxonomies reported from across the world, where the genera and species of animals that are identified generally correspond to certain cultural and ecological interests, as well as being used in symbolic systems when certain kinds of animals are used to convey assumed patterns in human characters and behaviour. Yet the positive outcome of Atran's work, especially, was to show that a wide range of similarities and differences is remarkably stable across most human populations. That finding, in my view, however, falls far short of demonstrating a cross-cultural implicit taxonomy, let alone one that tallies with the findings of modern biological research. Rather, to the contrary, what modern biology has shown is that both for animals and for plants no one definitive taxonomy is within reach. The phenomena are, as I put it, multidimensional. But that does not legitimate a purely relativist, Feyerabendian, claim that any classification is as good as any other. On the contrary, according to any given criterion, there will be more, and less, accurate classifications. It is rather on the prior question of which criterion, or set of them, to apply, that the ambition to give a definitive solution comes unstuck.

Since, as we said, there is no evidence, in this case, that our cognitive equipment as such varies in any significant way, to that extent a thesis concerning the psychic unity of humans is plausible enough, though the support for that general claim provided by this instance is quite meagre. Yet when we consider, not our potentiality to understand animals and plants, but the actual understandings reached, they vary to a remarkable degree.[21] In part these variations predictably reflect cultural, including linguistic, factors and on occasion ideological ones. Yet the historical record makes it abundantly clear, here as elsewhere, that views are subject to change, and common assumptions can come to be challenged and revised. As that process continues, indeed, in the very latest studies in microbiology, we come to learn that the phenomena that we have all along been struggling to comprehend are more complex, more open-ended, more multidimensional, than our predecessors of even a decade or so ago imagined.

---

[21] I shall be returning later, in Ch. 7, to the thorny question of how far animals are consistently viewed as belonging to a domain of *nature* as opposed to *culture*.

4

The Emotions

Up until the early 1970s, comparatively little work was done, in psychology at least, on the emotions. Since then they have been the subject of intensive study, by neuroscientists (such as Changeux), by developmental psychologists (such as Izard), by social anthropologists (such as Lutz or Rosaldo), by evolutionary psychologists (such as Tooby and Cosmides), by philosophers (such as Harré or Griffiths) and by linguists (such as Wierzbicka). Yet while there is general agreement on a number of fundamental points, such as that certain measurable neurophysiological and biochemical changes are broadly correlated with the emotions, very considerable confusion still exists including on what emotion is and how it should be defined.

Thus, in an influential handbook dating from a couple of decades ago (Izard, Kagan, and Zajonc 1984b), we find the following attempts to grasp what is essential about emotion. 'Human emotion is conceived to be a motivation-laden feeling resulting jointly from shifts in arousal and from the meaning attached to those arousal shifts' (Dienstbier 1984: 486). 'Emotion is seen as a sensory-feeling state that acts as a motivator, categorizer, and selector of perceptual and cognitive events and behaviors' (Moore, Underwood, and Rosenhan 1984: 464). 'Emotion is held to be a differentiated action set, often context bound, based on a specific information structure in memory' (Lang 1984: 222–3). Finally Schwartz and Trabasso (1984: 416) adapt Dahl's definition which was that emotion is an 'integrated unit . . . of experience consisting of (1) a distinctive perception; (2) an implicit wish and implied action (motive); and (3) a typical expression (facial and/or postural) that is species-specific (and in man also culturally adapted)' (Dahl 1979: 211).

None of the writers in that volume endorsed the extreme behaviourist view of John Watson according to which the dominant factors in emotion are a matter of profound changes in bodily mechanisms, especially the visceral and glandular systems (Watson 1931: chs. 7 and 8, esp 165), but several cited William James to the effect that emotion is 'a bodily sensation caused by some environmental event that is then consciously labeled' (e.g. Masters and Carlson 1984: 438). Most of the contributors agreed that the view taken on what emotion is has profound implications for the investigations subsequently carried out on its basis. Yet several backed off from committing themselves to a definite concept. Some argued that 'it may not be useful to debate the meaning of emotion' (Kagan 1984: 41), or that 'formal definitions may sometimes do more harm than good' (Izard, Kagan and Zajonc 1984a, 4) or otherwise resisted an attempt to give a unifying theoretical definition (Masters and Carlson 1984: 439 citing Skinner 1950). Subsequently some have denied that emotion is a useful concept for psychology. Griffiths, who took that negative view (Griffiths 1997: 14 ff.), argued that some emotional responses are socially constructed pretences, which he likened to socially constructed illnesses such as 'ghost possession' or 'the vapours'.

Radical disagreement continues on at least six fundamental issues (cf. Ekman and Davidson 1994; Griffiths 1997). First, are there certain basic emotions, and if so, which are they? Fear and anger are most frequently cited as prime candidates, but distress, surprise, guilt, shame, anxiety, contempt, and even joy and sadness figure in some, but are absent from other, lists (compare Izard 1977: 46 ff.; Panksepp 1982; Kagan 1984: 39; Campos and Barrett 1984: 229; Ortony, Clore, and Collins 1988: ch. 2; Changeux and Ricœur 2000: 113–17). Hume even thought that pride and humility are basic (cited by Kagan 1984: 47).

Second, and relatedly, should the emotions be viewed as distinct species, or do they form a continuum, with one emotion shading more or less smoothly into the next as in the spectrum of hues, though there is the further complication, in the emotions case, that they may be experienced not as singletons, but as bundles of more or less conflicting feelings (Ortony, Clore, and Collins 1988: 146)? Some would go further and treat the emotions in general as syndromes (Griffiths 1997: 45).

Third—the key question for developmental psychologists—do infants and young children experience emotion in the same way that adults do? That takes one fourthly to the elements of cognition in emotion (cf. Ortony, Clore, and Collins 1988): are emotions to be equated with, or reduced to, propositional attitudes? Fifth, and relatedly, there is the question of the role of emotion in the development of a moral sense.

Sixth, there is an issue that is frequently bypassed by the psychologists, though it is a principal concern both of social anthropologists and of linguists, namely how adequate or applicable English terminology is for the task of the study of emotion. The question of the universality of emotion can be distinguished from that of whether those recognized in English—or some of them at least—are universal. It has often been pointed out that concepts that figure prominently in some cultures' understanding of the emotions are not represented at all in normal English usage, though I have remarked before that not to have a word for a concept does not necessarily imply not having the concept. One important Japanese term for which we have no exact equivalent is *amae*, which Kagan (1984: 39) translates 'mutual interdependence', Wierzbicka (1999: 217) 'sweet dependence'. In Ifaluk the term *song* is used to register that a community norm has been violated (Lutz 1988: ch. 6, 155 ff.; cf. Wierzbicka 1999: 274, 287–8). *Naklik* in Utku Eskimo signifies wanting to nurture and protect (Kagan 1984: 39). Wierzbicka (1999: 3) pointed out that in Russian, German, and French there is no term that corresponds exactly to English 'emotion' and argued that the more promising candidate for a cross-cultural universal is 'feeling', even though 'feeling' covers many sensations in which there is no emotional component. Drinking a tepid drink does not necessarily give you a 'warm glow'. I shall be returning to Wierzbicka's universalist position later.

My tactics in this chapter will be to start at the biological end of the spectrum and from there move on to tackle some of the issues associated with cultural diversity. First, I should review some of the studies that have shown how certain elements of emotional experience are susceptible to physical, neurophysiological, or biochemical analysis. Neuroscientific data can be obtained, for example, via the use of positron emission tomography (PET scanning), functional magnetic resonance imaging (fMRI), magnetoencephalography (MEG), or electroencephalography (EEG) (Changeux 1985: 68, 163–4). These techniques can establish with some precision which parts of the brain are active (at least) in various types of mental, including emotional, experiences. Detailed investigations have been undertaken to describe the functions of the limbic system taken as a whole, and of the amygdala in particular (see Changeux 1985: fig. 37; Damasio 1994; 2000; LeDoux 1996). The findings are impressively specific and localized, though there is always the problem (to which I shall be returning) of *matching* what brain scans reveal with the subjective reports of the feelings experienced. Differences in the latter are not necessarily picked up on brain scans and conversely not everything that brain scans record correlates with specific modalities in the emotions reported. Nevertheless the information obtained, by such techniques, about an individual's reactions, is far greater than with such other tests as the measurement of heart-beat or of skin tension or resistance, or that of the concentration of cortisol in the urine (Izard, Kagan, and Zajonc 1984*a*: 1–2), although these too provide, to be sure, objective data that can be correlated, at points, with the self-reports of subjects.

A second type of evidence comes from the study of patients who have suffered brain lesions leading to disruptions in their behaviour. This goes back to the mid-nineteenth century. In 1848 there was the case of Phineas Gage, who had an iron bar go right through his brain, causing acute lesions to the frontal lobe. He survived but suffered from severe emotional disturbances and aphasia: the detailed report of this case by his doctor, J. M. Harlow, is reproduced with an introduction by Edgar Miller in Harlow (1993) (cf. Damasio 1994: chs. 1–2). Then in 1861 Paul Broca showed from a post-mortem examination of a patient who had suffered from aphasia that this had been caused by a lesion to the left frontal lobe (Changeux 1985: 19).

Third, the roles of specific chemical mediators and transmitters, such as acetylcholine, endogenous morphine, dopamine, adrenaline, noradrenaline, serotonin, are now reasonably well understood, as also are the effects of drugs that influence affect, such as amphetamines, barbiturates, and chlorpromazine (Changeux 1985: 114; Dienstbier 1984: 487). Using neurophysiological and biochemical interventions, researchers have been able artificially to induce in animals behaviour associated with certain emotions in humans. The implantation of an electrode in the brain of a rat has enabled it to trigger a 'pleasurable' experience for itself—which it repeats several hundred or even thousand times if allowed to do so (Olds and Milner 1954). Similarly the external manifestations (at least) of 'rage' have been artificially induced in cats (Hess 1964: ch. 2).

In the wake of Darwin (1872), fourthly, facial expressions have been studied both in humans and in animals (Ekman 1980; 1982), although Darwin thought that they were produced by mental states, while others have argued that they are the origins of mental states (Kagan 1984: 57). Expressions of aggression and of submission are usually particularly distinctive. Yet as Bateson (1990) and Hinde (1972; 1981) especially, have demonstrated, there are many intermediate expressions that are ambiguous, combining elements that belong to the 'aggression' register with others that suggest 'submission'. In such circumstances the animal is, as it were, hedging its bets. The message conveyed is open to interpretation and even, one might say, to negotiation, between the sender and the receiver.

But facial expressions may not only be ambiguous: they can be manipulated. We are swept along by the actor's convincing portrayal—of rage, or despair, or love. It has been shown (Chevalier-Skolnikoff 1982; Wiley 1983; Bond 1989) that some animals are capable of deceiving others, not just members of other species (their predators or their preys) but fellow-members of their own. Evidently the interpretation of facial expressions or other body language poses problems for those who would base decisions about their own behaviour on them.

The biological studies I have mentioned show that it is possible to make objective analyses of a wide range of emotional experiences. But as soon as we start dealing with the subjects' own reports of how they feel we enter a different territory, and have to pay attention to the very considerable diversity in the ways in which the emotions are described in different cultures. Michelle Zimbalist Rosaldo (1980) produced a much-cited study underlining the unfamiliar map of the passions among the Ilongot. Catherine Lutz (1988) is another anthropologist who has made a detailed study of terms for affects among the Ifaluk. As noted already, they use the term *song* to describe a reaction to the violation of a community norm. Again *fago* is a distinctive expression to convey a particular combination of compassion, love, and sadness. More controversially, Lutz argued that the Ifaluk did not distinguish between thinking and emotion, using *nunuwan* to refer to 'mental events ranging from what we consider thought to what we consider emotion' (Lutz 1988: 92, cf Wierzbicka 1999: 278).[1]

---

[1] Rosaldo (1984) similarly denied that the Ilongot drew a distinction between 'thinking' and 'feeling' as did Howell (1981) for the Chewong.

However, that Ifaluk term is interpreted very differently by Wierzbicka, the scholar who has undertaken one of the most comprehensive recent cross-cultural studies of a considerable range of natural languages, both comparatively exotic ones, such as Ifaluk, Ilongot, and Kayardild, and others closer to home, Russian, Polish, German, Spanish, and French. Wierzbicka's own position is an interestingly complex one in which she combines sensitivity to the variety in the vocabularies used in different languages to talk about the emotions, with a universalist thesis, namely that all emotions can be analysed in terms of what she calls the 'natural semantic metalanguage'. There are, she claims, shared universal concepts, the 'bedrock of cross-cultural understanding', that include feel, want, know, think, say, do, happen, good, and bad (Wierzbicka 1999: 34 ff., 273 ff.).

Thus, on the issue of the variety found, she undertakes a detailed analysis of the German term *Angst* (ibid. 123–67), charting the shifts in meaning in the last three centuries, and pointing out that it is far from the exact equivalent of the English 'anxiety', which has so often been used as its translation. Again, she calls attention to such items as the distinctive Russian term *toska*, which she glosses as meaning, roughly, 'melancholy-cum-yearning'. Yet even *toska* can be analysed or decomposed into its elements, using the natural semantic metalanguage. There its core component comes out as 'it is how one feels when one wants some things to happen and knows that they cannot happen' (ibid. 8 citing Wierzbicka 1992).

Now Lutz's understanding of the Ifaluk term *nunuwan* as both thought and emotion would be a counterexample to the universalist part of Wierzbicka's thesis. But having praised Lutz's fieldwork as careful and scrupulously presented, Wierzbicka says (1999: 278) that her data 'are compatible with a different analysis: namely that *nunuwan* means "think" rather than "think or feel" and that its frequent emotive connotations are due to context rather than to the word itself'. Meanwhile 'feeling' in Ifaluk is conveyed, according to Wierzbicka's reassessment of Lutz's reports, by *niferash*. This was glossed by Lutz herself in physical terms as 'insides', though she recognized that it can refer to psychological feelings as well as to physical ones. 'To say "my insides are bad" (*ye ngaw niferai*) may mean either that one is feeling physically bad or experiencing bad thoughts and emotions, or both' (Lutz 1988: 92; cf. Wierzbicka 1999: 277).

This dispute illustrates not just the diversity of emotional vocabulary but also the problems of interpretation that it poses. They are compounded by the fact that the lexicon may not be a reliable guide to the concepts recognized. Certainly the existence of lexical items may indicate the salience of certain concepts, but conversely the non-existence of the concept is not necessarily shown by the non-existence of a term for it. Yet Wierzbicka's universalist thesis is open to criticism first on the grounds that the core terminology of the shared universal concepts she identifies is less transparent than she allows, and secondly for the extreme reductiveness of the analyses she offers.

I am in no position to adjudicate between her and Lutz's interpretation of Ifaluk *nunuwan*. But Wierzbicka uses English to outline her universal concepts even while insisting that there are equivalents in every natural language. Yet two of her basic English concepts pose problems of translatability even within European languages which Wierzbicka is aware of, but whose importance she underestimates. The work of English 'want' is divided up between two (at least) Spanish expressions, namely *quiero* (which also means 'love') and *me hace falta* or *necesito* (I lack or need). Conversely one Spanish word for 'feel', *siento*, is used most often to express regret. Again the work of English 'know' is divided up between *savoir* and *connaître* in French and *saber* and *conocer* in Spanish. The trouble about 'good', 'bad', 'very good', and 'very bad', which have a key part to play in Wierzbicka's analyses of actions and events as well as thoughts and feelings, is rather different, namely that they are opaque, and their modalities (if not their valency) vary with context.

The explication of 'indignation' (Wierzbicka 1999: 90) will illustrate the first difficulty and also the second weakness of Wierzbicka's position, namely its reductiveness.[2] 'X felt indignation' is unpacked into nine components which she sets out as follows.

---

[2] Other difficulties come to light in the analysis of 'happiness' and 'shock' (Wierzbicka 1999: 53–4, 97). In 'happiness' the two key components are (d) 'I wanted things like this to happen,' and (e) 'I can't want anything else.' In (d) 'wanted' means 'desired' or 'liked', but if that is the sense of 'want' in (e), that seems too strong. For happiness is compatible with having other likes and desires besides the current experience. If it has the other sense of 'want' in English, namely 'lack' (have a deficit), that may be nearer the mark, but reveals the ambiguity of the English term that is treated as a key element in the core metalanguage. Where 'shock' is concerned, the problem is one of an apparent incompatibility. Here the elements include, 'I didn't think that something like this could happen' and 'I can't think now', the latter evidently in the sense that the person is at a loss. Yet if the experiencer cannot think, in any strict sense, then he or she is not in a position to have the thought

(a) X felt something because X thought something
(b)   sometimes a person thinks:
(c)   'I know now: someone did something bad
(d)   I didn't think that someone could do something like this
(e)   I don't want things like this to happen
(f)   I want to say what I think about this'
(g)   when this person thinks this, this person feels something bad
(h) X felt something like this
(i) because X thought something like this.

But at stage (c) it makes a considerable difference whether the 'something bad' that 'someone did' stems from an error or from malice, whether it was a misdemeanour, or unjust, or even vicious. Nor does the following component (d) ('I didn't think that someone could do something like this') resolve the indeterminacy and it seems, in any case, to limit the thinking to novel experiences. Yet we register indignation also at behaviour with which we are already familiar.

English is not the only language in which the resonances of the terms used to convey emotions and feelings are very rich, exhibiting what I call exceptional semantic stretch, resonances that are lost in the reductive translation to a supposedly basic universal language. Many nuances are indeed likely to be lost in any translation into another natural language, however sensitive that may be. On the other hand, it is not as if *no* comprehension is possible, as if *all* understanding is barred by the translation process. Wierzbicka is certainly right that intercultural understanding is possible, even though more difficult than her translation protocols into her universal language may suggest. Here, as in several of our other studies, we find that the thesis of cross-cultural universals tends to come unstuck in the face of the multidimensionality of the data—in this case the emotions and the diversity of the conceptual schemata that are used to map them.

Any ambition to construct a single universally valid metalanguage into which all human cognitive and affective experience can be parsed involves a massive idealization. The first problem is that it goes far beyond the possible biologically based justification for the analysis of certain human responses, and secondly it leaves out of account

that corresponds to the feeling of shock ('X felt something like this because X thought something like this').

how the child acquires new sensitivities—including moral ones—as it becomes incorporated into the group to which it belongs.

I mentioned at the start of this chapter some of the complexities of the underlying neurophysiological and biochemical processes to which common emotions such as fear and anger (at least) may be related. But how far is 'thinking' or 'feeling' revealed every time the brain-scan records activity? The problem is that the variety of the information those scans offer does not easily correlate in detail—beyond a very limited point—with the range of thoughts and feelings that the subject may describe.

If biology can provide some determinate answers to questions concerning the neurophysiology and biochemistry of emotional experience, there is still a shortfall between those findings and the varied concepts found in different natural languages to register those experiences. The processes of social incorporation have also to be factored in. An Ifaluk child will learn to talk about, to identify, and indeed to experience, *fago*, as the Russian child will do with *toska*. The precise modalities of those experiences will not be registered *as such* by the English-speaking child, even though they will certainly recognize compassion, love, and sadness and may even on occasion feel all of these together. Again, children learn what is acceptable behaviour in every society without necessarily using a term quite like Ifaluk *song* to express their reactions to what deviates from the norm. Neither the associations of the word 'naughty' in English, nor yet those of 'transgressive' or 'deviant', provide an exact equivalent, for the first suggests a childish peccadillo, while 'transgressive' and 'deviant' imply culpability and abnormality.

To draw on my own experience to illustrate the point further, my father's first language was Welsh, though in London, where I was brought up, we all spoke English at home. However, he introduced me early on to two Welsh terms for which no simple equivalent exists in English, namely *hiraeth* and *hwyl*. *Hiraeth* is the longing for Wales that exiles feel—and in many circumstances 'nostalgia' will do as a gloss, though most Welsh would deny they are simply nostalgic for their country. *Hwyl* is the inspiration that certain performers are recognized to possess, not always, but in some of their performances, where the reactions of the audiences are an important contributory factor. This is not just a matter of 'the gift of the gab', although it certainly includes that, but also one of the passionate conviction of the speaker in what he or she is saying.[3] Here I learnt the meaning of the term by first-hand experiences in chapel services, for example, though the performers who exhibit *hwyl* include poets and politicians as well as preachers. Both terms became a part of the idiolect I acquired—English with a smattering of Welsh for use within a closed group of family and Welsh friends.

In part the cultural diversity I have spoken of reflects the diversity in the values inculcated by the groups in question. It may be instructive, in this regard, to turn now to the historical evidence from ancient societies to review not just how different conceptual maps of the emotions were in play in ancient Greece and China, but also how these interrelated with value systems and were, indeed, subject to change as those values came to be challenged and modified.

Two distinct types of controversies surround the ancient Greeks' conceptual maps of the emotions.[4] First, ancient Greek writers themselves took very different views of many of the key questions—and this provides us with our opening for, among other things, a diachronic investigation of how that diversity arose. Second, the correct interpretation of those views is a matter of dispute among modern commentators. Some remarks on the second group of problems will serve to indicate the radical nature of some Greek attitudes.

One focus of scholarly controversy has been the correct interpretation of the view that is ascribed to certain Stoic philosophers in general, and to Chrysippus, the third head of the school, in particular, namely that we should eliminate the *pathe*. Some take that to be a recommendation to get rid of the passions, that is the extreme emotions. They point to the fact that certain feelings, such as joy, appear to be allowed. They are called *eupatheiai* (which we can gloss roughly as 'well-reasoned impulses') in our sources (Diogenes Laertius 7. 116), although whether that was a term the Stoics themselves

---

[3] A standard Welsh Dictionary (*Geiriadur Prifysgol Cymru*, Cardiff, 1987: ii. 1937–8) starts its four-column entry on *hwyl* with the concrete sense 'sail', leading next to 'journey, progress, revolution' and then to this: 'healthy physical or mental condition, good form, one's right senses, wits; tune (of musical instrument); temper, mood, frame of mind; nature, disposition; degree of success achieved in the execution of particular task, etc; fervour (especially religious), ecstasy, unction, gusto, zest; characteristic musical intonation or sing-song cadence formerly much in vogue in the perorations of the Welsh pulpit'.

[4] There is now an authoritative survey of the problems in Konstan (2006), who has drawn attention to particular differences between ancient Greek accounts of the *pathe* and the map of the emotions in English.

used is unclear.[5] But others have argued for a more radical line of interpretation, namely that Chrysippus recommended eliminating the feelings as a whole.

Pathos, in its most general sense, can refer to anything that happens to you. The cognate verb *pascho* means 'suffer' or 'undergo' in that general sense. Although not everything we undergo is negative, *pathos* was often used interchangeably with *nosos*, *nousos*, or *nosema*, for disease, where the Greeks, like ourselves, distinguished between physical and mental diseases, diseases of the body, and those of the soul, though again like ourselves they acknowledged a class of complaints where both body and soul were affected.

The association of the main general term for 'feelings' with diseases has far-reaching implications and immediately suggests a map of what we might call the 'emotions' that differs appreciably from our own. How those implications were worked out in Chrysippus' theory is particularly surprising. Clearly there would be nothing to take us aback in a policy to eliminate physical disease, though there the problem would be how that is to be achieved, for it certainly is not always within our power to do so. But Chrysippus' target is much wider. The *pathe* he wishes to extirpate are certain impulses (*hormai*). But all impulses imply assent. That means that the *pathe* do not just incorporate judgements (*kriseis*): they *are* judgements. Yet the kind of mistake they make is not a mere error of fact. Rather it implies a conation that is—temporarily at least—out of the control of reason. In principle, reason should arrive at true judgements. The *pathe* he suggests we should get rid of are disturbances when the rational faculty is not in total command. Indeed 'irrational' (*alogos*) enters into the definition of each of the four main species of *pathe* (distress, fear, appetite, and pleasure: Long and Sedley 1987: i. 411, 65B) as well as into that of *pathos* itself (ibid. 410–11, 65A).

The Stoics hold that the Sage would be in complete control. The Sage's judgements are never at fault: there is no question of the Sage being deceived. Where the ordinary human being might be in the grip of fear or anger—thinking that a harm had been done or was

---

[5] Long and Sedley (1987: ii. 407). *Sumpatheiai*, another term that might suggest a positive role for certain *pathe*, relates in the first instance to the resonances between physical objects (as in musical harmonics, or in referred pain) rather than to the fellow-feeling among human beings (as in our term 'sympathy'), although it is true that Zeno stated that we should regard all humans as our fellow citizens (ibid. i. 429, 67A1).

about to be suffered—the Sage knew that for one who is secure in virtue there is nothing to fear or to be angry about. The Sage is thus invulnerable to misfortune and immune to disturbance of any kind. Health, for instance, was not a good, only a 'preferred indifferent' and so physical disease did not count as an evil. So the Sage would not be concerned at its occurrence, nor upset at a failure to be restored to health. Where mental disturbances were concerned, the Sage's rational faculty ensured that there was no room for error, for false judgements, or any of those impulses that were liable to upset lesser humans.

The picture that emerges—the 'emotional keyboard' as such writers as Shweder (1985: 200) and Wierzbicka (1999: 31, 46) have called it—seems at first sight quite extreme and it is tempting to dismiss it as aberrant, the product of idiosyncratic speculations on the part of an isolated and quite unrepresentative group of intellectuals. Yet that would be a mistake. First, the Stoics were not the only ancient Greeks to advocate the repression of most of the experiences we associate with the emotions. Second, and more fundamentally, the view they adopted exploits, even if it goes further than, tendencies that are already present in the use of the generic term *pathos* in discourse about what we call the emotions.

One feature of Stoic psychology that is exceptional is their insistence on the unitary nature of the soul. For them the soul just is the rational faculty and wayward impulses have to be located within it, when we fall short of perfect rationality. Yet for many earlier Greek writers, and not just philosophers, disorder in the soul was interpreted primarily as a conflict between its several parts or faculties. In the *Republic* Plato developed arguments to distinguish the reasoning faculty (*logistikon*) from both the spirited (*thumoeides*) and the appetitive (*epithumetikon*) parts. Aristotle rejected that tripartition and identified a greater number of faculties of the soul, often with an emphasis on biological function. They included reason, locomotion, desire, perception, and most basically nutrition and reproduction. This was used to stratify living things in a kind of Scala Naturae. Humans have all those faculties, most other animals all but reason, while plants have nutrition and reproduction alone. In his ethical writings, however, for the purposes of his analysis of the virtues and of responsibility, Aristotle uses a simple dichotomy, between the rational and the irrational: the tension between those two is at the centre of his analysis of self-control. It is also worth noting that even in the more complete psychological theory in his *On the Soul*, the introduction of imagination, *phantasia*, complicates the picture. It is a separate faculty: yet it depends on perception and memory. Locomotion and desire, in turn, depend on it, for the animal uses imagination, the ability to have a mental representation, to set itself goals and so guide its movements.

Both Plato and Aristotle consider reason to be the supreme faculty with which humans are endowed. But the theory that the soul has three or even more parts means that reason has those other faculties to deal with. What it has to contend with is, however, construed rather differently by different writers. The notion of conflict within the soul is already strongly thematized in Homer. In a famous passage in the *Odyssey* (20. 17–18) (twice cited by Plato in the *Republic*, 390d and 441b) Odysseus, newly returned home to Ithaca, has to restrain himself when he sees the dissolute behaviour of the women in his palace. He has to stop himself from killing them on the spot. 'He struck his breast and thus reproved his heart: "Endure, heart, for you have endured worse than this, on the day when the shameless Cylops ate your brave comrades . . ." '

The Homeric epics have a rich vocabulary of terms to express psychic functions, many localized to physical parts of the body (as *kardie/kradie* and *etor* are to the heart, *phrenes* to the lungs) or to the blood or breath of the living body. We are left in no doubt as to the violent reactions that the heroes experience in the face of misfortune and especially shame. The *Iliad* as a whole is the story of Achilles' *menis*—his anger, fury, wrath—at the insult he receives from Agamemnon. When Agamemnon is forced to return his prize, Chryseis, to her father Chryses—for that is the only way, so the prophet Calchas tells him, in which Apollo will stop the plague that is afflicting the Achaian army—Agamemnon's reaction is to take Achilles' prize, Briseis, away from him—thereby causing Achilles' fury and withdrawal from the battle, triggering the events the epic describes. Yet there is no single term in Homer that is the equivalent to emotion, no single part of the body responsible for all and only what we would call emotional experiences. *Thumos*, associated in certain passages with breath and with life, is the seat of desire and appetite, but it is also where deliberation may occur (*Iliad* 1. 193) as well as pleasure (*Iliad* 7. 189). The entry in the Greek lexicon, Liddell-Scott-Jones, illustrates its range. It begins with the gloss 'soul, spirit, as the principle of life, feeling and thought, especially of strong feeling and passion', and goes on eventually to include 'breath', 'soul', 'desire', 'inclination', 'heart', 'mind', 'temper', and 'will' among the various subcategories it lists.

That term provides the root for the second of Plato's three psychic faculties, namely *thumoeides*. But this now becomes more specialized. In presenting his arguments for tripartition, he first contrasts reason with appetite, *epithumetikon*. But a third faculty has then to be introduced to account for the spirited part, one that is identical neither with the appetites (which indeed it often opposes) nor yet with reason (for it does not stem from the exercise of reason). An association with anger—as in Homer—remains, but the focus is now on the noble indignation a person feels when a wrong has been done (*Republic* 440cd) and with courage or manliness, *andreia* (Hobbs 2000). The spirited part comes to the aid of reason in the battle to control the appetites, seen as the potentially disruptive element in the psyche. It is important to note, however, that although the function of reason is deliberation, Plato acknowledges that reason has *its* pleasures, different from those enjoyed by the basic appetites for food, drink, and sex, and again from those of the spirited part, but pleasures nevertheless. The philosopher is, after all, the person who *loves* wisdom.

Plato thus produces a complex picture of the psyche which Aristotle forthwith criticizes and emends. He begins by rejecting Plato's view of the relation between the soul and the body, the one, according to Plato, an invisible, indeed immortal, substance, the other a visible, physical one. Aristotle says that it is absurd to ask whether the soul and body are one or not. That would be like asking whether the axe and the ability to chop are one or not. On his view the soul is the activity of the body, not a separate substance inhabiting it.

Introducing his own unified faculty of desire, Aristotle protests (*On the Soul* 432^{b}3 ff.) that that should not be broken up, as it would have to be on the assumption of Plato's tripartite soul. On that view wish would end up in the rational part, and appetite and spirit (for which Aristotle uses *epithumia* and *thumos* respectively) would be in the irrational. Whatever has perception experiences pleasure and pain, and whatever experiences pleasure and pain also experiences appetite, which is the desire for the pleasant. So, while desire may be for a variety of objects, it serves a crucial biological function throughout the animal kingdom, being the faculty that motivates the animal both in nutrition and in reproduction.

There is, of course, far more to the range of Greek psychological theories than this brief sketch indicates: in particular a more complete account would exploit the rich sources of information that treatises on rhetoric, from Aristotle's onwards, provide concerning how individual emotions and their interrelations were represented. But from the cross-cultural perspective I am interested in, three main features at least are clear. First, there is a negative point. We do not find in either the philosophers or other writers a clearly demarcated unified faculty of the emotions as such. Greek literature is full of graphic portrayals of heroes and heroines and just ordinary people gripped by passion and grappling with conflicting desires. Aristotle indeed famously considered the main function of tragedy, performed on stage, to be to rid the audience of the strong emotions, pity and fear, that they experienced as they saw the destinies of the characters on stage unfold. This secured what he called a purification, *katharsis*, of those feelings, where again in the background the medical analogy of purging (also *katharsis*) is clearly present and may be the dominant idea (cf. Lloyd 2003: 187 ff.). But if we take some concrete examples, Medea, slighted by her husband Jason, is overcome by the desire for revenge on him and kills her own children by him. Her *thumos* (passion), she says in Euripides' play (*Medea* 1079) overcomes her *bouleumata*, her wishes.[6] In the *Hippolytus*, Phaedra falls passionately in love with her stepson after whom the play is named, but when rejected by him, commits suicide, though not before accusing him falsely to her husband Theseus—and thereby causing Hippolytus' own eventual death. But as we have seen, the main generic term, in this context, namely *pathos*, may, in different contexts, cover far more than just the emotions or the feelings, comprising also physical and mental diseases and indeed sufferings of any type. So from that point of view, the Stoics, with whom I began, were not so much out of touch with common Greek sentiments as might at first sight appear.

But then the second feature that should be remarked is the variety of analyses that were produced. One might have imagined that, once reflection and analysis got under way in the philosophers and rhetoricians, the outcome would be simply to make explicit what was already implicit in the Greek language. In practice, however, that

---

[6] Quite how this verse is to be interpreted is the subject of some dispute (see e.g. Dihle 1977): but that Medea is expressing the internal conflict she suffers is clear.

was very far from being the case. Different theorists, as we have seen, proposed quite divergent views on the structure of the psyche and on the interrelations of its various functions and activities. The pluralists, such as Plato and Aristotle, distinguished separate parts or faculties—though that then left the problem of what united them—of what made Socrates Socrates and not just a bundle of disconnected capacities. The monists—such as the Stoics—postulated a single rational faculty with the consequent difficulty that I have mentioned of accounting for every kind of negative impulse as a disturbance of reason.

The third recurrent feature, in ancient Greek theorizing on this subject, is the mixture of the descriptive and the normative. The prime influence on the psychological theories the philosophers proposed often comes from their moral philosophy, though to be sure these two are generally interdependent. The accounts of the soul that were put forward did not just purport to say what is the case. They carried implications for how we should conduct ourselves. One point on which Plato and Aristotle were agreed was that reason should be in control. They saw happiness and the good life in positive terms, as the exercise of reason as the highest faculty that humans possess. But in the period after Aristotle most philosophers took a more defensive, if not negative, stance, describing the goal as freedom from anxiety, *ataraxia*. But on both positive and negative types of view the attainment of true welfare was liable to be threatened by the prospect of the desires or the appetites running amok. Even the Epicureans, for whom the good was identified with the pleasant, were careful to distinguish between desires that are natural and necessary (such as drinking when thirsty), those that are natural but not necessary (such as for expensive foods), and those that are neither natural nor necessary (illustrated by a desire for statues, Scholion to Key Doctrines 29; Long and Sedley 1987: i 116, 21I).[7]

For the Stoics, with their unified psychology, everything depended on good judgement. But for Plato and Aristotle quite how one faculty, reason, was to exercise control over another, whether the *epithumetikon* or Aristotle's *orexis*, desire, posed a problem. When Plato

---

[7] The example is interesting in view of the argument proposed by Frischer (1982) that the iconography of the statues of Epicurus and his followers served the purpose of propaganda for the school—to convey the idea of the tranquillity that adherence to his doctrines brought with it (cf. Zanker 1988 on Augustus).

represented the three parts of the soul with the image of the chariot team in the *Phaedrus* (254c), reason is pictured as the charioteer and the other two faculties as two horses, one good (the *thumoeides*) the other wayward (the *epithumetikon*). The vocabulary in which this human exercises control is—as Ferrari (1987: 185 ff.) showed—surprisingly violent. True, the situation envisaged is when a person is reminded of his beloved, a positive experience since it can lead to an appreciation of true beauty, but a threatening one since passions are aroused. The charioteer is described as pulling on the reins 'so violently that he brings both horses down on their haunches'. When the bad horse again exerts itself, in its expression of desire to have sex with the beloved, the driver's reaction is even more extreme. He 'jerks back the bit in the mouth of the wanton horse with an even stronger pull, bespatters his railing tongue and his jaws with blood and forcing him down on legs and haunches delivers him over to anguish'. Evidently reason here acts in anything but a cool, calm, and collected fashion. It matches force with force indeed.

In the similar image in the *Republic* (588c–e) reason is represented by a human, while the other two parts are imagined, the one as a lion, the other as a many-headed monster. Again the analogy works as a graphic representation of conflict, where one element is trying to control and needs to control the others: yet this is at the cost of a certain recursiveness. The desires have to be curbed, and this is the work of reason. But when the attempt is made to explain how one faculty can indeed interact with another quite distinct one, reason tends to be pictured in human terms. Conflict within the psyche is then represented on the analogy of conflict between humans and beasts. Many Greeks seem to have felt threatened by the wild animals they imagined inside their own souls.

If we turn now to our evidence for ancient Chinese thought, there is as much disagreement among Chinese writers on questions ranging from human nature and the correct attitude towards desires, to the ideal of the Sage, as there is on analogous issues among the Greeks. But none of the principal generic terms used to speak of the feelings in Chinese carries with it the potentially pejorative undertones of the Greek *pathos*, even though particular strong emotions were considered disorders that needed treatment in traditional Chinese medicine. Sivin (1987: 287 ff.) identifies seven of these, *xi* (喜, joy), *nu* (怒, anger), *you* (憂, sorrow), *si* (思, 'ratiocination', or worry), *bei* (悲, grief), *kong* (恐, apprehension), and *jing* (驚, fear or fright). Elsewhere we find fivefold classifications, often though not always associated with the notion of the five interacting phases, though it would be a mistake to suggest there was a single orthodoxy on the question. Joy, anger, fear, and sorrow figure in most accounts, but sometimes another term for 'grief', *ai* (哀) replaces *si*, 'worry'. In some more extended lists, love (*ai*, 愛), hate (*wu*, 惡) and desire (*yu*, 欲) are treated as coordinate with joy and anger.

One of the generic terms used, *zhi* (志, 'impulse'), puts the emphasis on conation and intention (in other contexts the term is rendered 'will'). But other terms also appear for feelings in general. *Qing* (情) is often used in connection with *xing* (性) to speak of humans' essential nature as a whole, but neither carries any pejorative undertones. No more does the pair *gan/ying* (感 應) used in many contexts (not just human ones) of stimulus and response. Quite the reverse valency appears in the positive overtones apparent in the use of the same graph, 樂, which read as *yue* means music, read as *le* means joy, and read as *yao* means to delight in. No Chinese philosopher presents a radically conflictual theory of a bi-, tri-, or multi-partite soul: no more do we find a stark dichotomy between soul and body conceived, as by Plato, as two distinct substances, the one invisible and destined for immortality, the other visible, the soul's prison.[8]

To be sure there are many writers who condemn excessive desires. In the third century BCE Xunzi, 8. 11, remarks that indulging the emotions or your inborn nature is a sign of the ordinary person, not behaviour to be admired. Yet in *Against the Twelve* (ch. 6) he criticizes each of two diametrically opposed attitudes, the one that gives free rein to the desires, and the second that represses them. He attacks Tuo Xiao and Wei Mou on the first score, and Tian Zhong (or Chen Zhong) and Shi Qiu as examples of the second tendency. Unfortunately their works

---

[8] In classical Chinese thought there are various notions of 'ghosts' (*gui* 鬼), and 'spirits' (*shen* 神), and of spiritual aspects of human beings (*hun* and *po*, sometimes combined in the binome *hunpo*, 魂魄) but while these are all the subject of concerned attention, they do not hold out hopes of immortal bliss. Some have argued that *hun* and *po* reflect dualist beliefs when, on separation from the body on death, *hun* goes to heaven and *po* to earth. But in a critical re-evaluation of the evidence, including that from grave stelai, Brashier (1996) cast doubt on this and pointed out that the departure of *hunpo* does not necessarily bring about death, and *hunpo* deficiency is associated with ill-health: cf. Lloyd (2005: 102, 162 n. 11 with further secondary references).

are not extant and so we have to rely on Xunzi and his commentators for their views. For Xunzi himself, human nature is inherently evil, by which he means that it requires education and acculturation (23. 1a). The emotions are an inescapable part of our inborn nature, shared by everyone from the 'mere gatekeeper' to the 'Son of Heaven', the Emperor (22. 5b). But they need to be rectified, he says at 8. 7. Even the Sage follows his desires and fulfils his emotions (21. 7d): having regulated them he is in tune with principles of order. This is a very different ideal from the Stoics' recommendation to extirpate the *pathe*, even though the wished-for end result, Sagehood, may look as if it were the same.

Similarly, in the great third century BCE cosmological synthesis, the *Lüshi chunqiu*, excessive emotions—here joy, anger, anxiety/sorrow, fear, grief—harm life (3/2/1). Yet heaven gave appetites and desires to humans, when it gave them life (2/3/1) and those that are essential are inherently self-limiting.

The Sage keeps these limits in good repair to make the desires stop at the right place: this is why when he acts he does not transgress the limits belonging to his essential nature (*qing*). Thus, the desire of the ear for the five sounds, of the eye for the five colours, and of the mouth for the five flavours, belongs to our essential nature. In regard to these three, the desires of the noble and base, the wise and stupid, the worthy and unworthy are as one.   (Knoblock and Riegel 2000: 84)

So far as those desires go, even Shennong and the Yellow Emperor are on a par with the tyrants Jie and Zhou—and so too, as a later chapter, 19/6/2, adds, are barbarians and Chinese. Not even the three Sage Kings could eliminate (*ge*, 革) their desires. The Sages selected those sounds, colours, and flavours that would benefit our natures (*xing*) and they rejected what might harm them (1/2/3). However, the vast majority of honoured and wealthy people of today are deluded in such matters and so their natures are damaged.

Similarly, a century or so later, *Huainanzi* remarks (ch. 1: 19a) that pleasure and anger can get in the way of the Dao, and sadness and joy upset virtue. Yet it is self-indulgence that causes the damage, rather than feelings and emotions in themselves. The Sage enjoys internal contentment (ch. 1: 20a, 21b–22a).

Most Chinese writers accept the emotions as part of human nature with equanimity. But in some the position is more ambivalent. The opening stanza of the *Dao De Jing* (Graham 1989: 219) famously begins, 'The Way that can be Way-ed is not the constant Way. The name that can be named is not the constant name. What has no name is the beginning of heaven and earth, what has a name is the mother of the myriad things.' There then follows the double recommendation: 'Therefore by constantly having no desire observe the sublimest in it, by constantly having desire observe where it tends. The two have the same source but different names. Call it the same, the "Dark". The darkest of the dark is the gate of the sublime in everything.' The paradox is that it seems that it is only by desiring that we can reach freedom from desire. The two have the same source but different names, but then what can be named is not the constant name and that must apply also to whatever it is that the last couplet enjoins us to 'call' the same, namely the 'Dark', whether that is the source of desiring and desirelessness, or that pair itself. The ideal is indeed one well beyond what we can hope to attain in ordinary experience and even well beyond what we can express in ordinary language. Yet, when it deals with the more mundane problem of government, the *Dao De Jing* (57) speaks of the Sage 'desiring not to desire' whereupon 'the people of themselves become simple like the uncarved block'. Evidently the idea is that the Sage governs thanks to the example he sets of transcending desire.

In the equally radical *qiwulun* chapter of *Zhuangzi* (2) both assertion and denial, stating that 'it is', or stating that 'it is not', are undermined: the Sage adopts, or relies on, viewpoints with no categorical commitment to them. Yet Zhuangzi is sometimes represented as accepting what happens with calm and equanimity. This is the case with the story that appears in *Zhuangzi* 18 (Graham 1989: 175–6), which describes his reactions to his wife's death. His friend Hui Shi comes to offer his condolences and finds Zhuangzi drumming on a pot and singing. That strikes Hui Shi as the epitome of shamefulness. But Zhuangzi replies: 'Not so. When she first died, do you suppose that I was able not to feel the loss?' He peered back into her beginnings; there was a time before there was a life . . . before there was shape . . . before there was *qi*. It was by the alteration of *qi* into shape and then into life that life came. 'Now once more altered she has gone over to death. This is to be companion with spring and autumn, summer and winter, in the procession of the four seasons. When someone was about to lie down and sleep in the greatest of mansions, I with my sobbing knew no better than to bewail her. The thought came to me that I was being uncomprehending towards destiny, so I stopped.'

As in the *Dao De Jing*, so too in *Zhuangzi*, the Sage practises 'no ado', *wu wei* (無 爲). But this is *ataraxia* of a different kind from that aimed at by Hellenistic Greek philosophers. For both Stoics and Epicureans the attainment of peace of mind is the end result of considerable philosophical application, including the realization of the equation of the good with virtue (in the Stoic view) or with pleasure (in the Epicurean). Even the Sceptics, for whom *ataraxia* supervenes on the discovery that there are no positive doctrines to be had concerning unseen reality or hidden causes, have to engage in the search—the *skepsis* from which they get their name—to get to that position. For the Daoist sage 'no ado' implies no such strenuous ratiocination or philosophical effort and is indeed incompatible with such. It is not just that the violent control of the desires, by reason, as in Plato's image of the chariot-team, is at odds with the Daoist ideal: the Sage achieves freedom from 'ado' of any kind.

It is perhaps particularly remarkable that in the dispute over whether human nature (*xing*) is inherently good (as Mencius held) or evil (as in Xunzi) or indeed indifferent between the two (the position of Gaozi reported by Mencius), it is common ground to all three positions that desires and feelings are part of that nature. I have mentioned Xunzi criticizing both those who tried to repress desires and those who advocated indulging them, but clearly holding himself that desires belong indeed to our inborn nature. Gaozi is said to have remarked (Graham 1989: 121) that 'eating and sexuality are from our nature' and internal, but righteousness (*yi*, 義) is external, a matter of relationships between one human and another.

That division did not satisfy Mencius. His counter was that human nature is intrinsically good and he based that claim on an appeal to the empathy that all humans feel towards other humans.

The reason why I say that all humans have a heart which feels for others is that supposing people see a child about to fall into a well they all have a heart which is shocked and sympathizes. It is not for the sake of being on good terms with the child's parents, it is not for the sake of winning praise from neighbours and friends, nor is it the case because they dislike the noise of it crying. Judging by this, without a heart which sympathizes you are not a human, without a heart aware of shame you are not a human, without a heart which defers to others you are not a human, without a heart which approves and condemns you are not a human.   (2 A 6; Graham 1989: 125–6, modified)

Even if we concentrate, as I have done, on some prominent Chinese writers in the period down to the end of the Han, there is considerable diversity in the views expressed on the feelings and emotions and on what our proper attitudes to them should be. As with the Greek evidence, attempts at global generalizations fall foul of that diversity. At the same time we may remark certain differences both in the focus of dispute in Greece and China, and in the range of positive recommendations that were made. *Xin* (心), for the Chinese, covers both heart and mind, and is the seat both of thoughts and of feelings. But this does not become the locus of philosophical disputes proposing a variety of analyses of the different parts or faculties of the soul, let alone suggesting alternative theories on the conflicts that arise within it.

Moreover, second, and relatedly, we do not find Chinese philosophers going as far as some Greek ones did in their advocacy of the need to stamp out the appetites. Many, as we have seen, warn against self-indulgence, and some were for repressing the emotions (as we discover from Xunzi's criticisms of Tian Zhong and Shi Qiu in particular). However, so far as our extant sources go, we have nothing to parallel Plato's paradoxical account of the violence that reason has to use to control violent emotions. Tian Zhong's position is just one end of the spectrum in which a diversity of opinions about the possible dangers of self-indulgence is expressed. But that was not in the name of the glorification of reason.

Third, and conversely, the association we find in Mencius, between human fellow-feeling and the sense of morality, goes further than any Greek philosophical text in recognizing the positive role of feelings as the source of goodness. The Greeks had their advocates of the common humanity of human beings, as potential citizens of the world, indeed. But that last was rather an abstract theoretical philosophical position which was in some tension with the perceived differences between Greeks and barbarians, free men and slaves. The Chinese too, to be sure, were also influenced by their perceptions of the distinctions between themselves and other folk (cf. Ch. 6 below). Yet Mencius, as we saw, builds on his understanding of common human feelings to suggest a basic goodness in all humans.

It is time now to take stock of our multifaceted enquiry. We have indeed learnt much, in recent years, from biology, and will no doubt discover a good deal more as research on the brain proceeds at an ever-increasing rate. Studies in developmental psychology, in social anthropology, and in linguistics have also made important advances. Yet these have often been orthogonal to one another. Nor can the results in these three areas be seen as complementing, or easily meshing with, those of the neurosciences. We are still some way away from a satisfactory synthesis on the question of the emotions. Nor shall I attempt one here, but rather limit myself to identifying some of the component factors that need to be taken into account.

Although, as just noted, so much remains obscure and disputed, certain biological universals are secure, as is also the fact of cultural diversity in the languages used to describe the emotions. Let me recapitulate these points before entering more controversial territory. Among the features that tell for our common humanity may be included the basic overall structure of our brains, for all our individual differences (cf. Ch. 2 above; Changeux 1985: 172, 202, 212), the normal functioning of our limbic system, and the effects of biochemical mediators and transmitters on those functions. That is to say there is no cause to postulate or suspect substantial differences in the properties and reactions of brains between different normal human populations that are alive today, nor should we suppose that our ancestors in historical times differed in radical ways from ourselves, even though everyone accepts that *homo sapiens sapiens* developed from earlier hominid species (Changeux 1985: ch. 8).

Then it is also obvious that human infants and young children all undergo processes of social incorporation and acculturation and that as they do so, they learn different things, and acquire different skills, depending upon the group into which they are integrated. All normal human children have the ability to acquire a language and obviously the actual languages they do acquire differ substantially, not least in the vocabulary available to describe feelings and emotions. But it is not just a vocabulary that a child will pick up. Keeping an eye on its mother's responses, it will learn which patterns of behaviour are acceptable, which not. It will come to register that some objects in its environment are alive, others not, some intentional agents and others not, even though there may be differences both in the stages at which those distinctions become well established and even (as we shall see in

Ch. 6) in how they are applied. Certain of the behaviour patterns that are learnt have neurophysiological correlates. Initially labile synapses become established (Changeux and Ricœur 2000: 112). The repetition of the behaviour confirms the connections, and a given stimulus is then more likely to produce the given response—not that such patterns become unavoidable in other than extreme, pathological, cases.

On the one hand, the plasticity of human cognitive structures allows for different patterns of development. On the other, which patterns will be developed differs between different groups. The question that then arises is whether or to what extent commonalities exist where the feelings and emotions are concerned. Are there *basic* emotions that are indeed universal, however much they may be masked by apparent divergences in the surface vocabulary used to describe them? The most favoured candidates—fear and aggression—correspond to what are believed to be part of our evolutionary inheritance. There is an obvious evolutionary advantage both in registering that a predator may attack, and in registering that a prey is there to be attacked. Those are feelings that humans will need in the struggle for survival in competition with other species of animals—a point that applies not just to individuals but also to groups. Tooby and Cosmides (1989, 1990, 1996), indeed, have argued, with some force and plausibility, that the development of the emotions in general, and of the sense of the need to cooperate with fellow members of the same species in particular, was crucial to the early evolution of human beings. It may well be that an expansion in the feelings registered and in their expression carried adaptive advantages for humans when dealing with co-specifics, not just other humans in the group to which an individual belonged, but also with others again in other groups.

But while in this context, too, the postulate of some basic cross-cultural universals seems justified, that does not take us very far. The potential range of sensitivities acquired by the growing child in *any* group far outstrips what it will need—or its ancestors would have needed—merely for survival. The commonality here is that it will become socially incorporated—but the modalities of its acculturation will vary with the society or the group in question. The influence of the natural language it first acquires is hugely pervasive—indeed we can detect traces of that in the ways in which even some quite sophisticated researchers in this field sometimes seem unduly swayed by particular features of the English language. But depending on where the child is brought up, it will not just pick up the vocabulary for certain emotions (such as fear and anger)[9] that it may register even before the acquisition of language, but also learn about 'guilt' and 'shame' and 'sadness', not to speak of *toska, song,* and *hwyl*. It will learn, too, about the body language of its culture, not just facial expressions that have been claimed to be well recognized across the world as signals of particular emotions,[10] but also those that are culture-specific. Those brought up in England, if they are unwary, may think of laughter as always expressing joy—until they travel to Japan and find that it may also indicate embarrassment.

Reference to ancient attitudes and terminology may serve a double purpose in our inquiry. First, like the fieldwork of contemporary anthropologists, it helps us to appreciate the possibility of alternative maps of the emotions, not just including those we easily recognize, but some that enlarge our conception of the possible world of the emotions themselves. In so far as we are able to arrive at an approximate understanding of the ideas in question, it reassures us that our understanding is not totally constrained by what is available in our own natural language, even though we have, of course, eventually to give some gloss to our comprehension of others' complex vocabularies using our, native, terminology.

Second, there is a particular advantage in the study of complex ancient civilizations that is not always mirrored in modern anthropology. This lies in the point I have insisted on for both ancient Greece and ancient China, namely that each society developed a range of different ideas—including some sophisticated explicit theories—concerning the emotions and advocated different policies about how to cope with them. The very fact of this diversity, within ancient Greek and within ancient Chinese, shows that *they* were not prisoners of their natural languages either, any more than we are of English.

By that I do not mean to deny that the basic vocabulary common to all the writers we can consult carries overtones and undertones,

---

[9] It is striking that Wierzbicka, who holds to the possibility of a natural semantic metalanguage, argues against 'fear' and 'anger' as such being cross-cultural universals, Wierzbicka (1999: ch. 7.)

[10] One of the most enthusiastic proponents for the thesis of universals in facial expressions is Paul Ekman (1980; 1982) though his work has attracted sharp criticism in particular for assuming that facial displays express discrete emotional states—the problem of how emotional states are to be individuated that I mentioned before (Fridlund 1997: 104; cf. Wierzbicka 1999: 172).

as *pathos* did for the Greeks, and *qing* and *xing* for the Chinese. Rather the point is that neither the Greeks nor the Chinese were limited to a single view of the emotions by their language or their culture. If human children have a certain plasticity and can learn about the emotions and their evaluation from the adults and the other children by whom they are surrounded, human adults enjoy a similar capacity for growth, and can modify and transcend received opinions, even those that are deeply entrenched in the cultures to which they primarily belong. After all, my whole study here of the emotions is predicated on the assumption that, using the English language but guarding against the influences on our analysis it may exert, it is still possible to express and explore widely divergent points of view about the emotions.

From what points of view, I may now ask in conclusion, are emotions a given, and from what others are they socially constructed? How should we adjudicate the strengths and weaknesses of the universalist and cultural-relativist positions? The urge to treat those two as mutually exclusive and exhaustive, and to plump for one while rejecting the other, should be resisted.[11] Some of those who have argued on other than purely biological grounds that there are clear-cut universals underlying the diversity of emotional vocabularies seem guided by their a priori assumption of the psychic unity of humankind. Those who insist on the diversity through and through, ignoring some of the findings of the neuroscientists and evolutionary psychologists, seem intent on resisting the potentially ethnocentric tendencies in the constitution of those 'universals'. It goes without saying that such ideological considerations, on the one side or on the other, militate against a measured cross-disciplinary study of the phenomena.

Both biology on the one hand, and social anthropology and linguistics on the other, have much to contribute to our understanding of this complex domain. We must certainly pay due attention to the immense diversity of the maps of the emotions that are attested in different

---

[11] Mallon and Stich (2000) somewhat optimistically develop an argument to reconcile the social constructivist, and the universalist, views of emotion by way of diagnosing a confusion in the meanings and references of emotion terms. The social constructivist relies on a 'thick' description of 'fear', for example, encompassing antecedent conditions, as well as culturally learned responses, and insists that this varies from culture to culture, while the universalist, on a narrow view of the reference of 'fear' as what Mallon and Stich relabel 'core fear', can concede some variety but counter that there is still a universal emotion prototype.

societies, ancient and modern, and in different languages. We can and should expand our own understanding of the subject by studying how other people in other places and at other times have behaved and what they have had to say about their feelings. Attempts to whittle down all that cultural diversity and reduce it to a set of basic, supposedly universal, emotions have so far failed to produce a consensus on what these are, and that is before we come to the weaknesses I identified in the bid to force a 'natural semantic metalanguage' to capture what is essential to each and every complex emotion or set of them. Besides, the very variety of the neurophysiological patterns that are revealed by brain scans strongly suggests that, at a certain level, our 'experiences' are more diverse than any natural language can, or would want to, express.

True, the open-endedness of the map of the emotions may be all very well, but children have to learn how to behave. They have to be given clear signals and learn to send clear ones themselves, while learning also, as senders and receivers, about ambiguous ones and their usefulness too. But if so, the socially constructed elements in those maps should be seen as serving, precisely, social and cultural purposes. They hand on the norms and values of the group in question. On the other side, some of the 'given' elements in this field are the result of biological analysis, and yet 'given' only in the sense that they are what neurophysiology and biochemistry inform us about. This does not help the universalist as much as many might suppose. Matching brain scans with subjective experiences reveals gaps where the impressionistic, even if not necessarily culturally determined, qualitative language we have to use for those experiences does not capture *all* the information that the scans provide: nor conversely do the scans necessarily pick up the precise modalities of the complex subjective response. The cultural relativists take as their starting-point the reported diversity in the vocabularies used to express feelings, but should not ignore both the inter-translatability of parts at least of those vocabularies and the common biology that underpins them.

We are faced here too, as in several of our other studies, with the multidimensionality of the phenomena. The realist taxonomist seeks a universal solution to the problems of classification, carving nature, as Plato put it, at the joints. But there is no single discourse that should have precedence over all others. What we need are different types and levels of analysis allowing indeed that at some points they may be difficult to reconcile as they may relate to different facets of those multidimensional phenomena. The vocabularies of the emotions are deeply embedded in cultures, and the divergences across cultures reflect not just (obviously) differences between different natural languages, but also different focuses of attention, different saliences, corresponding more or less closely to differences in the norms and expectations of each society. Yet the emotions so labelled are never merely arbitrary. They are never purely imaginary. Most languages have direct enough ways of expressing the responses that evolutionary biology suggests to be essential. But as the experience of actors on the stage imitating the emotions shows, beyond a certain limited point, correlations between biology and subjective feelings will break down. In particular the values that the subject registers when he or she registers a complex emotion cannot be expected to show up as such either in the data of neurophysiology or in those that relate to the biochemical processes that he or she is undergoing. Yet it has to be by making the most of the various styles of investigation that we can undertake that we can hope to get clearer on a subject that is so obviously important in education, in morality, in interpersonal relations, and for our personal well-being. It is to well-being that I turn for my next enquiry.

5

Health and Well-Being

A BROAD distinction between 'disease' and 'illness' has long been accepted as a useful analytic tool, at least as a first approximation, to distinguish between the objectively determined biomedical condition (disease) and the subjective feeling ('I don't feel well') (illness). How far that is applicable in the absence of reliable biomedical diagnoses is problematic. But further difficulties arise in the use of the pair of terms that seem, on the face of it, to be the straightforward antonyms of 'disease' and 'illness', namely 'health' and 'well-being'. I have my reservations on that score. It would assign 'well-being' to the domain of subjectivity, and that may not be difficult to accept.[1] But is 'health' merely a matter of the absence of any recognizable biomedical complaint? On one, minimalist, view, that is the case. But following the lead of the World Health Organisation, Black's *Medical Dictionary* in its 41st edition (Marcovitch 2005: 317) puts it that 'the state of health implies much more than freedom from disease, and good health may be defined as the attainment and maintenance of the highest state of mental and bodily vigour of which any given individual is capable'.

That sets the stage for my investigation here. What are the boundaries between the objective and the subjective, and again between the cross-culturally universal and the culturally relative, in this area? How do those two oppositions relate to one another, for they surely do not exactly coincide? In particular, are there commonalities in human perception and understanding about health and well-being that we can trace across cultures, or are different societies' attitudes and views

---

[1] However, Diener and Suh (2000a) attempt to *measure* subjective well-being and indeed to do so across cultures to compare their contrasting 'qualities of life', although they underestimate, as it seems to me, the problems that any such project poses. I have already criticized Wierzbicka's natural semantic metalanguage for treating 'well' as a transparent concept, and two of Diener and Suh's own collaborators, Kitayama and Markus (2000), insist that both 'well' and 'being' are culturally relative terms.

irredeemably society-specific? If disease is the purview of biomedicine, then health, on the minimalist view I cited, will also be. But if the wider definition of health is entertained, there will be a case for saying that notions of health are to that extent socially constructed, though those notions will generally have one feature in common, namely a positive evaluation.

As for well-being, my argument will be that although it is up to the individual to register whether they feel well or ill, they will do so in the light of the assumptions and values of the society to which they belong, or to some sub-group within it. Yet while the specific values adopted certainly vary as between one society and another, all societies have some notion of values, about what is to be preferred or is beneficial and their opposites, and those ideas correlate closely with the conception of well-being that is entertained. That conception may play a crucial role, indeed, in one respect, in connection with the notion of values in general. At least we shall see that in both ancient Greece and ancient China, the idea of the *objectivity* of values drew heavily on an argument based on the analogy of the presumed objectivity of health and disease. How far we can dispense with the notion of well-being with the advance of biomedical understanding of disease is a question I shall tackle in conclusion, where I shall argue that such a notion still has an important part to play, both in general and in relation to those areas where biomedicine is still not able to provide adequate answers. Even when being well or ill is recognized to belong to the realm of the subjective, there is a difference between their mode of subjectivity and that, for example, of pain. The subject's experience of pain is not liable to contradiction, as Ryle (1954: ch. 4) pointed out long ago. Even when someone accuses someone else of merely imagining a pain, the imagined pain is still experienced as a pain (unless, of course, the subject is misreporting his or her experience wilfully or otherwise). But where illness is concerned, someone who is accepted as knowledgeable in the field may contradict the patient who reports not feeling well and indeed persuade them that they are in fact mistaken. The verdict that 'there is nothing the matter with you', backed, it may be, by sufficient *auctoritas*, real or perceived, may be enough for the patient instantly to feel better, though of course that is not always the case. Conversely, medical authorities may move in to diagnose not just a physical disease, but madness of some degree of severity, where the patient is normally in an even weaker position to contradict an 'expert' opinion.

Not every society possesses experts in the field. It is worth rehearsing some of the findings of medical anthropology in order to remind ourselves of the differences that exist in the ways in which different societies cope with illness and understand its origins and causation. Gilbert Lewis' (1975) account of illness in a Sepik society, the Gnau, is exemplary and his reports are all the more authoritative since he could compare what the Gnau said and did with what his own professional training as a qualified Western medical practitioner told him about the patients concerned.

The Gnau have no medical experts. It is up to the sick person to decide that they feel ill. They generally indicate this by stripping, covering themselves with ash and withdrawing from human company, usually at the back of the hut. Of course their friends and relatives are concerned to try to help. When a major ritual is called for, to counter the influence of an angry or malign spirit, this is carried out by the village as a whole, and the patient registers the group's support. But there are no health professionals, no self-styled doctors or specialist healers, who take charge of the diagnosis of the patient and are then responsible for treatment. To a large extent, the patients decide their own treatments: when they feel better, they have a wash, get dressed, and rejoin society.

Plenty of ideas are, however, on offer as to what went wrong. That can be a comparatively simple matter. The patient sprained an ankle and that was all there was to it, or ate something that disagreed with him or her. Plenty of conditions are not explained by being assigned a cause (ibid. 293). But often spirits are implicated. Lewis (ibid. 244) notes that there is plenty of variety in the accounts that may be offered and he remarks on the mismatch between the Gnau's accounts of causes and those he associated with the complaints in question. Thus first, a given spirit cause is not linked to a particular clinical kind of illness. A spirit called Malyi, for instance, was invoked as cause in different cases where Lewis diagnosed renal failure, arthritis, and pneumonia. Conversely, a given clinical condition does not imply a specific kind of cause. Lewis encountered some twenty-five cases of pneumonia which were assigned to some ten different types of cause. Third, a given clinical condition may be attributed to a variety of causes. Different explanations were given for one old man's pneumonia and they proliferated as his condition deteriorated. Similarly, if a case ends fatally, that often sparks retrospective revision of who or what was to blame. Indeed illness in general often leads the Gnau (as Lewis points out, ibid. 247) to reconsider recent events, activities, and social relations with a heightened awareness that features of them may have been missed. They are on the look-out for clues as to what may have gone wrong or which spirit may have been at work and they may revise their view of events in the light of the illness that later occurred.

When we compare the situation Lewis described among the Gnau with the evidence for our two ancient societies of Greece and China, two points immediately stand out. First, both ancient societies had what we may call health-care specialists or 'doctors', indeed, as we shall see, both had several different categories of these. None had legally recognized qualifications, such as exist for modern biomedical practitioners, who receive licences to practise only after they have finished their training in approved medical schools. But they had clearly defined roles in treating the sick and were marked out from other lay people by their—supposed—greater knowledge and skill, certainly their greater experience in the matter. Second, in both ancient societies some such specialists at least (not all) moved away from any assumption that sickness was brought about by spirits or demonic forces or could be cured by prayer or ritual alone.

Let me now go over some of the key features of the notions of health and well-being so far as ancient Greece goes. There the problem was not so much a lack of experts in health matters, as a proliferation of them, working with very different concepts of disease and its causation and accordingly with very different styles of care and treatment.[2] The idea that the gods are at work, both in bringing about diseases and in curing them, was deeply entrenched and indeed remained so until the end of pagan antiquity. But that general notion came in many different forms, and was subject to explicit attack from those who denied that personal gods have anything to do with disease or health and who asserted that all diseases have natural causes.

Sometimes diseases were represented as sent by gods as punishment for human wrongdoing, one's own or even, maybe, one's ancestors'.

---

[2] That applies to the diagnosis and therapy of physical diseases, and the problem is substantially greater where the understanding of madness and its treatment is concerned: see further below.

In the *Works and Days* 225–47, Hesiod contrasts the just with the unjust city and claims that Zeus brings famine and plague down from heaven on the latter. Elsewhere (*Works* 100 ff.), his picture is rather that of quasi-personified diseases roaming at random among humans and striking them arbitrarily. The best-known text in the whole of Greek literature, the *Iliad*, opens with Apollo sending the plague on the Achaians in response to a request from his priest, Chryses. The Achaians had taken his daughter captive and refused to accept the ransom he had offered. Now Chryses prays Apollo to punish them in return for all the sacrifices he has made and temples he has built for the god. There the operative 'diagnosis'—to identify which god is harming the Achaians and why—is in the hands of a prophet, Calchas (cf. Lloyd 2003: ch. 2).

Poetry is just poetry, for sure, though its influence on ordinary people's perceptions can be far-reaching. But we have evidence from archaeology that establishes the existence, from the eighth century BCE at least, of shrines dedicated to local gods or heroes to whom particular powers of healing were ascribed.[3] Similar cults are common throughout the ancient Mediterranean—let alone across the world—and call for no special explanation. Even in societies that can call on the most advanced biomedical techniques today, prayer continues to appeal to many as a source of comfort in the face of disease, and people still make great efforts, including travelling great distances in pain and discomfort, to show their devotion to a particular saint and pin their hopes for a recovery on the healing powers claimed at some shrine.

But two features of fifth-century BCE Greece are exceptional. First, there is the growth of the cult of Asclepius across the Greek-speaking world. It became an international, that is an inter-state, phenomenon almost as important, in its way, as the Delphic oracle, and perhaps like it, reflecting a new sense of Hellenic unity in that century in the wake of the threat posed by the Persian wars.[4] By the end of that century shrines to Asclepius were flourishing, at Epidaurus, at Cos and elsewhere. His cult appears to have been introduced at Athens—thanks

---

[3] The cases dealt with at the shrines were far from limited to those where the patient's psychological states were concerned. They range across the gamut of diseases and illnesses both physical and mental and indeed the shrines were also consulted in other types of cases of misfortune, such as the loss of treasure or a child.

[4] Not all Greek cities chose to resist the Persians, however: indeed many fought on the Persian side in those wars.

in part to the sponsorship of the playwright Sophocles no less—around 420 BCE and some have connected its popularity there with the despair engendered by the plague that struck the city first in 429. But caution on that score is necessary. Thucydides' contemporary report (2. 47) emphasizes that those who were taken to the temples and pinned their hopes on the gods were no better off than those who relied on lay medicine. Neither style of treatment produced any results. Thucydides' scepticism was, no doubt, exceptional. We simply do not know whether it was because of their misfortunes in the plague, or despite them, that his fellow Athenians decided to introduce the cult of Asclepius.

That takes me to the second more exceptional feature, the rise, precisely, of naturalistic medicine, it too a development of the fifth century BCE especially. Three points in particular need to be taken into account to get this into proper perspective. First, not all naturalistic doctors were antagonistic to every style of appeal to the gods. Asclepius and Apollo himself are invoked in the *Oath* in the Hippocratic Corpus as the patrons of medicine, although we should not imagine that all the doctors represented in that Corpus signed up to the provisions of that oath. Furthermore we find prayer recommended in some other treatises. In an otherwise naturalistic discussion of dreams, *On Regimen*, for instance, discusses which deities should be prayed to in which circumstances.

There were, however, secondly, explicit polemics against some assumptions of divine intervention. The most famous is in the treatise *On the Sacred Disease*, but this attacks not the work of the well-established shrines of Asclepius, so much as the practices of 'purifiers' whom we also hear about from Plato, individuals who went from door to door selling charms and incantations. *On the Sacred Disease* heaps abuse on these characters, labelling them 'magicians', 'quacks', and 'charlatans'. They have no basis for their claim to be able to diagnose which deity is responsible for which variety of the 'sacred disease'—or epileptic fit—let alone for their pretensions to be able to produce the corresponding cures by way of a combination of prayer and abstention from bathing or from certain foods. We do not know what the 'purifiers' might have said in their own defence, but we do have inscriptional evidence from the shrines of Asclepius at Epidaurus and elsewhere that displays an unshaken confidence in the ability of the god to deliver cures and perform other miraculous feats such as finding lost children or mislaid treasures. The inscriptions proclaim a 100 per cent record of success—provided the patients showed due piety towards the god and paid their dues. If they did not, indeed, the inscriptions suggest the god is just as capable of inflicting disease as Apollo had been in the *Iliad*.

The third key point is that the pluralism of Greek medicine in the fifth century BCE and later encompasses not just those who asserted, and those who denied, the efficacy of divine intervention, but several different styles of practice on either side. In addition to the doctors represented in the Hippocratic Corpus, we hear of 'root-cutters', 'drug-sellers', and those who were usually named *maiai* by the male writers who constitute our chief source. This is conventionally translated 'midwives' but these women were undoubtedly called in to deal with women's complaints other than those associated with childbirth. Moreover, we learn from inscriptional evidence of women healers who were highly respected and successful. One named Antiochis was officially congratulated by the Council and people of her home town, Tlos, in the late first century BCE, for her skill in the medical art and set up a statue to commemorate being thus honoured (Flemming 2000: 391).

Positivist histories of medicine have been keen to see the naturalistic trends we find in classical Greek texts as forerunners, even anticipations, of modern biomedicine. But from several points of view that would be quite mistaken. First, the ancient doctors were generally in no position to identify the pathogens of the diseases, especially the acute diseases, they were faced with. There was no shortage of theories about the assumed causes at work. Many saw the 'humours' as chiefly responsible. But there was no orthodoxy about humour theory in the classical period, neither about which humours are the important ones, nor indeed on whether the humours were the causes of diseases, or signs of them, or indeed just their products. Other theorists identified elements such as earth, water, air, and fire, or powers such as hot, cold, wet, and dry, as the responsible factors. Alternatively acute diseases were classified by their observed periodicities, as quartans, tertians, semi-tertians and so on, a classification that could be made exhaustive by the addition of a default or residual category, namely those of 'irregular' fevers. Again with regard to mental disease or madness, all that the naturalistic doctors agreed on was that they too had naturalistic causes, but how the usual physical ones were to account for psychological symptoms was a matter of pure speculation.

Second, as regards therapies, the record is very mixed. We may distinguish first, surgical from other interventions. The treatment of fractures and dislocations described in the Hippocratic treatises has been praised. According to some Greek writers themselves, their surgical practices were much milder than those of, for instance, the Egyptians. That was a claim that Herodotus (3. 129–30) makes concerning Democedes' treatment of the Persian king, Darius. Yet the evidence of those treatises shows that some practitioners used drastic procedures, strapping the patient upside down on a ladder and 'succussing' them (bouncing them up and down) a treatment used astonishingly in cases of difficult childbirth as well as for dislocations.[5] In general pathology the chief remedies were, in order of severity, the control of diet and regimen, the use of herbal and mineral drugs, venesection and cautery. But many of the Hippocratic writers speak honestly of their own helplessness in the face of difficult cases: many warn their colleagues against dangerous remedies and sometimes they accuse them of using the more spectacular surgical interventions just for show.

The topic of analgesics can be used to illustrate the problem of assessing the efficacy of most of the treatments described. The sedative effects of opium may well have been known already in the third millennium BCE in Sumeria, although the point has been disputed. The opium poppy is duly included among the plants used as pain-killers in Greek medical texts from the fifth century BCE onwards. But the first difficulty of evaluating this evidence stems from that of identifying the plant species in question (cf. Raven 2000). As Theophrastus, among others, makes clear, the same Greek term was sometimes used of quite different plants, and the converse problem, of a single species being known by widely different names, is a recurrent motif in Dioscorides, the chief first-century CE writer on materia medica. One example of the first type is the name *struchnos*, used of three different plants, according to Theophrastus (*History of Plants*, 7. 15; 9. 11), one a

---

[5] Drastic remedies are especially common in dealing with those deemed to be mad. Those reported in our sources include chaining patients up, starving them, keeping them in the dark, and flogging them. It is true that some doctors criticized these, especially among the so-called Methodists of late antiquity. But some of them too endorsed physical restraint, venesection, and the use of rapidly dripping water (purportedly to induce sleep), even though in principle they favoured milder treatments, such as massage, warm fomentations, listening to music, or getting the patient to fall in love (Caelius Aurelianus, *On Chronic Diseases* 1. 144 ff., 158 ff., 171 ff., see further Lloyd 1987: 25–6).

foodstuff, another a sedative, and the third a poison capable of giving a person delusions. Although Theophrastus gives brief descriptions of these three, his accounts are indeterminate and their identifications remain controversial (Lloyd 2002: 111).

Then the second difficulty relates to the Greek penchant for poly-pharmacy. Many plants were used in combination—one particularly famous remedy called 'theriac', the subject of a treatise by Galen, could consist of anything up to 400 different ingredients. That contributed to obscuring the question of which plant possessed which prop-erty. Among the pain-killers, a plant named *huoscuamos* (probably henbane) was often used in conjunction with one called *mandragoras* ('mandrake': sometimes the description tallies with atropa belladonna). Plants of both these families contain certain tropane alkaloids, atropine, hyoscyamine, scopolamine, in various degrees of concentration, but it has been suggested that the analgesic properties belonged rather to *huoscuamos*, even though 'mandrake' also acquired that reputation (Lloyd 1983: 132 sets out the evidence).

Finally there was always the problem of the individual patient's reaction to the drug. Greek medical writers were in fact very conscious of the need to take the patient's age and constitution into account, often warning against the use of strong purgatives, for instance, for certain classes of patient, pregnant women, children, the old. Here, as elsewhere throughout their medical practice, everything depended on the individual doctor's judgement, based on his clinical experience rather than on anything like scientifically controlled experiments.

Up to a point at least we can follow and trace the efforts of ancient Greek doctors both in the matter of determining the effects of drugs and more generally in their attempts to anticipate the courses or likely outcomes of particular types of diseases. In the first area we have some exceptional evidence not of scientifically controlled experiments, to be sure, but certainly of deliberate tests. Mithridates II is reported to have tried out a variety of poisons on human subjects, criminals in his prisons.[6] This was in connection with a programme whose aim was purely egocentric—to establish what a 'safe' dose of each drug was so that he could build up his own immunity to it and so protect himself against any plot to poison him. But this is not the only case in Graeco-Roman antiquity where human subjects were treated as

[6] See Galen K xiv. 2. 3 ff. and cf. Pliny, *Natural History* 25. 5 ff.

expendable for purposes of 'research'. The best-known case is that of the practice of human vivisection by Herophilus and Erasistratus in Alexandria—though that was to discover relevant anatomical and physiological data that the proponents of such procedures claimed would be relevant to medical practice and could be used to save lives.[7] That end was supposed to justify those means—an argument that has had gruesome echoes in modern times.

In general, however, the process of acquiring knowledge of drugs and poisons was haphazard and unsystematic. There was no reliable, standardized, way in which a doctor could record and pass on the information he had gained in his own clinical practice. Such knowledge was handed on largely by word of mouth, although the subject was discussed, as we have noted, both by natural philosophers such as Theophrastus, and by doctors such as Dioscorides. The accounts of the effects of drugs that we have in our written sources all suffer from the indeterminacies I have mentioned, starting with the problem of identifying the plants in question, and including also vagueness in the accounts of how to collect and prepare the drug and even the lack of standardization of weights and measures. The root-cutters were often secretive and they surrounded their procedures with myths and rituals. Theophrastus often expresses his doubts as to whether to believe their stories about the precautions needed to be taken when collecting poisonous plants, though he is clear in rejecting some of them as what he called pure 'superstition' (Lloyd 1983: 122–6, 129–30). Yet no one was ignorant of the lethal effects of *koneion*, hemlock, for instance. That was the drug used to execute Socrates when he was condemned to death by the Athenians in 399 BCE: according to Plato's *Phaedo* 117b, when Socrates asked whether he might make a libation with some of the drug, the jailor replied that he had prepared no more of it than he judged to be the right dose.

It is in relation to attempts to chart the course of diseases that we have the most sustained efforts made by the naturalistic doctors to build up a reliable database in the treatises called the *Epidemics*. In this context they took and recorded detailed case histories of individual patients, setting out their signs and symptoms day by day, in some cases continuing up to the 120th day from the onset of the complaint. The terms used are, of course, all more or less theory-laden and some

---

7 The chief source is Celsus, *On Medicine* 1 Proem 23 ff.

presuppose a good deal of previous medical experience. The reader is expected to know what 'thin' urine is, and to recognize urine that is 'like that of draught animals', and of course to understand such terms as 'crisis' and 'exacerbation', the key expressions used to describe the ups and downs of the patient's condition. Yet at the less theory-laden end of the spectrum, recognizing chill in the extremities was not problematic, even though interpreting its cause was.

The compilers have, of course, selected what to record. Yet while there are occasional references, for example, to 'bilious' discharges, no overall diagnoses of these diseases are offered in the case histories in the *Epidemics*.[8] There are some generalizations in the so-called Constitutions that accompanied them (accounts that included the climatic as well as health conditions at particular seasons in particular locations in Greece), but the case histories themselves do not reveal what theory or theories of diseases the compilers subscribed to. Future doctors could and did read these accounts both to learn about previous medical practice in general, and to match them with their own experience. In the latter context they would certainly be put on their guard if one of their own patients presented combinations of signs that looked similar to those of any one of the many cases in the *Epidemics* that end in death. Elsewhere in the Hippocratic Corpus, in *Prognostic* ch. 1, the practice of prognosis is recommended in part so that the doctor may warn his patients and their families that he anticipates a fatal outcome—and so not be blamed if that indeed happened: that at least was what was claimed. But even in the absence of secure causal diagnoses, the case histories evidently could and did provide useful information that could guide other practitioners.

Every style of healing for which we have evidence from Greek antiquity obviously fell well short of modern biomedicine, both in the therapies available and in the understanding of the pathology of diseases. That applies even to the naturalistic traditions represented in the Hippocratic Corpus and continuing down to Galen in the second century CE, though I have stressed that their treatments included the use of plant-drugs many of which had powerful active ingredients, and I have argued that clinical case-histories could be a useful aid in

---

[8] The retrospective biomedical diagnosis of the cases described has been attempted, but the author of the most sustained discussion, Grmek 1989, often has to admit the Hippocratic descriptions are too indeterminate to permit secure conclusions.

prognosis even in the absence of causal understanding. That being the case, we should not be surprised that the competition between those naturalistic traditions, and the healing that was practised in the shrines of Asclepius and elsewhere, was far from being straightforwardly resolved in favour of the former. Right down to the end of pagan antiquity, temple medicine remained a popular—maybe even the most popular—mode of treatment (cf. Lloyd 2003: ch. 8).

From one point of view, what both naturalistic and supernaturalistic medicine could offer was far closer than some of the antagonisms between them might lead one to expect, given the clear gap that opened up between them on the question of whether personal gods could or could not intervene in diseases and their cures. The healers in the shrines of Asclepius certainly presented a confident front, claiming, as I noted, plenty of cures, including some frankly miraculous ones.[9] For any sick person who was a believer, that was bound to be reassuring—especially as the inscriptions also record cases of initial scepticism eventually giving way to the relief of the acknowledgement of the power of the god. But Hippocratic naturalistic medicine could and did offer precisely the converse style of reassurance. Those who accepted that the gods had nothing to do with diseases could rest assured that their complaints had not been sent to punish them, for their crimes or indeed for those of their ancestors. Yet relief from any possible feelings of guilt would only come to those who were already committed to the Hippocratic position.

The explicitness of the antagonisms between rival styles of healing varied, depending on the rhetorical skills, or at least the levels of articulateness, that the main proponents displayed.[10] The pluralism did not just reflect different values: it arose in the first place because of the challenge to traditional views that was mounted in several areas of Greek thought and belief from the sixth century onwards. I shall be returning to this in Chapter 7. But meanwhile I may note that one of the side-effects of the rivalry in medicine was to weaken the psychological

---

[9] This applies particularly to the accounts of the god's 'surgical' interventions, where he opens up patients to remove the causes of their diseases, in one case cutting open the belly of a patient named Aristagora to get rid of a tapeworm and then stitching her up again (Epidaurus Stele B, 23, discussed in Lloyd 2003: 55, 77).

[10] There are implicit criticisms of some standard Hippocratic therapies, such as cautery, in the inscriptional evidence from Epidaurus, and in the second century CE Aelius Aristides often compares merely mortal physicians to the god Asclepius, much to the disadvantage of the former.

comfort on offer, since those who had some sense of that rivalry might always reflect that their own side did not necessarily have a monopoly of the truth.

Surprisingly enough, however, while the healers disagreed among themselves fundamentally about both diseases and their treatments, outside the circles of the medical writers health was repeatedly invoked as a paradigm case of what is objectively good and objectively determinable. The urge to find universally valid truths in this domain far outstripped any ability to deliver them. Plato especially uses the medical analogy in support of recommendations both in ethics and politics. We all want health: that is an unquestioned good. So we should also want virtue, the good of our soul. If we have done wrong, we should accept punishment. It is better for us to be punished than to escape punishment, just as it is better for the sick patient to be treated than not, even though the treatment may itself be painful.

More remarkable still, in view of the lack of confidence that the naturalistic doctors often honestly expressed, Plato repeatedly holds up the doctor as the model of the expert whose opinions ordinary people should trust and whose advice they should follow. Very much in contrast to the actualities of Greek medical practice, Plato constructs an ideal of a doctor who has secure knowledge not just about the causes of diseases but also of their treatments. His claim is that there can be similar experts also in the fields of ethics and politics, philosopher-kings whose decisions on right and wrong should be accepted as authoritative by everyone else. Just as lay people in medicine may well be mistaken, thinking they are healthy when they suffer from a serious disease, so too in politics what ordinary folk believed might be good for the state might be a recipe for disaster. The solution was to put your trust in those who—the claim was—were in a position to be able to determine objectively what the right policy for the state and its component parts should be. In one further application of the medical analogy that others had used before him, Plato pictures the state as the body politic, and argues that those who disagreed fundamentally with the policies the experts laid down were pathogens who had to be purged from the state by exile or by death.

I shall be returning at the end of this chapter to try to tease out the implications of this amalgam of ancient Greek ideas from the perspective of my strategic problem of the commonalities and culturally relative aspects of the topic of health and well-being. But first it will be instructive to compare the rich evidence on this question that comes from our other ancient civilization, namely China.

Four features immediately stand out as offering analogues for what we have found in ancient Greece. First, there is the development of a certain pluralism in medical styles also in China, and second, these included some that emphasized, while others generally disregarded, the role of demonic forces. Third, there are the beginnings of the systematic recording of the details of individual cases. Fourth, there is the use of health and disease as the analogue for order and disorder in politics and in cosmology. Let me highlight each of these four points in turn, while acknowledging that there is much on the complex subject of Chinese medicine that we shall have to leave out in the process.[11]

Our main early Chinese medical sources fall into three main categories. First, there are the medical texts that have recently been excavated from tombs, at Mawangdui and Zhangjiashan and elsewhere. The tombs themselves were sealed in the mid-second century BCE (in two cases in 168 to be precise) and that gives us a *terminus ante quem* for the texts they contained. Second, there is the biography of the doctor Chunyu Yi in the *Shiji*, composed by Sima Tan and his son Sima Qian around 90 BCE: Chunyu Yi himself lived in the middle of the second century. Third, there are the writings that go to make up the great medical classic, the *Huangdi neijing*, the *Inner Canon of the Yellow Emperor*. Our two earliest recensions, the *Ling Shu*, or *Divine Pivot*, and the *Su Wen* (*Basic Questions*) give us access to texts compiled, it is thought nowadays, some time in the first century BCE. But in addition to these medical sources, we also have, as in Greece, non-medical writings that throw light on ideas about health and disease, notably the great cosmological compilations, the *Lüshi Chunqiu* (the *Springs and Autumns of Master Lü*) assembled under the auspices of Lü Buwei before 236 BCE, and the *Huainanzi*, put together by Liu An, King of Huainan, some hundred years later.

The evidence for the pluralism I mentioned is both implicit in the divergent styles of medicine adopted in our different sources and explicit in some of them. It is apparent from the medical texts from the

---

[11] This includes the detailed study of plant drugs and their properties, for which our chief texts date from after the main period I am concerned with. See e.g. Sivin (1987); Hu (2005).

tombs that treatments such as acupuncture and moxibustion did not originally take the form they have in later canonical writings. Harper (1998) has argued convincingly, for example, that acupuncture points were at first treated as points for cauterization. Pulse lore too took some time to develop. Chunyu Yi tells us he learnt it from his teachers and from some books that are now no longer extant, but so far as our existing evidence goes, it is Chunyu Yi himself who was responsible for the first complex classification of pulses and their being used as the chief tool in prognosis. Moreover, Chunyu Yi also refers directly to other doctors present at his cases. They were evidently his rivals. They contradicted his diagnoses and recommendations for treatment, and he theirs.

Chunyu Yi's opponents are other doctors, *yi* (醫), and in some cases were evidently, like him, members of the literate elite, with a clientele from the upper echelons of society, including nobles and their courts. But a different strand of medical practice is represented by the mediums, *wu* (巫), who dispensed advice on a range of non-medical as well as medical problems. The main subdivision of types of illness, those from external causes, and those from internal ones, is common throughout Chinese medicine, but the first, especially, comes in different forms. The idea that the invasive forces at work are demons or spirits of some kind occurs in the tomb texts and reappears in many later writings. Chunyu Yi does not explicitly attack demonology in the way in which the Hippocratic *On the Sacred Disease* polemicizes against the 'purifiers'. No more does any Chinese source invoke an overarching category of 'nature' in order to define the area of inquiry over which the 'physicists' or the 'natural philosophers', as the Greeks called them, claimed expertise. But in Chunyu Yi's cases the external forces that disrupt the body are not demons but such factors as wind, *feng* (風), or hot and cold. In one text in the *Ling Shu* 58. 9. 2a (cf. Harper 1999: 99) when Qi Bo is asked about the activity of demons and spirits, he rationalizes this. The forces at work are invisible—and so they had been compared with demons and spirits. Yet he does concede that the *wu* had some knowledge of medical matters.

The third feature of similarity with Greece that I mentioned was the beginnings of the systematic recording of individual case histories, where the biography of Chunyu Yi provides our first Chinese evidence (cf. Hsu 2002). This sets out the details of twenty-five cases, but the context in which it does so is very different from that of the Hippocratic

Epidemics. Chunyu Yi had been accused of some offence the details of which are not clear from any of our sources. He was subject to official investigation and his case histories form part of his justification to be a competent medical practitioner. As noted, his chief diagnostic tool is the pulse where he develops a sophisticated vocabulary to distinguish the 'quick', the 'muddy', the 'strung' and so on. This provides him with the crucial information he uses to determine the internal processes of the body. Although he several times identifies the factors that led to the patient contracting the illness (often a matter of their self-indulgence in the matters of food, drink, and sex) he is more concerned with whether or how the natural functions of the body are impaired. These are associated with the liver, heart, and spleen, and so on, although attention is concentrated on the processes associated with these body-parts rather than on the anatomical organs themselves. But health is conceived as a matter of the free flow of *qi* about the body, disease as one of its impediments when disrupted by what was called 'deviant' or 'heteropathic' *qi*, *xie qi* (邪 氣).

Some of the patients Chunyu Yi describes die, though not when in his care or because of his treatment. But his prognoses prove to be correct on every occasion. He is, after all, out to establish his medical credentials, though when asked directly whether he is infallible, he says that he is not. In certain other respects, too, his account differs from those in the *Epidemics*. Pulse lore as he practises it certainly requires more previous medical expertise than the interpretation of most of the signs the Hippocratic doctors identified. Chunyu Yi expects the doctor not just to be able to recognize a 'strung' pulse when he felt one, but to interpret its significance correctly. But even though his account of the internal processes within the body is as far from modern biomedical knowledge as the Greek descriptions are, that did not undermine the usefulness of his case histories. Even lay people could recognize that some patients were severely ill. The description of their complaints and their outcomes could prove a useful source of information to other physicians as they sought to extend their clinical experience. Yet there was just as much of a mismatch between Chinese causal accounts and biomedicine as there was in the case of Greek ones.

That did not prevent the Chinese any more than it did the Greeks from basing important ideas about values in general on their understanding of health and well-being. The human body, the political state, and the cosmos as a whole were all represented in terms of the same set of images. We may think of these as microcosm–macrocosm analogies, but they are not so much comparisons as all exemplifications of the same patterns at work throughout the universe. As in Greece, so too in China, thinking about health was an important resource: it was a source of ideas for dealing with many other problems as well.

I may illustrate this first from a medical text, then from a cosmological one. In the *Suwen* recension of the *Inner Canon* (8. 1–2, cf. Sivin in Lloyd and Sivin 2002: 221–2) the body is imagined as a complex bureaucratic system. 'The heart system is the office of the ruler: consciousness issues from it. The lung system is the office of the ministers; oversight and supervision issue from it. The liver system is the office of the general: planning and strategy issue from it'—and so on for a total of twelve systems. But the text does not limit itself to picturing the body as a bureaucratic state: it spells out the lessons for government. 'It will not do for these twelve offices to lose their coordination. If the ruler is enlightened, all below him are secure. If he nourishes his vital forces in accordance with this, he will live long and pass his life without danger. If he governs all under heaven in accordance with this, it will be greatly prosperous.' So if the ruler secures his own health, both the state and indeed the cosmos itself can be expected to be in good order.

But what if not? The text proceeds: 'If the ruler is unenlightened, the twelve offices will be endangered; the thoroughfares of circulation will be closed and movements will not be free. The body will be greatly injured. If he nourishes his vital forces in accordance with this, the result will be calamity. If he governs all under heaven in accordance with this, he will imperil his patrimony. Beware! Beware!'

The implicit moral here is that the body provides the model for well-being in the empire. What both depend on is free flow, of *qi* in the body, and of information and advice in the state. The message is that the ruler should pay attention to his counsellors. We have analogous ideas in play in my second text, from the *Lüshi chunqiu* (20/5/1, Sivin in Lloyd and Sivin 2002: 223–4 and cf. Knoblock and Riegel 2000: 527). Just as Plato had no compunction in setting out what we should call anatomical and pathological theories, so this Chinese non-medical text talks first about the body and then applies its lessons to the state.

Human beings have 360 joints, nine body openings and five *yin* and six *yang* systems of functions. In the flesh, tightness is desirable; in the blood-vessels, free flow is desirable; in the sinews and bones, solidity is desirable; in the operations of the heart/mind and will, harmony is desirable; in the essential *qi*, regular motion is desirable. When this is realized, illness has nowhere to abide, and there is nothing from which pathology can develop. When illness lasts and pathology develops, it is because the essential *qi* has become static.

The next move is to cite other physical cases of the dangers of stagnation. 'Analogously, water when stagnant becomes foul: a tree when [the circulation of its *qi* is] stagnant becomes worm-eaten . . .' and so on. And then the application to the state follows:

States, too, have their stagnations. When the ruler's vital power does not flow freely [that is, when he is out of touch with his subjects] and the wishes of his people do not reach him, this is the stagnation of the state. When the stagnation of a state abides for a long time, a hundred pathologies arise in concert, and a myriad catastrophes swarm in. The cruelty of those above and those below toward each other arises from this. The reason that the sage-kings valued heroic retainers and faithful ministers was that they dared to speak directly, breaking through such stagnations.

Although some of these ideas are appreciably less familiar to us than those from our own Western traditions, we can see that just as in Greece, so too in China, the way in which health and disease are represented had implications well beyond the purely medical context. One key Chinese notion (not so far from a common Greek idea) was that of the importance of order. Indeed the very same Chinese term, *zhi* (治), was used both of ruling or governing in the political domain, and of curing in the medical one. Its antonym in politics is *luan* (亂), chaos—and everyone agreed that that was to be guarded against. Its antonym in medicine is *bing* (病), disease, and again there was no doubt about its undesirability. As in Greece, the agreement that disease is bad provides a spring-board to gain agreement that political disorder is calamitous, even though what, in detail, constituted political disorder was just as controversial (or a matter of individual opinion) as was the corresponding notion of political deviance in Greece. Yet in both civilizations *health* provides the basis of an argument by analogy for the objectivity of values.

I began by noting the claims of biomedicine to be in a position to deliver objective truth in the matter of disease and on the subject of health as well, at least on the minimalist view where that is equated with the absence of disease. Over a range of conditions, biomedicine reigns, or would have us believe it reigns, unchallenged. Yet much still lies beyond its control, even its competence. This is not just that it is unable to deliver cures in certain pathological cases. There are far more extensive indeterminacies that surround psychiatric practice. Many patients suffering today from mental health problems face a situation that is far closer to that reported in the historical and ethnographic records for illness generally. There is a general consensus today, to be sure, on the relative severity of psychiatric disorders, bipolar disorder, neurosis, psychosis, schizophrenia.[12] But there is much that remains poorly understood about the physical and mental causes at work and even when treatment is recognized to be effective, why that is so is still often unclear: we may parallel ancient Greek use of analgesics. Meanwhile the perceived or imagined need for the social control, including the institutionalization, of the mentally ill, mirrors analogous problems in the treatment of those, in the ancient world, who passed as mad on one or other understanding of 'madness'.[13] In the modern, as in the ancient, world, those who are considered undesirables by those in authority still risk being labelled not just deviant but sick.

Besides, on the wider definition of health, much more than just the biomedical state of the individual is implicated. For those of us who live today in modern industrialized societies, as for many other modern and ancient peoples, there are social dimensions, not to say metaphysical and cosmological ones, to a feeling of well-being, of being one, as we say, with society, with nature, even with the world. Can we, for instance, enjoy that feeling in a society that we consider unjust? What is the relationship between our feeling good and the possibilities, or the lack of them, of other people doing so? Well-being

[12] Even when the psychiatric profession sees the need to develop reliable general diagnoses of mental illness, and devotes considerable efforts to that end, as witnessed by the standard handbook used in North American practice, the *Diagnostic and Statistical Manual of Mental Disorders* (American Psychiatric Association, 3rd edn., revised, 1987), that goal is still elusive. Wakefield 1992, for instance, undertakes a radical critique of the definitions of mental disorder and dysfunction themselves (cf. Cooper 2002).

[13] The issue of who was of unsound mind in ancient Greece and Rome was often a matter of arbitrary decision. Schulz (1951: 198) noted that while the Greek doctors had accumulated a certain amount of experience in dealing with mental as well as physical complaints, and some of their writings were available in Rome, the Roman lawyers paid no attention to them. Who was to be regarded as 'furiosus' was left to magistrates to judge. The consequences for those so diagnosed included a severe curtailment of their legal rights. They were, for example, disqualified from making a will.

is universally prized. Yet what that will consist in will reflect the views and values of different societies and groups—and those of different individuals within them which may or may not coincide exactly with those of their particular group. Evidently the advances of biomedical science have done little or nothing to diminish our need to appeal to the rich but fuzzy concept of well-being in our attempts to determine what goals of life we should set ourselves both as individuals and as members of the collectivities to which we belong.

Thus health and disease are at one and the same time topics which biomedicine will claim can be handled objectively and scientifically, and ones on which both ancient and modern societies have held extraordinarily divergent opinions. However, there are two important ways in which those divergences are circumscribed. First, whatever is recognized as health or well-being is ipso facto acknowledged as a good and conversely however disease is defined, it is generally to be avoided.[14] Even though some Greek thinkers, the Stoics, denied that it is an evil, they still thought it was preferable to be free from disease. Even though some Christians argued that plagues are sent by god, and should be greeted with joy since by that means the saved went more quickly to heaven and the damned to hell,[15] they still saw the plague as a chastisement even while it served god's purposes.

Second, over a limited range of biomedical conditions at least, sick people are recognized to be sick in whatever culture they live. This is true despite the qualifications that have to be entered, in the first instance in the matter of how that sickness will be understood and the accounts that will be given of its origins and causes. Mistakes too are often made, which an individual may recognize with or without (more often with) the help of whatever experts are on hand in the society in question. Some who suffer from severe conditions that will later show themselves may initially appear perfectly healthy. Conversely, some who complain they feel unwell may be free of any pathological condition, though again there may or may not be experts to tell them that that is so.

---

[14] An exception should perhaps be made for the awe in which certain abnormal states, such as possession, may be held. Even the arch-rationalist Plato spoke of the 'blessings' of madness (mentioning poetic inspiration in particular in this context) in the *Phaedrus* 244a (Lloyd 2003: 150–1).

[15] Cyprian, in his *On Mortality* ch. 9, advised his congregation to accept a plague with joy on such grounds (Lloyd 2003: 233).

While cultural variability in this domain is remarkable, it should not be exaggerated. In two respects, the conclusions we should reach on health and well-being resemble the mixture of commonalities and relativities that we found where the emotions are concerned. On the one hand, there are certain biological factors at work liable to affect humans everywhere, even though different human populations will show greater susceptibility or resistance to certain diseases than others (cf. Ch. 6 below). Thanks to biomedicine many of the causes of diseases are now far better understood than they were even a hundred years ago, even though there are still limits to our knowledge both of physical and more especially of psychological complaints.

On the other hand, as is the case with the emotions, we cannot understand the particular highly diverse ideas that have been entertained about health and disease without taking into account other aspects of belief and especially of values. These are indeed culturally relative, and in every case pose problems of interpretation that anthropologists, sociologists, or ancient historians, must do their best to resolve. What is common across the board is the positive evaluation of whatever is represented as health and well-being and the generally negative one of their opposites. But we have seen that what passes as health, what passes as disease, and the ideas entertained on the causes of either, vary very considerably, as different individuals and groups all strive to appropriate this discourse as a resource for basing their ideas not just on physical and mental conditions, but about morality, politics, and cosmology.

My final observation emerges from a particular feature of both ancient Greek and Chinese notions in this area. Even while in both ancient societies we find evidence for quite different ideas about health and disease among contemporary groups, in both the medical domain also yielded models for what is objectively true: they provided the template for ideas about the state and even the cosmos as a whole. The idea that health and disease are subjects on which experts can be expected to pronounce with authority is put forward even without the array of modern biomedical arguments to back it up, and that idea is then used to justify the notions of authority and objectivity in the matter of values in general. The irony is that the ideal that there should be objective universal truths in this area got a grip on some humans' imaginations long before the limited justification for it provided by modern biomedicine was available. But maybe that should not surprise us, given that we have found other occasions when what is at stake in a given controversy between universalists and relativists in a particular field of enquiry turns out to be a second-order issue of the very possibility of authoritative answers.

6

The Self, Agency, and Causation

THE topics I have chosen for discussion in this chapter appear more abstract and philosophical than those I have considered so far and seem to pose particularly severe difficulties of interpretation, given some of the apparently exotic ideas that have been reported in this area. If notions of the self, agency, and causation are not cross-cultural universals, how we are to discuss them? The spectres of incommensurability, of mutual unintelligibility, and of apparently irrational beliefs loom large. What vocabulary, other than one that already presupposes our own assumptions, is available to arrive at some comprehension of the variety of ideas that we encounter? How can radically divergent viewpoints on questions such as these be compared against one another?

I shall first sketch out some of the major difficulties that relate to these three concepts and their interrelations, pointing to the apparent divergences that exist between the reports of the social anthropologists on the one hand, and the findings of developmental psychologists on the other. I shall then, as usual, turn to ancient civilizations to see what light they can throw on the issues, where it is worth reflecting on the diversity of views that can be found as between different periods and even within writers of the same period. These correspond, in part, to different world-views, to different values, and to the varying contexts in which the relevant notions are put to work. While our own ideas on causation are much influenced by certain dominant models, especially those from classical physics, our conceptual framework offers greater resources for understanding than some commentators seem to have allowed. Puzzles, of course, remain, but it is clear that qualifications are needed to both extreme positions, both that of the universalists in so far as they may make the claim that the psychological development of children everywhere is directed at a uniform set of adult conceptions, and to that of extreme relativists in so far as they run the converse risk of ignoring certain commonalities in those conceptions.

Ideas of the self, first, cannot be discussed except in relation to conceptions of what is other, including ideas about other humans especially. That immediately implicates the concept of race, one that certainly exemplifies a potent and confused mix of biological and cultural elements. In a wide variety of societies across the world the borders of humanity—of who counts as a truly human being—stop at the frontiers of the group in question. Others, with their strange languages and customs, fall short in what it takes to make a human a proper human being. Many collectivities see themselves as 'us', the people (Viveiros de Castro 1998: 476–7). The names we know those groups by are sometimes labels that others have attached to them, quite often with marked pejorative undertones. To the members of the collectivity itself, they are just 'the people'. Others do not speak, eat, dress, marry, or die correctly.

In many cases, Viveiros de Castro argues, that contrast is not to be interpreted in terms of a difference in substance, that is of membership of the human species, but rather in terms of personhood. Using the linguistic model of deixis, he suggests that it is a pronominal contrast, one between we/us and they/them, rather than a substantival one, and that certainly fits the evidence he cites where the same term for 'the people' can be used of other agents besides the members of the collectivity itself. But, of course, some groups have gone much further and treat others as essentially subhuman, flawed specimens inferior to those who belong to the real race of humans. As the experience of the twentieth century, more than any other period, showed (Traverso 2003), racism has repeatedly been used to justify not just the extermination of whole populations, but torturing them and carrying out biological experiments in the name of 'scientific' research. Evidently it was assumed that, subhuman though these people were, they were sufficiently human for the experiments to throw light on the biology and psychology of the members of the master race. But apart from those Western societies who ironically prided themselves on their civilization and culture, other groups have generally lacked the power to wipe out their enemies even if they wanted to do so, and they certainly have not had the technology of the gas chambers to do so on an industrial scale.

The boundaries of what are perceived as different races do not necessarily, and may not even usually, coincide with biological distinctions. The markers appealed to are mostly, sometimes entirely, cultural ones, a matter of language, custom, religion. Yet biological differentiae do exist between populations, in skull shape, skin colour, and more importantly blood group and DNA profile. So far from being factors that should *always* be discounted—to forestall their prejudicial use in any one of a number of public policy contexts—they have a useful and positive role in, for example, health care. It is important to ascertain and bear in mind these differentiae when assessing, for instance, the degree of susceptibility to particular diseases. Hacking (2005) who has made the point with some force recently, exemplifies it with sickle cell anaemia.

While the living current members of any particular group are naturally the chief focus of attention, it is often the case that neither agency nor personhood is limited to the living. In many societies the dead too have wishes and moods that cannot be ignored. The deep sea, or the forest, or even the area just outside the village may be inhabited by spirits, who may be anthropomorphic, or theriomorphic, or who may be able, like Proteus, to take on whatever shape they like (their 'clothing', as Viveiros de Castro calls it, cf. Ch. 7 below). Then too there are the fully fledged gods whose shrines or holy places must be maintained, whose rituals must be observed, and to whom prayers may be addressed to obtain favours or merely to ward off misfortune or malevolence. All of these may be intentional beings whose activities may be more difficult to interpret than those of your fellow human beings, but whose effects it would be folly to disregard.

Other people's deities may not impress you. But then there are your own, the ones that your own group worships and that you were brought up to believe in—unless you were born into a quite exceptionally atheistic family, and where do they exist in any numbers? Certainly not in most societies. Your own gods are not all just charming fantasies, like fairy stories or the belief in Santa Claus, that any normal adult will be assumed to grow out of. Their nature may be hard to comprehend, and why they act, if and when they act, in the ways they do, may be even more mysterious, especially if they are believed to be just and yet allow injustices to occur. But then mystery, if not sheer mystification, is of the essence of religion, even while it recycles ordinary aspects of mundane beliefs (the cognitive constraints discussed by Boyer 1994). If your god works in a puzzling way to achieve his or her ends, then you must try harder to understand. If in the process your ordinary beliefs about selfhood, agency, causation have to be revised—to accommodate a godhead who is both three and one, for instance—then you must learn to do that.

Whether we consider the reports of anthropologists or merely reflect on aspects of Western Christian belief, we are, I said, faced with severe problems of cross-cultural interpretation. But maybe even more intractable difficulties surface when we attempt to square those reflections with the findings of those who work in developmental psychology. Here the initial impetus came, of course, from Piaget. Intensive subsequent research has modified his theses in substantial ways, but generally remains within the paradigm that he developed. There is plenty of disagreement, as I have noted before, about the precise stages through which, and the ages at which a child's grasp of agency or causation develops. But the notion that development takes place in a definite sequence, even if it is one that still has to be charted in detail, is common ground.

One controversial issue that I alluded to in Chapter 3 relates to just how far we are born with innate domain-specific cognitive modules and which those modules might be. Do we need such to cover, for example, persons in particular as well as living beings in general? Should we postulate modules for number, as well as for physical objects, in addition to a module governing language acquisition, which provided one of the initial stimuli to develop the notion of modularity itself? Fodor's original idea was limited to perceptual, as distinct from conceptual, cognition, but Sperber and others have proposed substantial extensions in what he has dubbed the 'massive modularity' thesis.[1] Yet Carey (1985), as I noted, argued controversially that children do not initially have a naive biology, for example, but rather an innate psychology (cf. also Carey and Spelke 1994, Bloch, Solomon, and Carey 2001). At first animal behaviour is understood in purely psychological terms—in terms of wants and beliefs, for instance—and only later does the child come to see that biological processes may not be psychologically driven. Carey and her colleagues share the view

---

[1] With Fodor (1983), compare Barkow, Cosmides, and Tooby (1992); Sperber (1994; 1996); Carruthers and Chamberlain (2000); Atran (2001*a*). But contrast the doubts and criticisms of modularity expressed by e.g. Karmiloff-Smith (1992); Tomasello (1999); Panksepp and Panksepp (2000); and Sterelny (2003: 177 ff.).

that human reasoning is guided by core domain-specific systems of knowledge, but allow that both children and adults can bring about changes in such systems, by constructing and using mappings across them.

But if both the data, and the explanatory hypotheses to be favoured, in some domains, remain hotly contested, a considerable body of evidence has been accumulated, in the last few decades, relating to the developments in children's grasp of naive physics, perhaps the key domain for the discussion of notions of causation. It takes time for the child to appreciate that the height and width of a container does not affect the quantity of liquid poured into it (the principle of conservation). It takes time to recognize that when an object is not visible—when it is hidden by the investigator, for instance—it does not cease to exist. Appreciation of how pushing and pulling work, or of the unlikelihood of objects being freely suspended in air, and of the distinctions between (as Leslie 1995: 122, puts it)[2] mechanical properties, actional properties, and cognitive properties, similarly develops in stages.

I have problems both with some of the experimental protocols, and with the Western bias, in these studies which I shall be airing in a minute. But for now let me concentrate on the chief difficulty. This relates to how to reconcile what the developmental psychologists say about the stages through which a child's cognitive faculties pass as it grows to adulthood with what some ethnographers report about the beliefs of actual adults in societies across the world. There is at least a superficial resemblance between those adults' attributions of agency to beings other than fellow humans, on the one hand, and the views that children in their early years are first reported to entertain and then later grow out of. Yet those adults are certainly in no sense childlike in their behaviour.

What are the interpretative options here? We can distinguish four distinct, if at points not mutually exclusive, lines of approach. First there are those who have been prepared to cite the cognitive developmental evidence to support an evolutionary hypothesis, despite the obvious ethnocentricity of the suggestion that large segments of

---

[2] Leslie uses these three types of properties to distinguish what he calls three subtheories of Agency. The behaviour of Agents is differentiated from that of other physical objects by (roughly speaking) forces, goals, and beliefs that ordinary physical objects do not possess.

humanity are as naive as Western children. What any such hypothesis flatly fails to account for is, among other things, the fact that those who are reported to see spirits at work in the forest are often brilliant hunters and trackers. They are generally far more skilled at finding their way through those forests than the anthropologists who observe them—as both Lévi-Strauss (1955/1973) and Descola (1996) have acknowledged. Nor is there any question of their being more simple-minded in the interpretation of other people's feelings and emotions (for example) than we are. They are generally well aware of hurting others' sensitivities, for instance. And as for responding to the spirits of the wild, we should not forget that Western society too has yielded many cases of people, some of them great poets, who have seen God in a puddle.

So a second line of attack at the opposite end of the spectrum would insist that the notions of self, agency, and causation that the anthropological reports reveal are strictly non-comparable with those that we normally entertain and that are certainly assumed by the cognitive psychologists as they devise their tests for their children subjects. Some cultural relativists will argue that we are dealing with incommensurable world-views each of which has to be assessed purely in its own terms. Yet the weakness of that position lies in its self-defeating nature. If the views in question are radically divergent, then the question arises of how from our perspective we can make sense of them at all. It would certainly seem an unpromising line of interpretation to save another society's notion of causation from an apparent charge of naivety or irrationality by suggesting that it has nothing in common with our own ideas on the subject in the first place.

Yet we can hardly opt either, third, for a reductive version of the principle of charity in interpretation that would explain the reports of apparently strange beliefs about agency and causation in the anthropological literature simply by insisting that they should not be taken literally, and that the people in question did not really mean what they said.[3] The question of the tropes used in speech acts of different kinds—and in different languages and contexts—is indeed a delicate one (Lloyd 1990) and there are all too obvious risks of

---

[3] The principle of charity in interpretation which has it that we should try to make others' beliefs come out true, as far as possible, in our terms, has been proposed in different forms by Davidson and by Quine. For an overview of these differences and on the underlying methodological principles, see Delpla (2001).

misunderstanding both on that score and in general. Yet to legislate a priori that they must mean something other than their words appear to mean merely on the grounds that they do not make sense to us is to be as much guilty of ethnocentrism—or of a lack of imagination—as the first option that I criticized on just those grounds.

A fourth line of approach proceeds by challenging just how far either the results of the cognitive psychologists or the reports of the ethnographers should be seen as implying *general* notions about causation and the self that apply across the board. The question for ethnography, first, is how far the agency of the spirits of the forest (for instance) provides a model for ideas of agency in general. When a particular event is assigned to some such cause, are we to understand that similar ideas will be in play *whenever* cause–effect relations are discussed? Attempts at causal explanation often, in our own society too, arise from a need to fill what we may call a cognitive deficit (cf. Festinger's (1964) notion of 'cognitive dissonance'). When we too are faced with the apparently inexplicable, an assignment of blame or responsibility is one of the commonest means of filling the gap. I shall be considering some instances later where different notions of causation and responsibility are invoked when dealing with different classes of events, or even with the same type of event in more, or less, 'normal' circumstances. But for the moment it is enough to note that in our own culture, too, we sometimes appeal to what we may call non-standard modes of explanation for exceptional events, as when people may believe that their prayers are answered.

As for the evidence from studies of cognitive development, it is the claimed great strength of those findings that they are based on controlled and repeatable experiments. Yet they are open to question on at least two grounds. First, a point I have already mentioned, the work has been carried out, to date, overwhelmingly on European or North American children. The results are often presented as if they were universally applicable, but as I noted in Chapter 3, some investigations on Israeli and on Japanese children suggest that their assumptions about the domains of animals, plants, and the inanimate are distinctive.

Then the second ground for doubt stems from the very feature of the experimental situation that lends an air of scientificity to them, namely their artificiality. In Baillargeon's studies, for instance (for example Baillargeon, Kotovsky, and Needham 1995), the children are regularly confronted by a pair of situations, one that corresponds to what the experimenter considers a possible event, the other one that incorporates a physical impossibility. Not every child reacts differently to the two types of event (but those who do not tend to be discarded from the investigation). But for those who do, the two types of events they have to discriminate between are both artificial in the sense that neither arises in their ordinary experience in quite the form in which the experimenter presents them.

The experience of Luria (1976) in his studies of Central Asian peoples' grasp of elementary logic provides something of an object lesson. Again it was the investigator who controlled the situation, providing the subjects of the experiment with the information to which they were supposed to react. In one group of studies (ibid. ch. 4) those subjects were first told that in the Far North, where there is snow, all bears are white, and secondly that Novaya Zemlya is in the Far North and there is always snow there. They were then asked what colour the bears in Novaya Zemlya were. Some of the subjects replied that they did not know as they had never been to Novaya Zemlya. One answered: 'You've seen them, you know. I haven't seen them, so how could I say?'

The inference was then drawn that such individuals were deficient in the ability to reason logically. Yet instead of concluding that the subjects in question were weak logicians, the investigators might have themselves inferred that they were brilliant pragmatists. When the investigator asked the question, what colour are the bears in Novaya Zemlya, that implicitly threw doubt on the earlier information that in the Far North all bears are white. Those who are familiar with syllogistic know that the sequences of propositions are designed to test for validity, and have nothing to do with truth. But in ordinary human exchanges, questions seek the truth of a situation: the interlocutors are interested in knowledge. From the pragmatist's point of view, the replies the subjects gave are, one might argue, both more honest and more intelligent. They are more honest, since they were not in a position to pronounce on the colour of animals in some country they had never visited, and more intelligent, since they were responding to a conversational implicature. The question they were asked implicitly cast doubt on the earlier universal proposition. I shall return to the question of the universality of logic in Chapter 8, but for now may simply note how the artificiality of the situations influenced the results that the tests were claimed to yield.

The situation of the children in Baillargeon's studies is of course in many respects very different from that of Luria's subjects. But they both have in common that the subjects being investigated were faced with the unfamiliar, where the performance of those subjects is judged by criteria of normality that the investigators have, with greater or less justification, already decided upon. To find out what a given child, or a group of them, believe about causation and agency it is necessary to set up an artificial situation for them to respond to. But while the experimenters are confident in the distinctions they draw between 'possible' and 'impossible' events, for the child all the events belong to the strange circumstances in which they confront . . . the experimenter.

The thrust of these comments is to underline the problem of the generalizability of results derived from specific, more or less artificial, circumstances. The child is being investigated by the psychologist, and the members of a particular society are often questioned by the anthropologist, in contexts which represent some departure from the normal experience of either group. We have to make allowance for the leading questions that the ethnographic investigations involved in the Luria example, and for the fact that children's inferred implicit notions of cause and effect inevitably have to be matched against adults' expectations. This is not to deny the validity of the findings *in the contexts in question*, only to raise doubts about what can be inferred in general on their basis. Those remarks will seem excessively cautious and deflationary to specialists in the fields in question. But they gain some weight, I believe, from a consideration of some historical evidence. I turn first to Greece and then to China before returning to the strategic question of the tension between the universalist and the cultural relativist positions on the issues.

Ancient Greek ideas on the self, agency, and causation present their distinctive problems of interpretation as well, in the first instance because our earliest evidence comes from works of high literature. Even some considerable scholars who have discussed what the Homeric poems say or imply on those subjects have sometimes been prone to forget that they are not dealing with historical figures, but with products of the literary imagination. What is attributed to Achilles or to Agamemnon in the *Iliad* is not the result of Homer doing fieldwork! That does not mean to say that the Homeric poems are useless sources of information concerning what the Greeks of the archaic period may have believed, only that in interpreting them we have to bear in mind that they are evidence not concerning real ancient Greeks, but rather about what some Greeks of the archaic period believed or assumed about humans.

Thus in an influential study, Snell (1948/1953) suggested that there is no unified notion of the self in Homer. As I mentioned in Chapter 4, the heart, the liver, the lungs, the breath, are the seats of various cognitive, conative, and affective functions, and one of Snell's arguments was that what we think of as a unified personality was fragmented and divided up between those various psychic centres. The text in the *Odyssey* (20. 17 ff.) in which Odysseus chides his heart was used, as we saw, by Plato to suggest conflict within the soul, where Plato himself was certainly advocating distinguishing between the reasoning, the spirited, and the appetitive functions—with the consequent problems for his psychology that I discussed in Chapter 4.

But as later studies (Vernant 1983; 1989; Padel 1992; 1995; Williams 1993) have pointed out, to suggest that Homer lacks any notions that correspond to the self or to the agent is to overinterpret the texts. It is after all Odysseus who upbraids his heart, it is Odysseus who decides not to kill the women in the palace then and there, when he see them behaving outrageously—although he does eventually take his revenge on them once he has got rid of the suitors (*Od.* 22. 457 ff.). Disgusted as he is at the behaviour he witnesses, Odysseus shows every sign of exercising his usual resourceful cunning, his *metis*, even under provocation. The graphic descriptions of heroes deliberating between different courses of action are often accompanied by vivid similes of storm-tossed seas or violent winds. They certainly convey the ways in which they are—as we too say—'torn' between different options. But that does not strip them of their capacity as agents.

That they are indeed able to act as such is not undermined by two other types of evidence, the texts that represent the heroes contending with divine forces and those that depict them wrestling with fate or destiny. In another famous text in the first book of the *Iliad* (188 ff.) (cf. Dodds 1951: ch. 1), which I have already had occasion to cite (Ch. 4), Achilles is furious at Agamemnon who has just said that if he, Agamemnon has to return the girl Chryseis to her father under the orders of Apollo, then he will take Achilles' prize Briseis from him—to show him who is the more powerful of the two. Achilles is so incensed that he contemplates killing Agamemnon on the spot—although he is described as deliberating between that and setting aside his anger. He is just about to draw his sword when Athena appears to him. She stands behind him and pulls at his hair: so he does not see her, though he is well aware of her presence even before, amazed, he turns round and recognizes her by her flashing eyes. As for the other heroes, the poet says that none of them saw her at all. She addresses him and dissuades him from precipitate action. The scene is a dramatic one, whatever we make of the role ascribed to 'Athena'. But her presence should not lead us to think of Achilles as no more than a puppet since he clearly has his wits about him. She is there to persuade, not compel, him. He parlays with her and it is his decision to obey her.

The other type of case, also discussed by Dodds (1951) and by Williams (1993: 52) especially, represents a hero struggling with fate or destiny. In the *Iliad* (19. 86 ff., 137 ff.) Agamemnon says that he was deluded when he quarrelled with Achilles at the opening of the epic. He says that he was not responsible, but puts the blame on Zeus and Delusion (*ate*) themselves. He was, as we might say, the victim of forces beyond his control. Yet by offering Achilles compensation, as he does in Book 19, he implicitly accepts that some of the responsibility was his. Fate may have dictated what he was to do: but he did it. Similarly, in Aeschylus' play, Agamemnon has to sacrifice his daughter Iphigenia, to fulfil the oracle and to allow the Achaian fleet to sail for Troy. Yet again it is his decision to take his daughter's life. As Aeschylus expresses it, Agamemnon 'put on the harness of necessity' (Aeschylus, *Agamemnon* 218).

So far from implying that Homeric heroes generally suffer from fragmented personalities, these texts could be taken to suggest rather that they have a heightened sense of the difficulties of reconciling conflicting feelings and motivations when trying to decide on the course of action to take. Most of the situations they face are indeed ones of high drama: this is epic, after all. But a further point of interest for our study emerges from another feature of the Homeric material. This relates to the possibility of different types of causal account, and different invocations of agency, for the same class of event as well as different ones. The gods are often represented as being involved in the action. Sometimes it is the poet who tells us about them: sometimes the heroes themselves are described as inferring their presence. In one typical passage in the *Iliad* (15. 461 ff.), the poet describes how Zeus thwarts Teucer, who is about to shoot at Hector, by breaking his bowstring. When this happens, Teucer shudders with fear (466 ff.)—and we are told why. The bowstring was one that he had fitted new that very morning. The causal account that would be appropriate—so we may infer—to the snapping of a well-worn bowstring differs from that which is called for when a brand new one breaks. It is especially in exceptional circumstances, if not solely in them, that the gods are thought to be at work. Thus several types of causal story are available and the register of the causal account can be modified to fit the different situations that arise. Sometimes a personal agency may be suspected: but sometimes, of course, the event may be put down to mere chance, even if chance and fate have a tendency to merge into one another.

As Greek reflection of different classes of phenomena developed, some radical moves were made to redefine what types of cause should be thought to be responsible for what types of effect. The best-known example of this is the one I have mentioned before (Ch. 5), namely the attempt by some of the medical writers to rule out any notion of personal intervention by divine or demonic forces in either causing or curing diseases. This is the line of argument mounted by the author of the Hippocratic treatise *On the Sacred Disease* against the views of the 'purifiers' whom he accuses of charlatanry. Yet as we noted before, we should not exaggerate the extent to which this author's contemporaries were persuaded. Some no doubt were, and accepted the view that all diseases, the 'sacred disease' or epilepsy included, had natural causes. But as I noted, there were plenty of other Greeks both in the classical period and right down to the end of antiquity who continued to believe that the gods were able both to send diseases and to cure them.

That was far from being the only development that took place once Greek speculative thought got under way. Although the associations of causation with responsibility remained strong in most Greek theorizing, there were radical disagreements between different theorists both on what types of causal account are legitimate, and on the definition of cause and the distinction between causal and purely concomitant factors.

Aristotle proposed one of the more systematic and would-be comprehensive analyses, but his views were far from having it all their own way. On his account there were four types of causes that should be considered, though not necessarily all four would be relevant to any particular explanandum. The four were the material, formal, final, and efficient causes, and Aristotle's claim was that his account subsumed and went beyond all his predecessors' thinking on this subject. Roughly speaking the matter corresponds to what a thing is made of, the form to the characteristic features that make it the thing it is, the final cause is its function or the good it serves, and the efficient cause picks out what brings it about. Thus in the case of an object such as a table, the matter may be wood, say: its form is what makes it a table (rather than any other wooden object, say a chair), its final cause corresponds to the function of table, and the efficient to the craftsman who made it. But Aristotle would offer the same type of analysis not just of objects, but also of events.

Aristotle holds that the four causes correspond to different, but equally valid, questions, asking in relation to things or events, 'because of what (*dia ti*)?'. The answers to all four may tell us something relevant to our understanding of what the thing or event is. But as noted, it is not the case that all four types of question will be given positive answers in every case. In particular, not everything has a final cause. Thus residues in the body serve no good and are just the end-products of natural processes. The residues themselves have no final cause, although the natural processes (e.g. digestion) certainly do (*On the Parts of Animals* 677^{a}11 ff.). Again having eyes of a particular colour serves no purpose, though *having eyes* certainly does (*On the Generation of Animals* 778^{b}16 ff.).

One important implication of Aristotle's fourfold schema is that it allows, even directs attention towards, different causal factors for the same object or event. The account appropriate to a particular question will vary with the focus of interest of the enquiry. Let me illustrate with a topic that particularly concerns notions of the self and other, namely what makes a human a human. Aristotle's general answer to that question refers to the faculties of the soul, from nutrition and reproduction, through perception, locomotion, imagination, and desire to reason itself. Thus far all humans are the same. Yet differences also emerge in the modalities of the rational faculty that Aristotle postulates, as I shall be discussing further in Chapter 8.

First, there is his notorious downgrading of both women and slaves. The latter, in his view, are deficient in their rational capacities—an ideological justification for an existing social institution if ever there was one. He even says that nature would have given slaves inferior bodies if it could. It has done just that where women are concerned. First, all females are marked out physiologically: their bodies are unable to concoct the blood, that is in the way males do, to produce semen. And women are inferior to men in their deliberative capacities too. Yet he does not deny that they are human beings, and indeed essential to carry on the human species. The move he makes where barbarians are concerned is similar. The definition of human, as 'by nature a political animal', where 'political' means 'living in a city-state', is a normative as much as a descriptive one. Ideally humans should live in city-states as the Greeks did. But Aristotle is well aware that most human societies are not so organized. Even so barbarians are humans despite their strange languages and customs.

Aristotle's was far from the only complex analysis of causation that Greek philosophers proposed. The Stoics introduced further distinctions with a technical vocabulary that may initially have seemed as strange to their contemporaries as it may to us. One source, Clement (*Miscellanies* 8. 9. 33) (Long and Sedley 1987: i. 336), reports: 'When preliminary (*prokatarktika*) causes are removed the effect remains, whereas a sustaining (*sunektikon*) cause is one during whose presence the effect remains and on whose removal the effect is removed. The sustaining cause is called synonymously the complete (*autoteles*) cause, since it is self-sufficiently productive of the effect.' This makes the sustaining/complete cause a sufficient condition, but then Clement proceeds to other types of cause, auxiliary (*sunergon*) and joint (*sunaition*).

The difference between the joint cause and the auxiliary cause lies in the fact that the joint cause produces the effect along with another cause which is not independently producing it [one illustrative example would be that of the harmony a choir produces, which is not the effect of any single voice, but of all together] whereas the auxiliary cause in creating the effect *not* independently but by accruing to another, is acting as auxiliary to the very cause which *is* independently creating the effect, so that the effect is intensified.

That in turn is illustrated by pushing an already rolling cylinder, which makes it roll faster.

Two major points of dispute involving causation arose between the Stoics and their main Hellenistic rivals, the Epicureans, relating to determinism and to providentiality. We could not have clearer evidence to illustrate how values and morality intervene to influence the positions adopted. Against the determinist view, the Epicureans defended their idea of free will with the notorious postulate of the swerve, a minimal deviation in the movement of an atom that is, by definition, uncaused. The idea was to break the nexus of cause and effect at *some* point, for only if that is the case can humans be considered free agents. Yet the expression of their capacity to deliberate will be a matter of their character and their reaction to the situation they are in: a swerving soul-atom will not achieve that result, since it is *ex hypothesi* uncaused.

On that issue the Stoics adopted a determinist, though not a fatalist, line. According to some reports, Chrysippus, the third head of the school, drew an analogy between human agency and the rolling of a cylinder. The person who pushed the cylinder gave it its beginning of motion but not its capacity to roll. So 'fate' is a 'preliminary' but not a 'complete' cause. As in the cylinder case, two factors are involved in human agency, not just an 'impression' that is external to us, but also our 'assent' which *is* 'up to us'.

The second dispute concerned teleology, which the Epicureans, like the earlier atomists, Leucippus and Democritus, rejected. All that you need to explain natural phenomena, they argued, are the mechanical interactions of atoms. They produce worlds at different times and places in the infinite void without any providential force intervening. They were indeed particularly concerned to exclude any idea that the gods—benevolent or otherwise—had anything to do with cosmogony, with natural phenomena or with the capacities of living creatures. Nothing has been engendered in our body in order that we may be able to use it, Lucretius wrote (4. 834 ff.): it is the fact that it is engendered in us that has created its use. It is not that ears were given to us so that we might hear: the ears came first, and the possibility of hearing developed later.

To this the Stoics countered by arguing for a thoroughgoing teleology. There is just one world and it is the product of an intelligent designing force at work throughout nature. They called this active principle by several names, the cause, reason, *pneuma* (breath or the vital spirit), soul, fate, god, and even Zeus. In this they were far closer than their Epicurean rivals to traditional Greek views of the divine though they did not, for sure, subscribe to anthropomorphic gods.

I have gone into some detail on the debates on agency and causation to illustrate the complexity of the analyses proposed. Two points in particular stand out. First, there was evidently nothing in either the ancient Greek language or in ancient Greek social or cultural institutions that determined the notions that would be entertained on this subject—by philosophers or by ordinary folk. On the contrary a wide variety of ideas was proposed from the classical period onwards, including new ideas that called for new coinages or a specially adapted vocabulary. However, a connection between causation and responsibility remains strong throughout: one of the terms for cause, *aition*, has as one of its cognates the word used for the guilty party in a law suit (*aitios*). Thus far causation and agency remain connected, though some theorists were clear that the first covered a wider field of physical interaction than the second, in which intentionality is generally involved.

As we have seen, however, there was no uniformity about what was to count as a cause in physics or cosmology, nor even on whether or not it is coherent to talk of uncaused events. As for the notion of responsibility in the more mundane, but important, legal context itself, again different ideas were entertained and we can pinpoint certain changes that occurred. One striking example relates to the belief that animals and even inanimate objects can be culpable, can be put on trial and if found guilty, should be punished. That is an idea that can be found in Athenian law (MacDowell 1978: 117–18): provision for it is made, indeed, in Plato's *Laws* (873de), and it surfaces again in the European Middle Ages (E. P. Evans 1906). Yet in the *Digest* of Justinian, in the sixth century CE, the idea that an animal can commit a legal wrong is dismissed as absurd on the grounds that it lacks reason (or 'sense', *sensus*) (Mommsen, Krueger, and Watson 1985: i. 276).

My second fundamental point is that the variety found reflected especially differences in values. What was at stake in the philosophical debate on teleology was whether or not one believed that the universe was the product of a benevolent intelligence, or simply the outcome of the random interaction of physical forces. Both sides in that dispute thought that their view of the matter was the only one that was compatible with a happy life, one free from anxiety and care. It is remarkable that what one group of philosophers construed as securing that freedom was viewed by the other as generating the very anxiety that they wanted to remove.

Although some Greek ideas appear and are idiosyncratic, several of the points that emerge from our discussion can be paralleled from other ancient societies, notably from ancient China. I have mentioned in Ch. 5 that the belief in demons and ghosts was common, in particular in relation to the accounts that were given of diseases. I also there pointed out that that belief was abandoned by some of the doctors, and was directly challenged by such writers as Xunzi in the third century BCE (*Xunzi* 21; Knoblock 1988–94: iii. 109) and by Wang Chong in the first century CE (*Lun Heng* 65). Thus as we saw happen in ancient Greece, so too certain Chinese traditional beliefs came to be the subject of critical scrutiny.

Again, as in ancient Greece, once explicit analysis of causal notions began in China several different schemata came to be proposed. The Mohist canon, mostly dating from between the late fourth and late third centuries BCE, is unfortunately badly preserved in our sources. But we find clear evidence of explicit definitions of certain key terms which will serve to exemplify the range of ideas on causation that were entertained. *Gu* (故) is often translated 'reason' or 'cause', though we shall see that in some contexts 'explanation' would be more appropriate. This word is glossed in the Mohist Canon A1 as what something must get before it will come about, and this is subdivided into first the 'minor reason' ('having this, it will not necessarily be so') and then the 'major reason' ('having this, it will necessarily be so; lacking this, necessarily it will not be so'). The chief modern commentator, Graham (1989: 162), remarks that this makes the minor reason the necessary condition, the major reason the necessary and sufficient condition. Similarly, another important term, *shi* (使) 'send, command, cause', is given two definitions (Canon A 77), 'to tell', and 'a reason', with the explanations: 'to give orders is to tell: the thing does not necessarily come about. Dampness is a reason: it necessarily depends on what is done coming about.'

As in Greece, there is a rich vocabulary of terms used in explanatory accounts. *Yuan* (原) 'source', and *ben* (本) 'root', focus especially on the origins of sequences of events, *you* (由) and *yin* (因) on the sources from which an effect stems, the means by which it is achieved, or the factors relied on to bring it about. In medicine, *yin* is used in drawing a general contrast between inner causes (*nei yin* 內因) and outer ones (*wai yin* 外因), similar, though not exactly parallel, to the Greek distinctions between external and internal, procatarctic and sustaining, causes. In medical and other contexts *gu* itself may be used either of the causes that are identified at work or of the explanations of the doctor's diagnoses or prognoses.

The case-histories of Chunyu Yi in *Shiji* 105 provide examples of both types. In case 1, the patient himself reported that he suffered from a headache. This is put down to the hot *qi* (氣) ascending to the upper parts of the body. It had reached the head and was moving around and causing disturbances there. Hence (*gu*), the text notes, the head ached (2797. 12–13).

In case 6, the *gu* relates not just to what happened, but to why Chunyu Yi said it would. This is a case of wasting of the lungs of some kind, where insanity is predicted after three days, death after five, a prognosis justified by the usual complex analysis of the signs in the pulse. At the end of the account Chunyu Yi first associates madness on the third day with an injury in one of the circulation tracts (the *yangming*) and then says (2802. 5–6): 'as for death after five days, the liver and heart [pulses] were distant from one another by five degrees:[4] hence (*gu*) I said, on the fifth day, exhaustion and after exhaustion, death'.

Yet another instance of *gu*, this time in case 15, can be used to introduce a further aspect of Chinese thought in this area. This is a patient where the diagnosis is an injured spleen and the prognosis the blocking of the diaphragm when spring came, followed by the passing of blood and death in the summer. Chunyu Yi first criticizes the faulty understanding of the case by other doctors and then comments that the reason for the fatal illness developing in the spring was that the stomach *qi* was yellow. 'As for its being yellow, that is the *qi* of earth. The earth [usually correlated with high summer] does not overcome wood [correlated with spring]. So (*gu*) [in such a case], when spring comes, one dies (2807. 4).' However, in circumstances that he goes on to describe, there are exceptions, as with this patient who was able to last out one further season until summer.

This is one instance of the much commented on Chinese fondness for so-called correlative thinking. As in this medical case, the notion of five interacting phases is often in the background, where in the mutual generation cycle wood is followed by fire, which is followed by earth, which is followed by metal, which is followed by water, which

---

[4] The correlation between the five days and the five degrees or parts is, no doubt, important, however the latter are to be measured.

is followed by wood to complete the cycle. In the mutual conquest cycle wood overcomes earth, metal overcomes wood, fire metal, water fire, earth water, and wood earth once again to complete the cycle. But with each of the phases many other objects are associated, so these two cycles can be used to give an account of many other transformations.

In the cosmological passages of *Huainanzi*, for instance, various such changes are introduced by the terms *gu* (thus, therefore) and *shi gu* (是 故, for this reason). The opening of chapter 3: 1b, 2a, 2b (cf. Major 1993: 62 ff.) reads: 'It is easy for that which is pure and subtle to converge, but difficult for the heavy and turbid to congeal. Thus (*gu*) heaven was completed first, and earth fixed afterwards.' Again, 'The Dao of heaven is called the circular: the Dao of earth is called the square. The square governs the obscure; the circular governs the bright. The bright emits *qi* and for this reason (*shi gu*) fire is the external brilliance of the sun.' Again, 'Fire flies upwards, water flows downwards. Thus (*gu*) the flight of birds is aloft, the movement of fish is below. Things within the same class (*lei*, 類) mutually move each other: root and twig mutually respond to each other. Thus (*gu*) when the burning-mirror sees the sun, it ignites tinder and produces fire.'

The general interpretative dilemma this usage poses for our investigation is the following. Should we say that the Chinese focused on correlations *instead of* causes? Or is it rather the case that the mode of causal explanation that they favoured was a matter of such correlations? Many commentators have argued for the first option, some suggesting a major contrast between ancient Greeks and Chinese on this score, the first attempting causal accounts, the second correlations. Yet that view is certainly open to objection first with regards to the Greek position, since many Greek thinkers show a developed interest in correlations, not least in such contexts as the Pythagorean Table of Opposites reported by Aristotle. In that Table limit, odd, one, right, male, at rest, straight, light, good, and square are associated together in one column, contrasted with unlimited, even, plurality, left, female, moving, curved, darkness, evil, and oblong in the other. As in Chinese sets of five phase correlations the guiding idea is the analogy between the relationships across the members of each column.

But leaving aside that objection, the range of application of the term *gu*, which can be used, as we have seen, in straightforward causal contexts, suggests an argument in support of the second option, namely that the mode of explanation the Chinese were interested in was sometimes, though not always, a matter of such correlations. The kind of understanding sought relates to what is connected with what, what belongs to the same class as what, where the term *lei*, class or category, is used to trace such connections and to give them systematic expression.

The interconnectedness of things is a recurrent motif in Chinese cosmology and once again values are in play, in the strong political and ideological overtones that went with this idea. The emperor, on whom the welfare of 'all under heaven' depended, was seen as having a mandate from heaven. Heaven, the state, the human body all exhibit (as we have seen) a single pattern, exemplifying the balanced interdependence of *yin* and *yang* and the orderly interactions of the five phases.

My final point concerning Chinese ideas of self and other suggests yet another general parallel with some Greek notions. The Chinese were generally as emphatic on the cultural differences that separated themselves and other, non-Han, peoples as were the ancient Greeks. Yet just as Aristotle is clear that humans are all humans, so we find ancient Chinese texts similarly expressing the point. In the statement of the hierarchy of beings in *Xunzi* (9. 16a; Knoblock 1988–94: ii. 103–4) water and fire have *qi* (氣) alone, grasses and trees also have life (*sheng*, 生) to which birds and beasts add knowledge (*zhi*, 知). But humans have *qi*, contain life, have knowledge, and also have righteousness (*yi*, 義) and that makes them noblest of all. There the term for humans is *ren* (人) the generic term, used, like Greek *anthropos*, for any human being and indifferently for both men and women.

We find explicit mention of barbarian tribes in just such a context in a passage from the *Lüshi chunqiu* that I have cited for the evidence it provides on attitudes towards feelings. Discussing the theme of 'using desire' in 19/6/2 (Knoblock and Riegel 2000: 497–8), the text puts it: 'The Man and Yi barbarians—despite their backward tongues, their different customs, and odd practices, despite their clothes, caps and belts, houses and encampments, boats, carts, vessels and tools, and despite their preferences of sound, sight and flavour all being different from ours—are one with us and the same as us in satisfying their desires.' It is precisely because we all have the same desires, that we are all humans, Han Chinese and barbarians, Sage Kings and Tyrants.

What lessons, I may now ask in conclusion, can be drawn from a review of some of the ideas that are reported from two sophisticated ancient civilizations? Let me highlight three points in particular. First, we are obviously dealing, in several cases, with notions that are as unfamiliar to us as many that are recorded in the ethnographic literature. We do not pay the attention to the resonances between things that many ancient Chinese did. Of Aristotle's four causes, only the efficient cause corresponds at all closely to what we would today consider a cause. The evidence of the terms used by the ancients themselves, of *gu, aition*, and the rest, suggests different conceptual schemata on these questions from those we are used to in the more mundane circumstances of physical cause–effect relations.

Second, the diversity of views expressed by different authors within each ancient civilization is remarkable. Sometimes the focus is on blame and responsibility: sometimes it is on the real or supposed links or connections between things or the similarities in the categories to which they belong; sometimes again the terms pick out what physically results from what. Evidently neither ancient language restricted its users to just a single set of notions on the subject. Shifts can be traced in the focus of interest at different periods and in different contexts. Certain traditional ideas were criticized—not that that led to their being abandoned completely either in Greece or in China.[5]

In both civilizations, thirdly, questions of values are at stake. The notions had implications for world-views as a whole, for the place of individuals or groups within the scheme of things, and for understanding of that scheme as a whole. In Greece there was a particularly clear-cut contrast between those who did, and those who did not, believe in providentiality. Teleology was not the issue in China, but the modalities of the resonances and interconnections between things was the subject of much speculative attention.

The nature of the historical evidence is, of course, very different from that of the ethnographers or of the cognitive developmentalists with which I began. Yet it too has its bearing on the disputes between

---

[5] If, naturally enough, the authority of the inherited belief-system counted for much, in ancient Greece and China, as in most other societies, it was not immune to challenge at least in certain respects in those two ancient civilizations. Does that constitute a major contrast with the evidence provided by ethnographic studies? That would be a rash inference to make. True, the diachronic dimension in predominantly oral societies is hard or even impossible to recover. But there is plenty of evidence of the possibility of scepticism about authority claims in such societies, even if the histories of critical reactions are not recorded in writing.

those who would support a universalist position on these topics and their cultural relativist opponents.

Unlike in our studies of the emotions and of health, we cannot here point to universal biological factors that underpin notions of the self, agency, and causation and provide the basic starting points for those ideas. However, to survive, any human group needs plenty of knowledge of its environment, including knowledge of what we would call causal relations, what you need to do to make crops grow, catch fish, hunt animals, and interpret the behaviour of fellow-members of that human group. Where secure knowledge runs out, guesswork must take over, and the more one is surrounded by the apparently imponderable, the more that will be needed, as in the case of the causes and cures of illness that I discussed in Chapter 5. Recall Gilbert Lewis' observation that as one patient's condition deteriorated, the diagnoses offered proliferated—an experience that could be multiplied many times over from the records of ancient medicine. When faced with puzzling events or those beyond our control, the urge to assign responsibility, even to blame when intentional agents are assumed to be at work, offers an easy, but all too tempting, means of reducing the cognitive deficit,—too tempting, because often well beyond any available means of verification. Yet that has not stopped accusations of wrongdoing being levelled at many different types of individual, from hostile shamans to witches, where the intensity of the obsession with deviants exhibits considerable variation from one society to another and from one period to another in ways that have been the subject of many scholarly studies but that are still poorly understood.

The cognitive developmentalists would have it that, as infants and young children, we all pass through more or less the same stages in the development of causal understanding. But as regards adults' beliefs, both the ethnographic evidence and that from ancient civilizations strongly suggest that we can *end up* with very different causal schemata. Other factors clearly have a role, both language in particular and culture in general. Yet the evidence from China and Greece shows, if it needs showing, that a particular natural language does not dictate a single particular conceptual map of causation, nor indeed restrict its speakers to just one such schema. True, society-specific values enter in, and yet they too may vary not just between societies, but within any given one. But if the universalist view has to make room for the diversity of notions that different cultures have entertained, the cultural relativist must acknowledge that variation is not indefinite.

The points that emerge from reflection on the ancient historical evidence that both extreme positions need to take on board are what I would call the plural registers of causal schemata, the sense that these may exhibit a range even within a single society. The types of causes and causal accounts appropriate to some explananda in some contexts will not be those needed in others. It may be a statement of the obvious to remark that, faced with the obscure or the mysterious, humans everywhere will use their imaginations to try to get to grips with what happens and why, exploiting some real or supposed analogy with the schemata that work in otherwise more mundane situations.

Some notions of causation build on the experience of biological phenomena, others on mechanical effects or on the patterns exemplified in technology, the arts, and skills, where other types of agency are at work, and yet others will use human social and political relations as a model.[6] Sometimes the work of sophisticated thinkers leads to the criticism, and in some quarters the rejection, of certain traditional beliefs. Yet sometimes, we have to add, the elaboration of new causal schemata may well have seemed obscurantist to all but those directly engaged in the philosophical debate. If we may think that some such ideas just exemplify the wild fantasies of the human imagination as it flounders in the face of the inexplicable, we should also bear in mind that each of these models has had a part to play in some of the more complex and sophisticated metaphysical systems produced by Western philosophy, and that all three are well represented in classical Chinese thought as well. But that all those ideas may be used, singly or in combination, is a point that has all too often been neglected by those who have attempted to offer global generalizations about human causal understanding.

---

[6] I attempted a review of the ancient Greeks' use of analogies from the domains of biology, technology, and social relations in Lloyd (1966).

7
Nature versus Culture Reassessed

THE dichotomy between nature and culture, or rather, we should say, for reasons I shall explain, *some* dichotomy between those two, constitutes a key element in the articulating framework of several intellectual disciplines. It is invoked in different ways, and with different resonances, in explaining what natural science is concerned with, as much as it is in the account of what sociology is all about. In other contexts too we often associate nature with the factual, the objective, what is investigable and explicable in general terms, while the realm of culture is the realm of values, the relative, the subjective, the personal.

The dichotomy is of particular importance for my study of the problem of the psychic unity of humankind in two distinct ways. First, nature may be taken to correspond to what is universal, and culture with what varies from one society or group to another. On that construal the cognitive unity of all humans lies in whatever we can put on the 'nature' side of the dichotomy.

But then the second point of relevance of the topic relates to the extent to which the dichotomy itself is a universal feature of humans' thought about themselves and their environment. On one line of interpretation it would be the nature/culture division itself that would be an underlying assumption common to all societies, though then it becomes important to consider whether or how far there are culture-specific differences in the apprehension of that dichotomy. The opposing line of argument would have it that that dichotomy is a typical example of the imposition of Western categories on other peoples' world-views, though that then raises the problem of whether those views are incommensurable with our own. Either way, a first observation would be that we seem to have to make room for a variety of view-points on the question for two distinct reasons. First, there are, as we shall see, societies where there is no explicit concept of 'nature' as such at all, though that should not be confused with a denial that they have an implicit grasp of that domain. Second, how 'culture' is interpreted also varies remarkably, even before we take into consideration the fact that primatologists and others claim that certain species of animals possess culture at least in a restricted sense.[1] There is plenty of evidence from anthropology to the effect that in many societies animals as a whole are believed to form communities like those of humans.

My tactics in this chapter will be first to examine the historical origins of one version of the dichotomy which has been enormously influential in European thought at least. I shall follow up earlier studies in which I have investigated the contexts in which an explicit contrast between two concepts corresponding, roughly, to nature and to culture, that is *phusis* and *nomos*, was proposed by certain ancient Greek thinkers. This investigation will bring to light both the polemical use of that dichotomy and the very contrasting values with which it was associated by different writers. Reference to ancient China, where there was no exact equivalent to the concept of *phusis*, will serve two purposes. First, it will show how investigations into what we call natural phenomena may be carried out in the absence of any explicit overarching concept to categorize them, and second, how, in the absence of that concept, the justification of the existing social dispensation proceeds quite differently

Those historical preliminaries will serve as background to my discussion of the major anthropological questions. To what extent is any such dichotomy made explicit in the world-views of societies reported in the ethnographic literature? Do 'nature' and 'culture' correspond to 'actors'' as well as to 'observers'' categories? If they do, how can we begin to account for the apparent variations in the application of some such dichotomy in different societies? If they do not, how far does the introduction of a Western construal of that dichotomy prejudice the interpretation of the world-views to which it has been applied? The nature/culture division turns out to be a far more problematic framework than is sometimes realized for the

---

[1] There is now a vast literature on this subject. Boesch, and Boyd and Richerson, are among the contributors to Runciman, Maynard Smith, and Dunbar (1996), who address the question with regard to primates especially. Cf. also Boyd and Richerson (2005).

discussion of the views in question, namely about what there is and about the different categories into which that falls.

I shall move rapidly through the salient points in the ancient historical part of my inquiry since I have gone into the question in some detail elsewhere (Lloyd 1991: ch. 18; Lloyd and Sivin 2002: ch. 4). So far as the explicit concepts go, the Greeks eventually made much use of the terms *phusis* (nature) and *nomos* (covering laws, customs, and conventions). Initially, however, that dichotomy was not available to them. True, the term *phusis* does occur once in Homer, in the *Odyssey* (10. 302 ff.) where the god Hermes indicates a plant to Odysseus, though whether the primary sense in that passage is 'nature'/'character', or more simply 'growth', is disputed. Even so, to have the idea of the nature of some particular object is not to have the general concept of the domain of nature as such, one that encompasses all and only what we call natural phenomena. In any case the plant in question, in the *Odyssey*, is a magic one, *molu*, with which Odysseus is able to counter the spells of Circe who tries to turn him—as she had turned the rest of his companions—into a pig.

Neither Homer nor Hesiod can be said to have had the notion of nature as a general concept. Of course no one should expect archaic epic and didactic poetry to deal with what we call natural scientific questions. But both poets are very free in referring to what look to us like cases of the suspension of the normal regularities of nature. This is high literature, to be sure, and Circe's turning Odysseus' companions into pigs has a symbolic appropriateness that transcends the difficulties that the literal-minded might feel when they ask the question of how precisely she did it: what kind of alchemy was this? Again Hesiod's *Theogony*, in telling the story of the generations of the gods and of the creation of the first woman, Pandora, goes into lavish detail about the birth of other creatures. In this account the world is populated with a wild array of hundred-armed beings, fifty-headed dogs, Chimaeras, Hydras, and the like, which no one is going to encounter in real life, but which belong rather to the vivid world of the imagination.

We should certainly not imagine that Homer and Hesiod and the audiences for whom they composed their poems were somehow unaware of the regularities of what we call natural phenomena. It did not take Aristotle to point out to them that a human being begets a human. It is just inconceivable that Hesiod's contemporaries (or anyone else) were somehow in two minds about the need to sow seed if they wanted grain, even though many no doubt believed that the success of the crop depended also on Zeus, and even though it was only sensible—Hesiod thought—to follow the advice he gave in his poems not just on when to plough or to shear the sheep, but also on how to keep the gods on your side. As I remarked in Ch. 6, some notion of causation—and we may add of the regularities of natural phenomena —is commonly assumed in every society that depends on them—as we all do—for survival. But first there is a fundamental difference between an implicit assumption and an explicit concept, and secondly we can certainly not take for granted a one-to-one correspondence between what is assumed and the concepts we use. That is precisely where the cross-cultural comparative problems lie.

It is not possible, on the basis of the available evidence, to identify exactly which Greek thinker or thinkers were responsible for introducing *phusis* as a general concept covering the domain of nature as such. But the evidence we have both for Presocratic philosophers from the sixth century BCE and for Hippocratic writers from the fifth makes it clear that they went in for naturalistic explanations of what we call natural phenomena in a big way. One of the general terms that Aristotle uses of many of those philosophers is, precisely, *phusikoi*, that is, 'naturalists'. The doxographic evidence attributes to them a bewildering array of theories, fifteen or so different explanations of lightning and thunder, eleven of earthquakes, twelve of comets and shooting stars, though we are generally not given the *grounds* on which they were proposed, only that they were put forward.

Many of the items in question, though not all, had been associated with gods or treated as themselves divine. Earthquakes, for example, were often thought to be the work of Zeus or of Poseidon the 'earth-shaker'—though we should not imagine that every time the Greeks heard a clap of thunder they thought that Zeus was sending a signal. However, it would appear that one of the main aims of these naturalistic accounts was to offer an alternative explanation, removing the role of personal gods and treating the phenomena as, precisely, works of nature.

We can see this in Xenophanes' statement about the rainbow, Iris in Greek, where a scholiast cites Xenophanes' own words (Fr. 32). Iris had been treated as a messenger of the gods. But for Xenophanes the rainbow is just an ordinary phenomenon, no omen for the future.

'She whom they [humans] call Iris also is a cloud, purple, and red, and yellow to behold.' Xenophanes is also famous for his attack on anthropomorphism: if horses and oxen and lions had hands and could draw like humans, they would draw the shapes of gods as like themselves, like horses and oxen and lions. Yet he was no atheist, for he proposed that god 'sees as a whole, perceives as a whole, hears as a whole' (Fr. 24), a god that is 'unlike mortals in body and in mind' (Fr. 23).

Again the polemical role of nature in early Greek medicine is abundantly clear. As I have discussed before, the Hippocratic treatise *On the Sacred Disease* is entirely devoted to the claim that the disease that had been called 'sacred' is natural. It has a natural cause, namely the blocking of the blood vessels in the brain that occurs especially under the influence of phlegm. That is pure speculation, of course, but the author would have insisted that it is the right *kind* of explanation, one in terms of nature, and not in terms of personal gods. Those who thought otherwise, who claimed they could identify the deity at work and bring about a cure through charms and incantations, are charlatans exploiting a gullible public.

The obvious but important point about the concrete evidence we have is that we are dealing with no merely intellectual debate, no mere abstract theoretical discussion about causation or nature. On the contrary, 'nature' was introduced in the context of a polemic in which new-style theorists—philosophers and medical writers—debunked a number of traditional ideas, offered alternative explanations of a variety of phenomena, and in the process carved out a domain of nature over which they would be the acknowledged experts.

But if the first feature we should notice about the introduction of the explicit concept of nature is the polemical function it served, the second relates to the disputes that arose over the values associated both with it and with one of its antonyms, namely *nomos*. For some, *nomos* was *mere* custom or convention, the rules and regulations that a person with the power to do so will ignore—or manipulate to their own advantage. Social codes in all their variety, Callicles says in Plato's *Gorgias* (492c), are a nonsense. They are set up by the weak, but according to nature it is *just* for the stronger to have more than the weak. One argument for this proceeds by reference to the behaviour of animals, and a second cites actual interstate relations in the Greek world to make the same point. Xerxes' invasion of Greece, and Darius' of Scythia were not just by the lights of *nomos* that 'we' the Greeks set up, but according to nature, indeed according to the 'law' of nature,[2] what they did was just. Similarly, Thrasymachus, in Plato's *Republic* (338e) has a different view of the origins of laws, when he says that each interest group, once it gets into power, fixes them to suit its own advantage. These are just two of a number of expressions of the common theme that the only universally valid principle is that 'might is right'.[3]

But against those who took that view there were others who evaluated *nomos*, in the sense of law, far more positively, seeing it as the guarantor of justice and as what marks out humans from other animals. Justice and shame, the sophist Protagoras is made to say in Plato (*Protagoras* 322c), are given to all humans, and it is those concepts that provide the basis for civilized social life. Among others who resisted too sharp a contrast between law and nature, Plato himself believed that the ideal human lawgiver should imitate the intelligence at work in nature and the cosmos as a whole.

What this makes clear is that, once the dichotomy between nature and law or convention had been made explicit, the validation of any particular set of customs or social roles became much more problematic. It was much more difficult to claim that the actual social dispensation went without saying. Yet 'nature' was often used not just descriptively, of what is the case, but normatively, of the ideal, and so of what carries positive evaluation.

We find such a use in Aristotle especially, both in his zoology and in his politics. What is picked out as 'natural' in the former case is what corresponds to the proper functioning (as Aristotle sees it) of the living creature. Humans provide the yardstick by which other animals are judged, though they deviate or fall short of that model in a variety of ways. As we saw in Ch. 2, Aristotle defines 'above' in animals as the direction from which food is taken in and to which growth is directed, and 'right' as the side from which movement begins. But he also thinks that it is *better* that these differences should be strongly marked. 'The starting-point is honourable and above is more

---

[2] The expression 'law of nature', *nomos tes phuseos*, is used in this context at *Gorgias* 483e, but by that Callicles means the principle that might is right: this has nothing to do with laws of nature as we now understand that expression in natural science.

[3] Other expressions of this view can be found in, for example, Thucydides 5. 85 ff. (the Melian debate) and the fragments of the fifth-century BCE sophist Antiphon.

honourable than below and front than back and right than left' (*On the Progression of Animals* 706^{b}12–13). Moreover, humans are 'of all animals the most in accord with nature. But naturally right is better than left and separate from it. And so the right is "most right-sided" in humans' (*On the Progression of Animals* 706^{a}19 ff.). In humans alone, he is prepared to say (*On the Parts of Animals* 656^{a}10 ff.) the natural parts are according to nature. He even accepts the consequence that plants, fed from their roots, are in a sense 'upside down' (*On the Progression of Animals* 705^{a}32–3).

This normative use of 'nature' spreads across from zoology to politics. Aristotle defines a human being as 'by nature' (*phusei*) a 'political' animal, by which he means specifically an animal that lives in city-states, *poleis*. Yet he knows very well that most human societies are not city-states such as the Greeks lived in. Such institutions were certainly not 'natural' in the sense of normal, regular, or usual. They were rather an ideal to which other social arrangements might aim, although in practice they all fell short.

It is, of course, not only the ancient Greeks for whom 'nature' is not just a descriptive term. In modern English usage, the normative associations of 'nature' and 'natural' are still very pervasive and not always recognized for what they are, namely covert value judgements presented as if they were statements of fact. We say that it is not natural for parents to neglect or to maltreat their children, and yet that often happens. We label as deviant or unnatural social or political or even sexual behaviour of which we disapprove, lying, stealing, racial abuse, although in many cases such behaviour is quite common. Those examples are from the moral domain: but outside it too, in the context of disease, we think of health (in some sense) as the *natural* state of the body, sometimes forgetting, first, that diseases are a common, and in that sense a natural or regular occurrence, and secondly, that diseases too have *their* natures.

My historical survey of Greek materials shows how 'nature' served to mark out a certain kind of investigation, and further how issues of values and of morality were deeply implicated in their use of the dichotomy of nature versus culture. We can examine what was, and what was not, distinctive in the Greek experience by considering another ancient civilization that did not develop an explicit concept of nature as such. How did the Chinese define the types of investigation they engaged in, and how did they deal with the problems of values we have been discussing from ancient Greece?

First the claim that the ancient Chinese did not have that explicit concept needs to be clarified to avoid misunderstanding. They certainly had a variety of concepts 性 for use in different contexts where it is not too misleading for us to employ 'nature' or 'natural' in translation. They spoke of the heavens, *tian* (天), or more comprehensively of heaven and earth, *tiandi* (天地), or they referred to the myriad things, *wanwu* (萬物), to indicate the diversity of things. They used the terms *xing* (性) and *jing* (精) to describe the characteristics of things and human characters (bravery, cowardice, and so on).[4] They were interested in the patterns or immanent order of things, *li* (理) (the term originally relates to the patterns in jade). They were concerned with what happens spontaneously (without human intervention and so natural in that sense) for which they used the expression *ziran* (自然), literally 'self so', the term that eventually came, in the nineteenth century, to be adapted to translate 'nature' and equivalents as used in European languages. They investigated the changes in things, using the expression *wuxing* (五行), the five phases, though these were not the elements in the Greek sense of the fundamental constituents of which everything else is composed, so much as, precisely, the phases in the transformations or cycles of change—a concept which, it should be emphasized, took some time to be fully elaborated (see Sivin in Lloyd and Sivin 2002: ch. 5 and Appendix). The five phases are named fire, earth, metal, water, wood, but they are not substances so much as processes. Water means soaking downwards, fire means flaming upwards, as one classic text puts it, namely the *Great Plan* (*Hong Fan*) from the treatise known as the *Documents* (*Shu*).

The fields of investigation they pursued include some that correspond more or less closely to those we are used to. They had two terms for their principal branches of 'astronomy', namely *tianwen* (天文) (the 'patterns in the heavens', including the interpretation of omens and portents—astrology in other words) and *lifa* (曆法) (primarily calendar studies, but also other quantitive enquiries for instance into

---

[4] What is called the *xing* (性) of a thing does not necessarily identify its principal physical properties. In the *Lüshi chunqiu* (1/2/2) the *xing* of water is said to be pure, and the *xing* of humans to be longevity

eclipse cycles). Similarly *yi* (醫) is used for medical doctor and for medicine, and *bencao* (本 草) ('roots and grasses') covers herbals or pharmacopoeia.

Elsewhere, however, the Chinese classification of the learned disciplines diverges from ours more strikingly (cf. Lloyd 2004: ch. 3). The term *shu* (數) can often be translated 'number', though it has a range of other meanings as well, including 'several', 'counting', 'scolding', 'fate and destiny', 'art' as in 'the art of', and 'deliberations'. When combined with another term *shu* (術) (roughly 'methods') it forms one of the most general rubrics: its subclasses included not just the two areas of the study of the heavens,[5] and five-phase theory, but also various modes of prognostication.[6] Five-phase theory itself (*wuxing*) comprised the study of changes not just in the physical world, but in every aspect of experience, including politics. As I noted before, the resonances and interactions they were interested in range from the seasons, musical notes, colours, tastes, smells, and living creatures all the way to rulers, ministries, sacrifices, and measuring instruments.

The Chinese experience makes it clear that you do not need a category of 'nature' as such in order to engage in extensive and in many cases sophisticated investigations into a wide variety of phenomena. Several such studies brought to bear mathematical analysis on the data (cf. Lloyd 2002: ch. 3). But we should note that some of those enquiries were not limited to what we think of as *natural* phenomena, and some move from the natural to the social field without marking any break between them.

On the question of values and ideology, next, there is an evident general similarity between Chinese and Greek thought in the common (if not, on the Greek side, universal) belief that the cosmos as a whole is steeped in values. Yet there are distinctive features in the way the Chinese express those values, and in the ideas they entertained on the question of the relationship between the cosmos as a whole and its parts. The Chinese treated all three domains, of the heavens, the

---

[5] The sixfold classification of *shu shu* owes much to the work of the scholar-bibliographers Liu Xiang and Liu Xin in the centuries either side of the millennium. The second of the two astronomical studies (after *tianwen*) was there named *lipu* (曆 譜), where the second element refers to chronologies. It also included the quantitative study of harmonics.

[6] Thus *shigui* (蓍 龜) referred to milfoil and turtle shell divination; there was a category of *zazhan* (雜 占) or miscellaneous prognostic procedures, and *xingfa* (形 法) was the study of significant shapes including geographical ones and physiognomy.

state, and the human body, as all exemplifying in principle the same order and dispensation. They did not construct analogies between these realms (like Greek macrocosm–microcosm comparisons) but rather saw them as interactive parts of a single complex whole (Lloyd and Sivin 2002: ch. 1). All three exhibit the interchanges of the five phases and the interaction of *yin* and *yang*. A key feature of that interaction, wherever it is to be found, is the interdependence of the two principles. Even when *yang* is at its strongest, *yin* begins to reassert itself: conversely at the moment of maximum *yin*, *yang* already starts to re-emerge. This opposition too spans natural phenomena and social ones (as we should say), from the interaction and interdependence of the seasons to those of male and female and ruler and ruled.

Divergent views were expressed on how the ruler should conduct himself and the various virtues he needed to exhibit. But all were agreed that on him depended the welfare of 'all under heaven'. It was an unquestioned principle that the ruler must stay in tune with the cosmos as a whole. Elaborate 'monthly ordinances', *yue ling* (月令), were drawn up—as we see in such texts as *Lüshi chunqiu* and *Huainanzi*—that set out exactly what the ruler and the court had to do in order to ensure not just good government, and good social management (the due administration of justice for instance) but also that the cycles of seasonal phenomena should be orderly. Any deviation from the prescribed rituals would lead to civil unrest and to ecological disaster—not that those two types of misfortune were distinguished as such. Once again the domains that the ancient Greeks and ourselves contrast as nature and culture form, for the Chinese, a seamless whole. On that view, the social dispensation did not require any special comment or justification. If the ruler's Mandate from Heaven was in good order, social order was guaranteed. Conversely, any failure in the emperor's virtue or weakening of that Mandate would, if left uncorrected, lead inevitably to droughts, floods, and storms, as much as to criminality and rebellion.

The material from China that I have thus cursorily reviewed already casts doubt on any assumption concerning the universality or the uniformity of the nature versus culture dichotomy. But it is time now to turn back to the ethnographic evidence, to which indeed that dichotomy has repeatedly been applied. My argument will develop in three stages. First, I shall press the importance of the distinction between explicit and implicit categories: in many cases the nature/culture dichotomy reflects interpretation rather than description, 'observers'' rather than 'actors'' concepts. Second, I shall evaluate the claim that, even if not explicit, the dichotomy correctly represents a fundamental contrast implicitly recognized in a wide variety of societies. That will take me, third, to scrutinize the possibility of a quite different analysis of the underlying ontological presuppositions at work, one that takes as its starting point the redefinitions of 'animism' and 'totemism' that have been proposed on the one hand by Viveiros de Castro and on the other by Descola.

One way of testing how applicable some nature/culture dichotomy is cross-culturally is by considering some of the rich evidence that has been assembled concerning dualist classifications. In a collection of essays entitled *Right and Left*, Rodney Needham (1973) brought together a great deal of material concerning such classifications where one strongly marked opposition was that between right and left. The tables of opposites that many of the contributors to that volume presented normally represented the anthropologists' own syntheses of the ideas and practices they encountered in the societies they studied. They were, indeed, 'observers'', not 'actors'', categories.

In one instance, however, in one of Needham's own contributions, dealing with the ideas of the Nyoro people of East Africa, 'nature' and 'culture' themselves figure in the table, 'nature' associated with left, 'culture' with right (Needham 1973: 328). Yet as Goody (1977: 64) for one was to point out, Needham did not provide any direct evidence to show that the Nyoro themselves explicitly distinguished that pair in those terms. Moreover, the list of items in the table he presented included both what *we* should call social pairs, and what *we* should call natural ones—which suggests some tension in the classification if indeed one column is held to equate with culture, the other with nature. Among the social pairs were king and queen, chief and subject, brewing and cooking, the Nyoro language and alien dialects. Among what we might think of as the natural pairs, were heaven and earth, moon and sun, life and death. Similarly, in the dualist classification of the Meru of Kenya, we find again *both* natural pairs, such as south and north, or west and east, *and* social or cultural ones, in that case co-wife and first wife, black clans and white ones, all included in a single schema of correlations that evidently spans *both* those domains.[7]

But might it not be argued that, even if not explicit, the nature/culture dichotomy nevertheless often provides an important articulating framework in many world-views? Is that not the case, for instance, with the corpora of South and North American myths collected by Lévi-Strauss? His first volume (Lévi-Strauss 1964/1969) was entitled, in its English translation, *The Raw and the Cooked*, and that might seem a concrete expression for, precisely, the contrast between the natural on the one hand, and the social and cultural on the other.[8] Yet the first problem is that in many of the myths in question any presumed boundary or distinction between 'nature' as such and 'culture' is not only not marked: it is ignored. Marriage is a cultural phenomenon par excellence, and so is passing on cultural knowledge. But in these myths not only do gods and goddesses marry one another, they marry humans as well. In one Sherente myth, for instance, the planet Jupiter (called 'Star') descends to marry a young bachelor who loved her, and in another she teaches humans what to eat. Humans are distinctive in that they have a particular diet. Yet in that myth that cultural rule comes from a deity who, in the shape of the planet Jupiter, belongs in one sense, in *our* terms, to the natural world.

Of course that myth about the institution of a human social practice relates to past times and one way of highlighting the importance of culture is to provide a story of its origins. All human societies have rules of behaviour that govern human social relations and that accordingly implicitly mark them out as the social phenomena they are. But *human* societies are usually not the only ones in question, for the relations between gods, or other divine beings, and even cosmic forces, are often imagined in social terms (as they were very vividly in ancient Greece, where the consequences of the anthropomorphic conception of divinity were elaborated in graphic detail). That is not, or not just, a matter of what was true in mythical time: it remains true of the current dispensation.

---

[7] Needham (1973: 116). Similar dualist classifications that span the nature/culture divide are reported for the Kaguru by Beidelman (1973: 141) and for the Lugbara by Middleton (1973: 373 ff.).

[8] This was how Greimas and Rastier (1968: 93) for instance took Lévi-Strauss, although their particular gloss was that 'culture' corresponded to permissible social relations, 'nature' to unacceptable ones. Lévi-Strauss himself insisted that one of his principal objectives was to show how the raw/cooked dichotomy was used to capture quite abstract ideas.

The question that this opens up is whether the analysis of other societies' underlying ontological presuppositions in terms of nature and culture does not distort them. Both Viveiros de Castro (1998) and Descola (2005) have tackled, from slightly different points of view, the question of the taxonomy of the possible ontologies that can be found in both ancient and modern, both technologically simple and technologically complex, societies. In Descola's schema there are four such ontologies, contrasted in terms of the notions of physicality and of interiority that they assume. Physicality relates to what is believed about bodies and physical objects generally: interiority concerns how one feels inside oneself, and beliefs about other persons or other intentional beings. Descola's taxonomy proceeds by way of a contrast, in each case, between a view that stresses continuity, and one that emphasizes discontinuities, between humans and non-humans. Thus on the physicality axis, one view maintains that all physical bodies are essentially the same, while the opposing one stresses differences and postulates that what marks out different kinds of entities is, precisely, the bodies they inhabit. Similarly, on the interiority axis, the emphasis may be on continuity (the souls of all beings are the same) or on the discontinuities (humans are a race apart).

This double differentiation yields a fourfold schema. Where, in the hands of Tylor and others, 'animism' had been used as a vague, general rubric covering any attribution of animate characteristics to inanimate things, that term is now reserved for an ontology in which other beings besides humans have spirits, but what differentiates them is their bodies. Interiority, selfhood, is common: physicality what distinguishes things. Where 'totemism' had been criticized by Lévi-Strauss (1962/1969) as an artefact of ethnography based on a confusion between, first, the identification of humans with various plants and animals, and second, the naming of kin groups with plant and animal terms, it is now applied specifically to an ontology in which the essences of particular animals, plants, and other objects are used as a model for human social distinctions: the unity or continuity between humans and non-humans is assumed both on the physicality axis and on the interiority one. 'Analogism', third, assumes discontinuities on both axes, postulating differences between humans and non-humans in both their physicality and their interiority, but setting up correspondences between the domains thus differentiated. Finally, there is 'naturalism', where physicality is unified, but interiority divided and discontinuous.

This view insists on differences between humans and non-humans on the interiority axis in respect of minds and cognitive faculties generally (humans alone have culture in the strict sense), but sees humans and non-humans as linked by their shared physicality. We are all made of the same stuff. This is the ontology that has dominated Western thought since the eighteenth century.

There are many aspects of this complex proposal that merit more attention than I can give them here, and one of its great strengths is the insistence that non-Western ways of looking at the world are liable to be distorted if the analyst imposes Western categories on them. Descola presents his four ontologies as ideal types, but in practice they are not mutually exclusive, although one will be dominant for one society, group, or collectivity at any one time. There is, to be sure, a specific difficulty with regard to how any ontology can change or be modified. Since the alternative attitudes with regard to physicality and interiority are not a matter of, and do not permit, degrees, any shift in ontology implies a polar switch. But how is that brought about in a society as a whole? How, in particular, did 'naturalism' arise? What processes or stages led to its eventual dominance in Western thought? Again, both ancient Greece and ancient China meet the criteria for 'analogism', and fall therefore in that category in Descola's schema: yet that might be thought to underestimate some of the contrasts between the two, and within ancient Greece in particular, that I have mentioned in this chapter.

It is enough for my present purposes to concentrate on the first set of assumptions, namely 'animism', where it is useful to supplement Descola's views with those of Viveiros de Castro who also speaks of animism but relates that to what, following Århem (1993), he calls 'perspectivism'.[9] This is a view he opposes to our own ideas concerning the nature/culture dichotomy. Where we hold that nature is universal, cultures diverse, in perspectivism it is culture that is universal, natures that are diverse. Where Descola stays with our concept of 'nature' at least where 'naturalism' is concerned, Viveiros de Castro contemplates a redefinition of the boundaries between 'nature' and 'culture', though both agree that in animism/perspectivism it is body or physicality that differentiates beings.

---

[9] On the relations between Descola's evolving ideas on 'animism' and the 'perspectivism' of Viveiros de Castro, see Viveiros de Castro (1998: 472); and Descola (2005: 196 ff.).

It is worth citing Viveiros de Castro on the question in some detail. Introducing his account (1998: 470) he first remarked that 'the initial stimulus for the present reflections' was 'the numerous references in Amazonian ethnography to an indigenous theory according to which the way humans perceive animals and other subjectivities that inhabit the world—gods, spirits, the dead, inhabitants of other cosmic levels, meteorological phenomena, plants, occasionally even objects and artefacts—differs profoundly from the way in which these beings see humans and see themselves.' He then explained as follows:

Typically, in normal conditions, humans see humans as humans, animals as animals and spirits (if they see them) as spirits; however animals (predators) and spirits see humans as animals (as prey) to the same extent that animals (as prey) see humans as spirits or as animals (predators). By the same token, animals and spirits see themselves as humans: they perceive themselves as (or become) anthropomorphic beings when they are in their own houses or villages and they experience their own habits and characteristics in the form of culture—they see their food as human food (jaguars see blood as manioc beer, vultures see the maggots in rotting meat as grilled fish, etc.), they see their bodily attributes (fur, feathers, claws, beaks etc) as body decorations or cultural instruments, they see their social system as organized in the same way as human institutions are (with chiefs, shamans, ceremonies, exogamous moieties, etc). This 'to see as' refers literally to percepts and not analogically to concepts, although in some cases the emphasis is placed more on the categorical rather than on the sensory aspect of the phenomenon.

Viveiros de Castro (ibid. 471) remarks that 'this perspectivism and cosmological transformism' have been 'only the object of short commentaries' and seem 'to be quite unevenly elaborated'. Nevertheless he is able to cite (ibid. nn. 1–3), for such a view, reports of the Campa, Matsiguenga, Wayapi, Araweté (his own fieldwork), U'wa and Akuriyo from South America, as well as Eskimo, Koyukon, Kaska, Cree, Ojibwa, Kwakiutl, Tsimshian, Haida, Chewong, and Ma'Betisék from other parts of the world. As for the notion that animals' bodies are 'clothing', he says that that is found among the Makuna, the Yagua, the Piro, the Trio, the Upper Xingu societies, and in north-west American cosmologies especially.[10]

---

[10] Thus Århem (1996: 190) wrote concerning Makuna beliefs: 'when animals roam in the forest or swim in the rivers, they appear as fish and game, but as they enter their houses they discard their animal guises, don their feather crowns and ritual ornaments, and turn into "people"'.

Clearly, first, social roles and cultural life are not limited to human beings, but are (in this view) widely shared by other animals and spirits. By the same token, second, there is no operational notion of 'nature' that describes a domain of animals and creatures other than humans as a distinct, non-social, category. Originally, indeed, animals and humans were undifferentiated, though it was not humans who then became separated off from other animals, so much as they who lost some of their human traits (ibid. 472). Moreover, the boundaries between one species and another, and those that mark individual membership of a species, are and remain unstable and subject to transformation. Shamans, especially, are thought to be able to cross those boundaries more or less at will.

Once again we face a hermeneutic crux, indeed a double one. One school of thought might seek to argue that, despite the appearances, the animist ontology aims to establish and validate the contrast between humans and the rest of the world, between culture and nature. Yet that does not just use observers' categories that go beyond those of the actors themselves. In this case those categories positively conflict with those that are in play in the beliefs reported, which apply social and cultural concepts indifferently and universally both to humans and to non-humans. That line of interpretation is subject to the objections I have mentioned in other contexts, namely that it runs the risk of overriding the actors' own reports about their beliefs in favour of the categories the observers themselves believe, a priori, must obtain.

The alternative is to grant, first, that our nature/culture dichotomy has to be suspended. On the 'animist' world-view, interiority (as Descola calls it) is common to humans and non-humans alike: what divides them is (just) physicality, the particular bodies these various intentional agents inhabit. What is common, however, both to this and to the other three ontologies in Descola's taxonomy, is the need for some account of the present dispensation. We are dealing with world-views, cosmologies, attempts to make sense of the complexities of experience, including not just what things there are, but also why events happen in the ways they do, why good or bad fortune strikes, why some efforts at controlling the environment are crowned with success, others not. Those attempts are often associated with a story of origins, of how that dispensation arose, where the distance between what the world was like then, and how it is now, may be more or less marked. And there are generally clear implications for how humans should behave, towards other members of their own collectivity, as well as to other humans and non-humans. The other three ontologies share with naturalism that they present themselves not just as descriptive accounts of how things are, but also normative ones, since how things are carries lessons for how we should behave. The divergences within the contrasting world-views for which we have ethnographic testimony have to be respected. It is certainly not as if our concept of nature is one that everyone possesses—we have already seen reason to doubt that—nor even is it one to which everyone aims, let alone is it the case that nature comes with ready-made joints to be used in its analysis.

Yet, if ontologies do indeed differ *radically*, we encounter the second hermeneutic problem: how is any mutual understanding between them possible? We have mentioned the difficulty before (Ch. 6) and suggested a guarded response. On the one hand, we should certainly not underestimate the challenge posed in evaluating what the members of a given society with an 'animist' or 'perspectivist' ontology are committed to when they talk of jaguars seeing human blood as beer. Ethnographers in the field may often be hard put to it to make sense of this in context, and a fortiori outsiders need to exercise caution.

But that is not to say, on the other hand, that there is no possibility of understanding whatsoever, for within limits at least that can be and is painstakingly built up by the ethnographer, making the most of the opportunities for bridgeheads that are provided by everyday discourse where less may be at stake. Nor does it preclude piecing together both mundane and more highly charged beliefs to suggest generalizations concerning the underlying ontological categories themselves. Besides, a group that sees jaguars as no different from humans in that they have souls, is still in no doubt that jaguars are jaguars in that they have different bodies ('clothes'). What it is to be a jaguar is conceived very differently in different world-views, not to be reduced to the DNA that the modern biologist may be interested in, nor even to their ethology. There is, to use the terminology I have introduced elsewhere in these studies, a multidimensionality in what it is to be a jaguar.[11]

[11] We have found multidimensionality relevant to colour perception and to spatial cognition, and we noted the same phenomenon in relation to modern zoological taxonomy, where in each case alternative theories reflect varying criteria and interests but do not thereby forfeit objectivity. What the plural ontologies of Descola and in particular his 'animism' and Viveiros de Castro's 'perspectivism' have in common with those examples

In this instance, our experience of our own society helps, in so far as it presents us, surely, with some analogous situations. What exactly a group of individuals may be committed to when describing their conviction that God became man, or that in the sacrament the wine is the blood of Christ, poses similar interpretative problems, even when we have the advantage of speaking the same language as our informants and of sharing much of their educational and social background. It will not cut any ice with the faithful to be told that they cannot really believe what they say they believe or that they do not mean what they say to be taken literally, but only, as it were, figuratively. After all, massive hermeneutic efforts have been expended down the centuries, by theologians, to show that the doctrine of the Trinity is, precisely, a literal truth. Of course attending Mass is no ordinary common-or-garden activity—but then no more are many of the rituals associated with 'animism' and 'totemism'. We recognize too that many communicants believe in the Trinity and in transubstantiation not because they have worked out robust reasons for themselves that lead to those beliefs, but rather on the authority of others whom they trust, their priests or simply their parents or anyone else they may respect.[12] But in other societies, too, in other contexts, what is believed is often, maybe even generally, accepted on authority, that of parents, elders, priests, though it will only be in literate communities, of course, that there will be appeals to the authority of a sacred text.

I do not mean to imply that there are exact parallels between the cases I am comparing. But it is worth reminding ourselves that in understanding members of our own society we have to bear in mind such points as the following. First, the level of commitment to a set of ontological, metaphysical, or religious beliefs may vary from one individual to another. Second, the values associated with those beliefs may also do so, and third, there may be significant differences in the connections between the values and the commitment and in the

is a recognition of the multiple points of view from which the same object may be apprehended, indeed seen, depending upon who or what does the seeing. But it should be emphasized that no reported—or reconstructed—ontology allows just *any* perspective to be adopted on a Feyerabendian principle that anything goes. On the contrary, there are obvious important constraints on such perspectives, not just interpersonal or social ones, but also from the side of what is there to be 'seen' whether by predators or prey.

[12] For Descola, our modern Western ontology is labelled 'naturalist'. But it is clear that that is not *just* what it is.

extent to which the latter underpins, or is believed to underpin, the former. We evidently have to pay careful attention to the contexts of utterance of a belief and to the mode of discourse in which it is presented. Are we dealing with anything that resembles a scientific theory, subject to certain accepted procedures of verification? In most cases, obviously not. But then what sort of justification, if any, is expected or appropriate?

Obviously, the problems of the anthropologist in the field cannot be resolved at second hand. How does the general view that jaguars are persons, or the particular one that this creature is such and such a shaman in disguise, relate to other, often very exact, knowledge of the behaviour of jaguars? Are there particular circumstances when it is appropriate to suspect that a particular agency is at work?[13] Does the general belief itself originate with shamans or with 'experts' in the matter, or is it transmitted as part of what everyone in the collectivity accepts? How far, if at all, is it subject to question and challenge, for certainly there is plenty of evidence in the ethnographic literature that the word of shamans themselves is frequently doubted?[14] In each case the resources for interpretation have analogues with those we have to call on in interpreting what fellow-members of our own collectivity maintain. Even though the ontologies Descola diagnosed may be more complex and less all-encompassing than his schema initially might suggest, the great merit of his proposal was to underline the dangers attached to the use of particularly highly charged Western categories, and my own historical studies of the invention of the notion of nature add support to the need for particular caution in that regard.

So what general conclusions does this survey suggest? The evidence seems to me to tell against there being any innate apprehension of the domain of nature as such. The acquisition of some notion of culture or society, on the other hand, would appear to be the inevitable result of any process of social incorporation, and so, on that score, universal, even while there is enormous diversity in the ideas that are entertained not only about the societies there are, but also and more particularly

[13] Cf. Ch. 6 above, on exceptional circumstances that may call for non-standard explanations.

[14] Cf. Lévi-Strauss (1958/1968: 175 ff.), who made famous the case of the Kwakiutl Quesalid, who had begun with the intention of showing that the ways of the local shamans were fraudulent, but who ended up being considered a yet more powerful shaman than they.

about the norm or ideal to which society should aspire. In that regard I have noted before that it is characteristic for many human groups to set up strong contrasts between 'them' and 'us', with wide differences in the ways in which the contrasts are represented, including some which deny humanity to those who are not 'us'. How far it is possible to find such a phenomenon of intra-species boundary-marking in other primates or other animals more generally is a question for the animal behaviourist. But so far as the human species goes, some notion of social interdependence is surely basic.

Yet what that notion is contrasted with may not constitute a well-defined category at all. What we may be tempted to assume has to be seen as belonging to 'nature'—the animal kingdom for instance—may well be thought to form societies quite like those of humans. That is principally what is suggested by the divergent attitudes towards physicality and interiority that Descola has analysed.

The conclusion we reach thus turns one of our starting assumptions on its head. I noted at the outset that for some, nature is the domain of the objective and value-free. When we got to the Greeks, however, we found that the term *phusis* that they introduced was not just a tool of polemic between rival intellectual leaders, but also strongly associated with disputes in moral and political thought. At the end of our study, we arrive at what may seem the paradoxical result that what has been claimed to be the value-neutral concept of nature is highly society-specific, while what is universal is *some* idea of the social group or collectivity—a concept that inevitably incorporates value judgements about how best to organize human interrelations. Of course for those societies, ancient or modern, who can call on the concept of nature, that can indeed in principle be invoked in order to stress, precisely, the common humanity of human beings. Yet in practice—as we said—nature has been, and continues to be, as much normative as descriptive, as much a way of introducing value-judgements as setting out what there is, as much a matter of ideology, in fact, as of identifying what all can agree is there to be investigated.

8

Reason

THE enquiry into the unity or diversity of human cognitive capacities faces one of its sternest tests where reason is concerned.[1] Some have confidently assumed and asserted that there are no fundamental differences between human groups or peoples in the matter of rationality. We all think 'in the same way', even though there are plenty of differences in the contents of our thoughts, including in whole sets of beliefs. How can there be different rationalities? That idea, some would say, is self-contradictory, since there would have to be a single mode or type of rationality by which other such modes were identified. As for the ideas that rationality is distributed unevenly across peoples or populations, that some are better endowed in this respect than others, that there are groups that exhibit an inferior rationality or are otherwise deficient in this faculty, those ideas look like the very worst kind of cognitive imperialism, namely one that underpins racism.

Fascist regimes used such ideas to bolster the denial of the true humanity of groups of whom they disapproved, Jews, Gypsies, the mentally retarded, and so to justify the implementation of programmes first of eugenics, then of extermination, to wipe them from the face of the earth.[2] Yet the notion that human rationality is unevenly distributed had appeared long before, when Aristotle claimed that Greeks were superior to Barbarians, males to females, masters to slaves, precisely in respect of rationality—even though Aristotle did not contemplate a programme of eugenics as his teacher Plato had

---

[1] While there are obvious differences in performance—we all make mistakes—the fundamental question relates to the underlying faculty, and I shall accordingly concentrate on that in this discussion.

[2] However, as Traverso (2003), pointed out, eugenic programmes go back to the 1890s, and the enforced sterilization of the mentally ill was practised in the period before the First World War and down to the 1920s both in certain states in the USA and in European countries, including Switzerland, Sweden, Norway, and Denmark.

done in the context of his ideal state, where who had the right to mate with whom was to be rigorously controlled. Aristotle's theory of the soul proposed that what marks humans out from other animals is precisely the rational faculty. Yet as I also pointed out before (Ch. 6), he also held that that comes in more or less perfect forms. The rational faculty of the slave is limited to the capacity to understand the master's commands (*Politics* 1254^{b}20 ff.). Although he considers the view that some had put forward, that slavery is an artificial, man-made, institution, and that no one is by nature a slave, he rejects it, precisely on the basis of the argument that some humans have only that limited, minimal, rationality.

Women, too, in Aristotle's view, lack the full deliberative skills that men can and do exercise. It follows that they cannot meet the criteria for full citizenship. In every Greek state, in practice, women's rights were limited, in some more than in others, to be sure, and influential as they may have been in many areas, their direct participation in the political process was zero. So Aristotle does not even need seriously to argue the case for his thesis that women's rationality, too, is imperfect. However, when it comes to such groups as farmers and craftsmen, to exclude them from citizenship, as he does when he sketches out his ideal city in *Politics* Books 7 and 8, he has to shift his ground. They lack the leisure to undertake full political and military responsibilities, and so while they were citizens in most of the democracies he was familiar with, that did not correspond to what he considered the best political constitution.

At one level, analysis of *what* we think may seem straightforward, although the relationship between conscious desires and unconscious ones, and between explicit attitudes, values, and beliefs and implicit ones, may prove problematic. The phenomena of rationalization are common enough, the ways in which the desire to reduce cognitive dissonance (as Festinger 1964 called it) operates have been studied, as also has that mode of rationalization that Elster (1983) dubbed 'sour grapes'. But what we mean when we talk about *how* we think is even less transparent. That expression has been used to cover a wide spectrum of possibilities. At one end of that spectrum we may be referring to exercises in logic, the capacity to make valid deductions from given premises, to see what follows from what, in other words. But 'how we think' may refer to more than just applying certain logical rules. It may and probably more usually does refer to the exercise of the imagination, grasping what a person intends even when they have not fully expressed their thoughts, or have not expressed them in words at all. The ways in which people think include also how they set about communicating their thoughts, persuading others, defending their own positions, justifying their attitudes and values. Extensive studies have been undertaken to discuss, for example, how decisions are reached under conditions of uncertainty and on the psychological factors that influence practical reasoning.

Meanwhile a major industry has come to be devoted to devising and applying tests to measure intelligence. Educators, employment agencies, and policy makers would all love to have procedures that are, and can be seen to be, both robust and fair. Yet that is hardly the case with those used at present, which largely underestimate the basic problem of saying what intelligence is. Very often it seems that all that IQ tests are testing is the ability to take IQ tests. The results are heavily influenced by the extent to which the subjects have learned what to expect, and better scores may reflect no more than greater familiarity with the tests themselves. Whether what they reveal is relevant to other situations where modes of intelligence do not readily lend themselves to formal analysis, let alone to multiple choice questions, is doubtful.

The problems that centre round reason, rationality, and intelligence are complex and elude easy, in some cases any, resolution. But we may explore, admittedly highly selectively, the different approaches that have been adopted, reflecting different interests, different methodologies and above all different starting assumptions. I shall begin where some of the modern debate started, namely with Lévy-Bruhl's proposal of a pre-logical mentality. That will lead me to some comments on the controversy that stemmed from that, on the question of apparently irrational beliefs. A very different set of—this time practical—concerns motivates those who carry responsibility, in our society, for dealing with deviant behaviour, discriminating, as our society insists, between the criminal and the insane.

Turning from the abnormal to the normal, that is to what is accepted as within the latter's range, we may consider the work of psychologists who classify personality traits, including the modes of intelligence associated with them, differentiating extroverts and introverts, divergers and convergers and even 'female' and 'male' minds. Those studies, Baron-Cohen's especially, overlap with the neurophysiological and biochemical investigations undertaken by Changeux and others, that I have already mentioned in discussing the emotions. Empirical research of a very different type, sociological rather than neurophysiological, has been claimed to support theses concerning the different ways in which 'Asians' and 'Westerners' think—as the subtitle of Nisbett's recent book (2003) puts it. Such studies are clearly of particular importance for assessing the universality or otherwise of modes of rationality. To evaluate them I shall undertake a detailed critique of Nisbett's methodology and results and bring to bear other investigations that throw light on apparent divergent competences in reasoning. Finally, I shall turn back to the early history of the subject, to see what an investigation of the origins of self-conscious logic itself can teach us concerning our strategic question of the psychic unity or diversity of reason and its products.

Lévy-Bruhl was initially convinced that the only way to account for what seemed to him to be the wide differences in the beliefs and thought patterns of different peoples that his reading in the ethnographic literature suggested to him was by way of the hypothesis of distinct mentalities, the 'pre-logical' one to be found especially in 'primitive' peoples, and the logical or scientific one exemplified by those who lived in civilized countries such as France. The former worked on an altogether different set of logical rules from the latter, not the laws of contradiction and excluded middle, but a law of 'participation'. This allowed a person to be identified with his or her belongings or name, and permitted a person to be in two places at once, indeed in two bodies at once. Although in his early publications Lévy-Bruhl correlated his postulated mentalities with primitive and advanced societies respectively, he came to recognize that both mentalities can be found everywhere in the world. He expressed his regrets concerning the label 'pre-logical', but never abandoned the notion of mentalities itself.

From the outset Lévy-Bruhl's ideas attracted severe criticism, but the type of puzzle that he had begun with continued to be at the centre of a furious controversy in which both anthropologists and philosophers participated. How was one to understand or interpret the apparently irrational statements, beliefs, and patterns of behaviour that ethnographic reports contained? Could a single logic, a single standard of rationality, be applied to the whole of humanity? Much of this debate now seems, in retrospect, like shadow-boxing. True, a number of useful points were made, about the conditions of mutual intelligibility of apparently radically divergent systems of beliefs, concerning whether it is coherent to talk of alternative conceptual schemas, on the limits of the determinacy of translation, and other matters. Yet the debate was not notable for the care with which the problematic items of belief were contextualized and located in relation to other ideas and practices from the society in question.[3] The famous Nuer statement that twins are birds, and the Dorze belief that the leopard is a Christian animal, were often taken in isolation from the sets of ideas and practices of which they formed a part (cf. Lloyd 1990: ch. 1). Nor were the skills that both Nuer and Dorze show in managing their ecologies and their day-to-day lives in their respective environments allowed to serve as reminders of their practical intelligence. The Amazonian peoples whose cosmologies have been studied by Viveiros de Castro and Descola exhibit a vastly superior knowledge of the ecology of their territories, the behaviour of the animals within them, and the properties of the plants that grow there, than members of industrialized societies are generally able to claim concerning *their* natural environment (cf. Ch. 3 n. 4 and Ch. 7 above).

A further striking feature of that debate was that it was seen as largely, if not solely, a problem that had been thrown up by reports from exotic societies. As I have insisted before, we cannot afford to forget that some extravagantly counter-intuitive beliefs are held in our own society. The Christian doctrine of the Trinity, that holds that God is three and that God is one, might have alerted the discussants to the point that the phenomenon they were concerned with is not confined to collectivities studied by ethnographers 'in the field'. Different interpretations of that theological doctrine will be favoured by different people. But one observation that it is easy to make is that paradox may serve as a marker of the special status of statements and beliefs about the very exceptional person who God is. On one view it is not the content of a belief that is being conveyed but the special nature of what it is a belief about. I do not suggest that such deflationary

---

[3] Gellner (1974) exposed the farcicality of outsiders discussing Zande attitudes towards their cows, when the Azande have no cattle: the discussants had taken what Evans-Pritchard had reported concerning the Nuer and applied it to a totally different society living hundreds of miles away in a different part of Africa.

accounts will capture what is at stake in the Christian any more than in the Dorze or the Nuer case. Indeed to capture everything that is at stake in each of those cases will demand, as I have said before, the most detailed and sensitive analyses of the roles of the people who assert the beliefs in question, the contexts in which adherence to them is expected, accepted, or demanded, and what maintains such beliefs in the societies in question.[4] But the comparison serves to block any claim that Western traditions of rationality are somehow immune to the types of problematic beliefs that led to the diagnosis of a pre-logical mentality in other peoples.

Certain modes of irrationality take on an altogether different significance when the problem is one of coping with the deviant behaviour of individuals. Faced with evidence of sufficiently disturbed behaviour or of apparent failures of rationality on the part of an individual, the first problem will be that of diagnosis. Is this a case that a welfare officer, a social psychologist, or a psychotherapist should handle? Or is the individual suffering from a sufficiently serious mental illness that he or she should be encouraged to submit to treatment? Or should the individual be sectioned and indeed confined—even against his or her will—in an asylum? Or is the matter one that the police and criminal justice system alone should deal with?

Much hangs on the decision taken. The individual's liberty is at stake. The modes of 'treatment' on offer will vary, though it must be said usually with little prospect of improvement in the individual's condition. Not even those fortunate enough to afford extensive psychoanalysis will necessarily benefit from the experience. Physical interventions, such as drugs and electric shock treatment, produce results in many cases, though the reason they do so may be little understood. Meanwhile punishment, meted out by the courts, merely serves to protect society.

The 'experts' responsible for the diagnoses often have to rely on inspired guesswork—or mere guesswork indeed—as much as hard evidence, even when they are not patently involved simply in an exercise of damage limitation. It is true that there are exceptions. The physical causes of certain abnormal mental conditions are sometimes

---

[4] Compare Fernandez's (1982) work on 'empty concepts' and Boyer's (1993; 1994) more general thesis that religion derives much of its strength from the combination of common or garden ideas (about persons, agents, intentions) with special, exceptional, initially counter-intuitive or even paradoxical ones.

identifiable, in many cases as the result of the study of lesions to the brain. Statistical evidence has been collected that suggests correlations between delinquency and deprivation, economic, social, emotional. Certain indicators of the gravity of psychiatric cases are generally agreed. If the patient talks of suicide, that cannot be ignored, if only because legal action might subsequently be taken against the authorities if it is dismissed. Sometimes the prospective patients are well aware of this, and use that knowledge to ensure attention. Yet there are still plenty of grey areas and conflict as between the advice offered by 'experts' of different types. Social welfare officers, psychiatrists, magistrates, come to the assessment of an individual's case from very different backgrounds and with very different primary concerns, and that is before we come to the individual's own family circle. They will be assumed to be familiar with his or her past behaviour patterns and will be called upon to give their views on the severity of the complaint and what should be done. But evidently they too, the immediate family or circle of friends, will have their interests, their agenda, and sometimes those will run counter to the interests of the 'patient' concerned.

The fundamental problem, not confined to our modern stressful industrialized societies, is that there is no consensus on what is to count as normal 'rational' behaviour. We have a rich vocabulary of terms to talk about the retarded, the mentally deficient, the handicapped, the deprived, the disturbed, the insane, the criminal.[5] Other societies do not necessarily draw the same boundaries—fuzzy ones, at best—as we do. And most do not have the institutions—the hospitals and lunatic asylums, the prisons—with which to implement whatever those in authority decide needs to be done in particular cases or in general.[6] But however the norm is decided, or however departures from it are recognized, no society fails to distinguish in some way between the more, and less, well-adapted individuals, between eccentric

---

[5] In some cases the creation of the category contributes to *producing* the very phenomenon it describes, as Hacking (1991; 1992a; 1995) has suggested in his studies of what he calls the 'looping effects of human kinds', citing the examples of child abuse and multiple personality disorder in particular. He has subsequently backtracked on the issue of 'human kinds', as well as modifying his views on 'natural kinds' and 'natural classifications', but the effects he described are well established however they are to be labelled.

[6] The transformations of attitudes that accompanied the institutionalization of the mad and of the criminal in the eighteenth century were highlighted—with some elements of exaggeration maybe—by Foucault's (1967; 1972) work especially.

and ordinary behaviour. Different individuals have different talents and abilities. While most of these are evaluated favourably (the gifted singer, the gifted hunter) some may well be viewed with some ambivalence, as may be the case with the gifted diviner, or the holy man whose close contacts with the spirit world may be greeted with a mixture of awe, admiration, and fear.[7] Why different persons have the skills and the characters they do may well not arise as a question at all. But that there are such differences will normally be taken for granted.

Our modern fascination with character and personality has given rise to a mass of studies attempting various types of taxonomies, if not also explanations. Extroverts are contrasted with introverts, divergers with convergers. Sometimes these are represented as character traits that we are born with, sometimes they are rather ones that we acquire. The educational psychologist Liam Hudson (1966) claimed that convergers naturally select subjects such as mathematics and Latin once at school, while divergers prefer art or English literature. But once those choices have been made, they influence the subsequent development, and confirm the character traits, of the pupils in question in an obvious feedback effect. But more often the determining factors are assumed to belong to the very earliest stages of an infant's experience, its relations with its carers, its mother, father, siblings, and in some cases, its extended family.

Two sets of recent studies have gone much further and suggested broad conclusions concerning the differences between 'male' and 'female' minds (Baron-Cohen) and between 'Asians' and 'Westerners' (Nisbett). The methodology and the results in both cases need examination, for both evidently have considerable potential significance for the overall thesis of the 'psychic unity' of humans.

Baron-Cohen's work (2003) originated in part in studies of the wide spectrum of conditions loosely labelled 'autism', and it uses modern techniques of brain scans as well as a battery of psychological tests. The hypothesis that these studies explore is that there are significant differences between what he calls 'male' and 'female' minds, though those terms have to be interpreted with some care. It is far from being

---

[7] The idea has been suggested that what is called shamanism can be explained in terms of our psychological categories of personality disorders up to and including schizophrenia. But that is on the flimsiest of evidence and without much attention to the wide range of phenomena that 'shamanism' has been held to cover.

the case that all men exhibit the one, all women the other. Rather, just about everyone will exemplify characteristics associated with both. The claim relates, then, to broad traits and tendencies across human populations. But the 'male' mind shows particular skills in a range of tasks, notably ones involving numbers: conversely, the 'female' mind scores more highly than the male in, for example, interpreting others' behaviour in interpersonal relations. Interestingly enough those diagnosed as suffering from one or other type of 'autistic' condition show the characteristics of the 'male' mind in an extreme form.

At first sight this might look like a revival of Lévy-Bruhl's hypothesis of mentalities, for did he not similarly contrast 'participation' with 'causality', in the terms Tambiah (1990) used in his survey of the question in his Lewis Morgan lectures? Yet that would be a very mistaken impression, since the differences are fundamental. Baron-Cohen's work is based not on second- or third-hand reports, but on extensive tests carried out in controlled conditions. Most importantly, the results are claimed to support not a theory of mutually incompatible mentalities, hermetically sealed off from one another, but rather certain characteristics that cluster in patterns that exhibit considerable overlap. Nor is it assumed that the character traits revealed are fixed for the life-span of the individual concerned.

Much further work no doubt needs to be carried out before a confident assessment of Baron-Cohen's work can be given. But the shape of its possible implications for the study of human rationality can already be discerned. With the exception of the extreme 'autistic' end of the spectrum, the picture that is emerging is one of a wide range of overlapping skills and competences. The differences found between individuals and groups correlate to some extent, but only to some extent, with given biological, including of course sexual, differentiae. It is not for nothing that the two main contrast sets have been labelled 'male' and 'female'. But the hypothesis being tested is certainly not a biological determinist one. Baron-Cohen allows for the complexity of other influences, social and psychological, that go to form personalities, as also for the plasticity of the personality once formed. We may conclude that this is one potentially fruitful, but by no means exclusive, way in which to try to bring order into the complex proliferation of recognizable character traits that humans display.

Both the methods and the results of the work of Nisbett and his team seem subject to more serious reservations and difficulties. As to methods, the first major problem relates to who is to count as 'Asian', who as a 'Westerner'. Under the former he includes not only Chinese living on the mainland and on Taiwan, but also Chinese of the diaspora, as well as non-Chinese Asians, Japanese and Koreans, two peoples who normally consider the differences between themselves and the Chinese to be far greater than any similarities. Recent Chinese immigrants to America, and American citizens of Chinese descent, are also brought into this category, though these are usually treated as an intermediate group, yielding results that are half-way between 'Westerners' and 'Easterners'. Moreover while some of the interviews were carried out in Chinese by Chinese members of Nisbett's team, others were conducted in English or through an interpreter. Some of the research he cites involved putting Chinese and Japanese children in quite artificial situations, as when they were tested in their ability to solve anagrams (Nisbett 2003: 58)—not a question that could arise in their mother tongues.

Although Nisbett mentions these points, even apologizing, in his introduction (ibid. p. xxii) for his global category of 'East Asian', their significance tends to be downplayed. Yet the differences in the groups so lumped together and in the techniques used to explore their attitudes might be thought to throw serious doubt on the viability of his generalizations.

As for 'Westerners', that category is just as problematic. 'When I speak of European Americans, I mean blacks [*sic*] and whites and Hispanics—anyone but people of Asian descent' (ibid.). Little or no attention is paid to the different countries of origin of 'European' Europeans. Using national categories still, he sometimes remarks on differences between 'Britishers', 'Germans', and 'French', but generally operates with his global antithesis between East and West.[8]

Indeed Nisbett argues that many of the key characteristics he associates with how 'Westerners' think originate in ancient Greece, to which he devotes a detailed discussion. Yet first the actual links between ancient Greeks and contemporary Europeans, let alone Americans,

[8] It is unclear to what extent the tests that Nisbett cites systematically checked for gender differences. But his remark at 2003: 100 that 'gender differences are always smaller than the cultural differences' may suggest a rather different view from that supported by Baron-Cohen's work.

are tenuous. Even the sense in which the ancient Greeks are the ancestors of those who live in what we know as Greece today is problematic. Moreover, secondly, Nisbett's account of ancient Greek thought—their mentality, as he calls it—is full of oversimplifications and plain errors. While I have been at pains to point out that there are different foci of interest, and styles of enquiry, among different Greek writers, as indeed also among Chinese ones, Nisbett ignores the major differences between Aristotle, say, and Democritus, or the Stoics and the Epicureans, and writes as if all Greeks shared the same basic atomist ontology. Thus he claims (ibid. 80) that 'the ancient Greek philosophers tended to see the world as being composed of discrete objects or separate atoms. A piece of wood to the Chinese would have been a seamless, uniform material; to the Greeks it would have been seen as composed of particles'—a remark that simply fails to square with Aristotle's view of wood as a homogeneous substance. But the more fundamental problem is that many of the attitudes Nisbett focuses on as typically 'Western' appear to reflect values that do not predate the industrial revolution, and in some cases seem to be peculiar to certain segments of contemporary American society in particular.

Several of these objections would, no doubt, be dismissed as quibbles. Nisbett and his associates are confident that differences show up between his two global groups in just about every investigation they have conducted. So we come now to the results claimed, where we may remark, first, on their heterogeneity. 'Asians' are held to differ with regard to their sensitivity to the interests and feelings of others, to their sense of group solidarity, in other words, where the contrast is with the aggressive individualism of 'Westerners'. Again representatives of the two groups are reported to respond very differently when told stories about some real or fictional crisis or disaster, a multiple murder, or a suicide, that is, in the answers they give when questioned about who or what they thought was responsible for how things turned out.

But in many cases the differences identified simply reflect the more or less deep-seated attitudes of the respondents who were questioned, including the values they may be assumed to have acquired in child-hood. No one will doubt that there are indeed important differences in such between different groups in different societies, even between different societies as a whole, even though generalization is always risky, and identifying the factors in upbringing or in the processes of social incorporation that might be responsible for particular characteristics is also likely to be speculative. But no one will deny the importance of such strongly-held values as influences on the assumptions that will be in play when a person is asked about the causal factors involved in those stories of crisis or disaster.[9]

Thus far 'thinking differently' would mainly be a matter of the differences in the values we possess and the assumptions we make when arriving at judgements about how we should behave or how others do. But what would it mean to say that modes of reasoning themselves differ, not just in the contents of the values brought to bear, but in the manner of reasoning conducted on their basis? At this point Nisbett's account runs into a problem of consistency that does not surface in his text. For him to sustain a thesis concerning the differences in the modes of reasoning as such used by his two global groups, he has to separate form from content. Yet *that* separation he considers to be characteristic of the West, indeed a 'Western ailment' (ibid. 203). The East does not separate these two, he claims, but adopts a holistic 'dialectical' approach. Where the West insists on the laws of identity and of non-contradiction (ibid. 176), the East seeks to resolve 'contradictions' and 'conflicts' (where logical and substantive issues are run together in Nisbett's account as well as in the views he ascribes to Easterners) and prefers 'both/and' to 'either/or'. It is clearly difficult to assess differences in the forms of reasoning used by Easterners when *ex hypothesi* they do not observe a distinction between 'form' and 'content' in this context.

Of course that does not preclude our applying our formal logical rules to evaluate different stretches of reasoning as we encounter them or as they are reported. So the next question relates to the appropriateness of doing so. A digression will serve to highlight some of the difficulties. The transparency of formal logic is, of course, its claimed strength, but that may be deceptive. It enables determinate answers to be given to the question of whether an inference is or is not valid, thanks to the fact that the reasoning proceeds by way of clear and

---

[9] Indeed, in my analysis of different styles of causal analysis in Ch. 6, I noted certain differences in the kinds of explanation or understanding sought, and in the different models of causation invoked, within both different Greek and different Chinese writers as well as between them. The chief difference between Nisbett's ways of thinking, and my 'styles of enquiry', is that the latter may and do vary with the aims and methods of particular individuals and groups—and with the subjects investigated—not just with cultures as a whole, let alone with global generalizations concerning East and West.

unambiguous propositions, well-formed formulae, to use the normal jargon. But very little of the ordinary reasoning we engage in, for practical purposes in everyday life, makes use of well-formed formulae. We need to decide whether we can afford to make a certain purchase, whether we have time to fit in each of two activities that compete for our attention, what to do to help a friend in trouble. Sometimes we may clarify the issue by appealing to a general principle, to the effect (for instance) that generosity towards friends is a good thing, or that truth-telling is, or paying our taxes. But the kernel of the reasoning will generally not lie in moving deductively from the given general principle to the particular case, but rather in determining whether or in what way the general principle is applicable. The key issues might relate to what counts as generosity in the case in hand, even to who count as our friends. Given that the principle that the truth should be told is subject to exceptions, is the case in hand one of the exceptions?

These examples are mundane to the point of being crass, but they serve to underline the contrasts between formal and informal reasoning, and the artificiality of the stock examples of valid inferences in the logic textbooks.[10] These are set out in schemata of the form 'all Bs are As, all Cs are Bs, so all Cs are As', or 'if p, then q: but p: so q', where the validity of the conclusions does not depend on what the symbols stand for (terms in the case of As, Bs and Cs, propositions in the case of ps and qs) nor on the truth of the premises. To set out sequences of argument in formal or semi-formal terms can certainly direct attention to what premises are needed to get to which conclusions, and the study of formal logic will serve to alert us to common mistakes. Judged by the canons of strict validity, arguments of the form 'if p, then q: but q: so p' commit what is known as the fallacy of the consequent. But the soundness of the reasonings we usually engage in more often turns not on the issue of validity (on what follows from what) but rather on that of truth. That is not problematic when we are dealing with what are called analytic truths, statements that are true in virtue just of the meanings of the terms (as in 'all brothers are males'). But of course the premises we need in practical reasoning are more often synthetic than analytic. The key question is, more often, do we have good grounds for holding to the truth of

---

[10] Nisbett (2003: esp. ch. 7, 165 ff.) uses a number of more or less formalized textbook examples of syllogisms.

the empirical propositions on which we rely? That may be no easy matter to decide. Errors of judgement there are easily made—and are undoubtedly more frequent than those where we mistake an invalid for a valid inference though some types of these, as we shall see, are common enough.

Individuals from other backgrounds and cultures besides those investigated by Nisbett and his team have been studied for their performance in exercises in formal logic, though the results have sometimes been overinterpreted. While they certainly show that there are variations in the ease and speed with which subjects adapt to what is, for them, a quite unfamiliar situation, whether the results reveal any more than that is a moot point. Let me return for a moment to the exchanges between Luria and his Siberians, which I mentioned before (Ch. 6), and then refer to some of the studies that have cast doubt on certain aspects of our, Westerners', abilities to reason correctly according to the standards of formal logic.

The Siberians who appeared not to grasp the rules of syllogistic logic may have been responding perfectly adequately when we consider the pragmatics of the exchanges between them and their investigators. First *told* that all bears in the Far North are white and then that Novaya Zemlya is in the Far North, but then *asked* what colour the bears there were, the respondents might well suppose that that question *put in doubt* what the investigators had first offered by way of what we call a universal major premise. So far from the subjects betraying some inability to reason well, I suggested that they were obeying the rules of pragmatics more meticulously than those who were questioning them.

But Westerners too are far from the regularly competent reasoners that some have tended to assume. Tversky and Kahneman (1974) have investigated various biases that may be involved in judgements under uncertainty, and Fischhoff's study (1975) showed that when people have been told the outcome of an event, they regularly overestimate the accuracy with which they would have predicted it if they had not been given such knowledge.

But perhaps the most relevant investigations, for the purposes of cross-cultural comparison, are those that involve the so-called Wason test, named after a set of experiments first described by P. C. Wason in 1966, then in greater detail in Wason 1968. These involved subjects being presented with four cards, each of which, they were told, had a letter (for example, A or B) on one side, and a number (for example, 2 or 3) on the other. They were then given the rule that if the letter is A, then the number is 2. Presented with four cards where the sides that could be seen carried A, B, 2, and 3 respectively, they were asked which card or cards had to be turned over to *disprove* the rule. While most saw that the card showing A needed to be turned over (to see whether or not there was a 2 on the other side, for if there was not, the rule was disproved), very few saw that the card showing 3 *also* needed to be turned over (for if it had the letter A on the other side, then the rule would equally be disproved). Instead subjects tended to choose the card with the number 2, where it is true that if the letter on the other side was A, that would *support* the rule. However if the letter was B, that would not *disprove* the rule they had been given. Yet when subjects were given the same test not in abstract form (with cards showing A, B, 2, and 3) but where the cards carried realistic content,[11] they performed rather better, though that did not help those same subjects avoid mistakes when confronted again with the abstract test.

Such tests have been the subject of considerable discussion and debate.[12] But three crucial points emerge. First, Westerners are no more immune than Luria's Siberians to errors in reasoning when these are judged by the canons of strict logic. Secondly, the subjects tested found the task somewhat easier not when it was presented in an abstract form, but when the information on the cards could be connected with a real-life situation. That suggests, thirdly, that the artificiality of the more abstract formulation is itself not a help but a hindrance. The conversion of universal propositions and issues to do with biconditionality are (as I noted) sources of some perplexity. Given that 'all As are Bs' or that 'if p, then q', there is no justification, in logic, for assuming that 'all Bs are (also) As', nor that 'if q, then p'. The rules

[11] The four items in the realistic test were (1) the back of a sealed envelope, (2) the back of an unsealed envelope, (3) the front of a correctly stamped envelope, and (4) the front of an envelope stamped incorrectly, and the rule to be disproved was that if an envelope is sealed, it had the correct stamp. Fewer in that situation failed to see that they needed to turn over not just the first card, but also the fourth, the envelope that had an incorrect stamp (cf. Johnson-Laird, Legrenzi, and Legrenzi 1972).

[12] Wason and Johnson-Laird (1972) diagnosed the source of the mistakes as a tendency to wish to verify rather than to falsify. J.Evans (1982; 1989) pointed further to a greater interest in heuristics than in deduction. Sperber, Cara, and Girotto (1995) maintained that relevance theory holds the key. Subjects pursue an investigation up to a certain point, but cease to do so when they believe (correctly or mistakenly) that they have examined all the relevant factors. Cf. also Fiddick, Cosmides, and Tooby (2000) and Atran (2001*b*).

of formal logic prohibit both moves. But in everyday reasoning, they are often made whether or not this is because they seem plausible in the light of other background data that may be brought to bear. When not doing formal logic, but engaged in practical reasoning, we draw on whatever resources of information are available to us, including assumptions that may need revision, and we do not limit ourselves to what may be inferred merely from the logical relations between the propositions we may express.

How does all of this bear on Nisbett's claims? It is essential to distinguish the different criteria by which skills in reasoning may be evaluated. The canons of formal logic provide one type of test, but that leaves out of account the pragmatics of intercommunicative exchange. In practical reasoning in real life, the skills that count include qualities such as clear-headedness in the appreciation of a situation in all its potential complexity, correct judgement as to which principles are the ones to apply and in what ways, and a sensitivity to the reactions of others affected by the decisions taken—more than simply an ability in formal logic. So far as that ability is concerned, the Wason tests showed that mistakes are not limited to those with little or no schooling, nor to those from a particular cultural background. Indeed some professional logicians were reported as making embarrassing errors (Wason and Johnson-Laird 1972: 173).

But over and above the types of formal mistakes that those tests revealed to be common, the ways we reason to decisions regularly exhibit the influence of a complex set of cultural, social, and psychological factors. Some of Nisbett's studies suggest certain patterns in these influences, as when greater, or less, attention is paid to the importance of group solidarity. But if we are right to suggest that the differences there relate principally to differences in the values and attitudes of the individuals and groups concerned, then that, maybe rather banal, point is what chiefly emerges from Nisbett's investigations, rather than support for the global generalizations concerning 'East' and 'West' that he then proposes on their basis (cf. Ortner 2003).

One final set of evidence remains, however, to be considered. The self-conscious analysis of reasoning has in its history, especially, though not exclusively, one involving the ancient Greeks. By investigating that, we can hope to throw some light on what needs that analysis served and what differences it made. The answers to both questions contain (I will suggest) some surprises. In Aristotle's hands, formal logic formed the basis of a theory of rigorous demonstration which, by showing how in principle certainty can be attained, could claim superiority over all other modes of reasoning. Yet the results of his analysis were of limited bearing in most areas of practical reasoning—with one notable exception, namely that once certain types of correct or incorrect procedures had been identified and classified, they could be cited *as such* in communicative exchanges, thereby facilitating dialectical moves with interlocutors. Otherwise, how far the introduction of formal logic improved standards of reasoning is difficult to say. It certainly did not mean that mistakes in reasoning thereafter ceased to occur, even among those who had mastered the new discipline.

Let me elaborate these points briefly. First, we should be clear that an interest in explicitly examining aspects of reasoning is not confined to ancient Greece. In ancient China, for instance, there are acute analyses of techniques of persuasion (as in the *shuonan*, Ch. 12 in *Hanfeizi*—a point to which Nisbett does not attend). These concentrate on the interpersonal aspects of persuasion, which are of course central to the task of bringing another person round to a point of view that he or she would not otherwise agree with. While in Chinese discussions, faults of reasoning are often laid at the door of the reasoner (as they are indeed in many Greek accounts), some are located in the arguments themselves. The topic of inconsistency (*bei* 誖) is not just illustrated by example, but discussed in so many terms.[13]

When Aristotle engaged in his exercise in formal logic in the *Prior Analytics*, that was in part with an eye to the theory of demonstration that he set out in the *Posterior Analytics*. The distinctive feature of that, historically speaking, was that it showed what was required in order to secure incontrovertible conclusions, namely true, indeed self-evident, premises and valid deductive inference. The Chinese too, of course, prized arguments that defeated those of their opponents, but they did so mainly by showing the weakness of their opponents' positions directly, not by claiming that their own were unassailable thanks to their logical structure. Aristotle was well aware that *informal* demonstrations, claimed as such, had frequently been set out in the

---

[13] The stock illustration of inconsistency related to the manufacturer of lances and shields who claimed that his lances could penetrate anything, but that his shields could withstand penetration by anything. For a brief discussion of the topic of inconsistency in the Mohist Canon, see Graham (1989: 185–6); cf. Harbsmeier (1998: 217–18, 342 ff.); Lloyd (2004: 42, 46–7).

law courts and in the political assemblies. But his analysis enabled him—so he thought—to outdo all rivals on the score of the certainty of the conclusions reached by rigorous demonstration—a certainty that depended, as I said, not just on the validity of the reasoning, but also on the truth of the premises. But then the fundamental primary premises were supposed to be self-evident axioms. I have argued elsewhere (Lloyd 1996a) that the exceptionally competitive situation in ancient Greece, that pitted one would-be expert in argument against another, often in open public debate, acted as an important stimulus to Aristotle's analysis, both to his development of a notion of strict, axiomatic-deductive, demonstration, and to his studies of inferior, including fallacious, modes of reasoning.

However, Aristotle himself makes two other valuable points in his discussion of the problems. Although he prides himself on the superiority of the rigorous demonstrations he demands in philosophy and mathematics, he recognizes that in rhetoric no one would attempt to argue in such a fashion. For strict demonstrations, you need premises that are true, primary, immediate, better known than, and explanatory of, the conclusions. But if there were an occasion when a forensic orator had premises that fulfilled all those conditions, the last thing he would dream of needing to do would be to proceed to such a demonstration. Rhetoric does not normally use necessary truths, but probable ones, propositions that hold for the most part. It is precisely when the facts of a case, or their interpretation, are disputed that the orator will need to use all his skills to make his case in what Aristotle is prepared to label *rhetorical* demonstrations. For that purpose the orator will use arguments, examples, analogies, enthymemes[14] especially: but he will be aware that he has other means to win his audience round, namely by presenting himself as a sincere, honourable, well-intentioned fellow, one who can be trusted—very much the sorts of consideration that Chinese discussions of persuasion also pay attention to.

The second astute observation that Aristotle makes relates, precisely, to the interdependence of reasoning and character in the domain of ethics. True intellectual virtue (what he calls *phronesis* or practical wisdom) presupposes moral goodness. He explains by considering what

---

[14] Enthymemes are the deductive arguments appropriate to rhetoric, though they do not meet the conditions (such as the reliance solely on necessary premises) that apply to syllogisms in the strict sense in logic: see Burnyeat (1994).

we should say if the one exists without the other. Skill in reasoning about ethical matters that is divorced from goodness of character is just *cleverness*. Conversely, goodness of character without the intellectual excellence of practical wisdom is mere *natural* excellence, not true moral excellence at all.

This insight may at first sight seem surprising, especially coming from Aristotle who had insisted on the possibility of the purely abstract analysis of argument schemata in his formal logic. But we recognize well enough, in the phenomenon of rationalization, that the way the stingy person *reasons* about the circumstances of a case where he is called upon to be generous reflects his character as the stingy person he is. Practical wisdom, in Aristotle's view, depends on taking all the circumstances of the problem into account. Being courageous, he points out, is first a matter of a settled disposition, but then it is one that is reflected in the right reactions to what is fearful when that is encountered. Not only must one know just how dangerous the situation is, and the consequences of different courses of action if one takes them, but one must also be *self-aware*, conscious, for instance, that one is inclined to be cowardly, or foolhardy, and ready to aim off for that tendency. We may talk about character, and reasoning, in abstract terms separately from one another, but in practice the two are importantly interdependent. There is something of a final irony, here, in that this interdependence is so clearly expressed by an ancient Greek philosopher, when, on Nisbett's view, such an insight looks distinctly 'Eastern' and conflicts with what he takes to be characteristically 'Western'.

The pursuit of diversity in human reasoning has been fraught with problems. Many different modes of diversity have been claimed, on the basis of many different types of consideration—or indeed not based on argument or evidence at all, but simply asserted in the light of assumptions of racial superiority. Clearly, when certain groups are labelled as deficient in reason, that can be used to justify denying that they had any political rights—as Aristotle did with women and slaves—or even denying them their right to live, as Nazis did with Jews and Gypsies. But even Lévy-Bruhl believed, initially at least, that whole populations lacked some basic ability to reason logically, though if he had been right, how they survived would have been quite a mystery, since they were certainly repeatedly faced with practical problems they had to resolve with skill and intelligence.

The issues have been bedevilled by lack of clarity on the very nature of logic itself. When formal logic was first introduced—as it may be said to have been by Aristotle—that did not mean that for the first time people were able to reason coherently. How much of an improvement it led to in performance in that regard is, I said, quite doubtful. What that introduction certainly secured was the possibility of analysing argument schemata in abstract, general terms. But that still leaves plenty of problems in the matter of the translation procedures needed to get from any stretch of informal reasoning to the underlying abstract schemata. In most informal reasoning, indeed, that translation is thwarted by the indeterminacy of the implicit assumptions in play.

But over and over again the differences in reasoning that have been pointed to turn out to depend to a greater or lesser degree on explicit or implicit attitudes and values. *They* vary, to be sure, as between individuals and groups, though as the groups get larger, the generalizations about their shared attitudes become riskier, and Nisbett's 'Asians' and 'Westerners' are global hypostatizations that go well beyond the evidence. But accepting Aristotle's point, that in ethics at least, character and reasoning are interdependent, the variations that we may agree occur should be said to be functions of the two together, rather than of reasoning as such on its own. If that point is taken, the issue of human cognitive diversity in this area is not a matter of the acquisition of skills in the formal analysis of reasoning, let alone of determining where performance comes on some imaginary scale of rationality/irrationality. Rather, differences in the ways individuals or groups reason should be seen as reflecting, especially, the diversity of human character traits, where, we said, we have good reason to make due allowance for the variety and complexity of the influences at work, and indeed the variability in their effects.

Conclusion

SHYLOCK: Hath not a Jew eyes? Hath not a Jew hands, organs, dimensions, senses, affections, passions? Fed with the same food, hurt with the same weapons, subject to the same diseases, healed by the same means, warmed and cooled by the same winter and summer as a Christian is? If you prick us, do we not bleed? If you tickle us, do we not laugh? If you poison us, do we not die? And if you wrong us, shall we not revenge?

Merchant of Venice, Act III Scene i

In a play that is full of racial stereotyping, Shylock is made to enter a plea for the uniformity of all humans, both physical and emotional. The issue of the psychic unity, or diversity, of humans has been controversial ever since antiquity. The moral implications of whatever answers are given are obvious, and a very great deal has been at stake particularly for those judged to be, on one score or another, whether religion, race, or skin-colour, in some way inferior human beings. Much worse treatment than Shylock was represented as eventually receiving[1] has been meted out on inferiors by those who judged themselves to be the master race, claiming to be superior in physique, in intelligence, and—the sickest point of all—in morality itself, indeed. If, down the ages, groups and individuals have often been strident in their endeavours to prove, or more often merely unwaveringly to assert, their own superiority, the opposite position, that all humans are essentially the same, has sometimes been stated more as an article of faith than a view supported by reasoned analysis and empirical evidence.

---

[1] For having plotted to take the life of a citizen of Venice, Shylock is condemned to death, though his life is spared by the Duke. However, he is fined half his wealth and forced to bequeath the rest to the Christian who has married his daughter—besides being compelled to convert to Christianity himself (*Merchant of Venice* Act IV Scene i).

I appreciate that my review of just some of the areas in contention has done no more than scratch the surface of the problems. It would be possible to include many other topics and to bring to bear the work of many more investigators. But on the basis of this selective survey, what conclusions may be suggested?

It is worth observing, first, that a good deal of the material that I have presented in my discussion represents the findings of research undertaken quite recently, sometimes within the last decade or so, in developmental psychology, in social anthropology, and especially in many different areas of biology, from neurophysiology to molecular phylogenetics. I have from time to time expressed reservations about some of these studies, in the first two areas especially. But robust results in all three have transformed our understanding. Thus, thanks to work by Mollon and others, the variability of colour perception in different individuals is now far better understood. The studies of Levinson's group have thrown important light on the different dominant spatial frames of reference used in different societies. The evolution of animals and their current groupings have been shown to be far more complex than most of our predecessors could have been aware of, and that is relevant to the claims that have been made that the underlying assumptions that drive folk biological taxonomy correspond pretty well with what biology confirms to be the case. Brain scans can reveal which areas of the brain are active during a subject's emotional experiences, and the role of many neurotransmitters is now well understood. All of this helps to illuminate different aspects of our cognitive and affective experiences and throws light both on how individuals and groups differ, and on what we all have in common.

Thus one simple-minded assumption that the evidence serves to refute is the idea that what is common in human cognitive faculties falls to the side of biology or neurophysiology, while diversity is a matter of culture. That straightforward correlation obviously fails first because the commonalities include not just biological data but also the fact that we all become socially acculturated and have the capacity to learn a language. We all acquire one or more spatial frames of reference, though not necessarily the same ones. We all adopt or modify the values of the collectivity to which we belong, though those values are far from uniform across collectivities as also are individuals' responses to them. Second and conversely, we have identified biological and neurological diversities, as well as cultural ones, that affect the cognitive performance of different individuals and groups. If as a physical organ the human brain exhibits certain anatomical and physiological characteristics, as a learning device it shows considerable plasticity. We have had many occasions to remark, in our discussion of ancient societies especially, both on the room for manoeuvre that we can enjoy, and on its limits, the tension between an individual's or a group's capacity for intellectual flexibility, and the social constraints within which it must be exercised.

Many problems indeed remain. What is responsible for the variability in human navigational skills? Can some of that be put down to the differential development of the hippocampus, for instance? The correlation between brain scans and the subjects' experience of emotions is imperfect, to say the least. If the understanding of physical disease has been transformed since the start of the twentieth century, the same cannot be said of mental illness, and there is much that is opaque in the relation between disease and illness.

But it is especially in the analysis of cultural input that doubts and obscurities persist. Partly stimulated, it may be, by an adherence to the general thesis of psychic unity, and partly inspired, no doubt, by the apparent success of Chomsky's theories on language acquisition, claims for the discovery of cross-cultural universals, on colour perception, in animal taxonomy, in the development of notions of agency and causation, and elsewhere, have been advanced. Yet many such findings have proved to be unfounded or premature. Avoiding circular arguments and Western bias in these investigations has turned out to be far harder than many researchers imagined. The application of the Western dichotomy of nature and culture to other peoples' cosmologies is subject to the criticisms I rehearsed in Chapter 7. Luria's study of divergences in reasoning ability underestimated the role of pragmatics. The lack of formal logic, among peoples unaffected by its development, implies no inadequacy in their powers of reasoning, just as its invention, by Aristotle, secured no automatic improvements in practice: it enabled diagnoses of validity and invalidity to be made, for sure, but only once argument schemata had been parsed in, precisely, abstract, formal terms. Conversely, Nisbett's claims concerning the differences in the ways Asians and Westerners think appear to reveal differences in values and attitudes more than they do in modes of reasoning as such themselves.

In every one of the subject areas I have explored, getting clear about the issues involves taking into account three different types of factors and determining their varying weights. First, there are cultural differences, especially linguistic ones and those that relate to values. Second, there are important physical, biological, and neurophysiological factors at work, where we can identify important commonalities and relevant variations between individuals and groups. Third, we have to use our best efforts to evaluate what is now known about what the belief systems are beliefs about, including especially recognizing what I have called the multidimensionality of the data. That is often reflected in differing, but autonomous, styles of enquiry though these differences carry, of themselves, no implications for differences in underlying cognitive capabilities. But if, undoubtedly, culture, language, and ideology frequently influence the outcome, in many cases indeed seeming to constitute the most important factors in what is believed, we have every reason to resist the strong thesis that they combine to determine thought. The study of past civilizations repeatedly shows both points, both how culture and language influence thought, and that they cannot be said to constrain it completely, since we often find divergent views expressed in the same language by different members of the same society—as remains the case, of course, with the English language today.

In general, to be sure, most members of most societies will tend to stay with the customs and beliefs of that society, the ones they learnt as children. In coping both with the practicalities of survival and with the problems of understanding that experience is bound to throw up, it is obviously more economical to make the most of the resources of tradition first, before setting about revising it. When the technology appears to fail or the customary accounts involve some massive suspension of disbelief, there is generally no shortage of excuses or ad hoc explanations available to shore up what traditional 'wisdom' dictates. But cognitive deficits may build up, and whether or not in response to them, critical or independent-minded individuals may branch out and suggest new solutions to the problems—though they will still be faced with the considerable task of gaining a hearing for their new ideas or practices. That will require persistence, persuasiveness, and a fair measure of luck. The history of thought is littered with examples of ideas that might have been found promising but were dismissed out of hand, and who knows what others there may have been that have left no trace in the record.

It is always particularly difficult, in any group, to break free from its deep-seated, implicit, often unconscious, ideological assumptions. I have devoted other studies to just that question, in relation to how scientific inquiries get off the ground especially.[2] But my historical investigations here too exemplify how basic values can come to be challenged and revised, even if it has always taken courage as well as clear-headedness to expose the fallacies of racist suppositions. Neither the ancient Greeks nor the ancient Chinese were at all tolerant towards those they considered barbarians. But Plato gives the division of all humans into 'Greeks' and 'barbarians' as an example of a wrong-headed classification (as wrong-headed as it would be to classify numbers into the number 10,000 and the rest, *Politicus* 262c) and we saw that the *Lüshi chunqiu*, 19/6/2, acknowledged that the Man and Yi barbarians and the Chinese themselves share a common humanity, linked by their desires.

We are all aware of the amazing diversity of human talents. Some people are superb musicians, others not, some good navigators, others not, and so on through the entire gamut of our intellectual and artistic skills. Without such diversity, there would be far less of the creativity that we naturally prize and celebrate. At the same time our basic membership of the same human species, a matter of our genetic make-up, is undeniable, and we also all importantly share the experience of acculturation in general and of language acquisition in particular, however much the cultures, and languages, in question differ. The relativist must make room for those latter common factors, just as the universalist cannot afford to ignore diversity.

Work on the detail of the problems I have tackled continues at an ever-increasing pace and intensity. We can expect to gain further insights, whether from scientists, anthropologists, psychologists, philosophers, or even from historians, about the variability of human colour perception, spatial recognition, the evolution and classes of living things, the emotions, conceptions of well-being and of agency and causation, the diversity of cultures, and the pragmatics of reasoning. In the past, discussion of particular issues, and especially of the strategic question of unity versus diversity, has often been marred by extremist

---

[2] I may refer to Lloyd (2002; 2004).

views. But all the simplifications of previous analyses, including the more innocent ones, will eventually, let us hope, come to be seen as just that, as simplifications of issues that have an important bearing on our understanding of what it is to be a human being and on how our great diversity is perfectly compatible with our shared humanity.

Progress has to be piecemeal and will depend on well-focused specialist work in particular areas, whether biological, anthropological, philosophical, or historical. At the same time we should not lose sight of the strategic connections between the investigations carried out in different disciplines. I am aware of how many questions remain to be resolved. But much recent work lays down important markers for future research. The overview of aspects of current thinking that I have here undertaken has sought not just to bring to light the pitfalls of global generalizations, but also more positively to encourage that piecemeal, but at the same time cross-disciplinary, approach and to draw attention to the solid results that it has yielded.

NOTES ON EDITIONS

Chinese texts are generally cited according to the standard editions, for example from the Harvard-Yenching Institute series, the University of Hong Kong Institute of Chinese Studies series, and the *Zhonghua shuju* dynastic histories. However, for *Huainanzi* I use the edition by Liu Wendian (Shanghai, 1923). For the *Huangdi neijing lingshu* and *suwen* versions I use the edition of Ren Yingqiu (Beijing, 1986). For *Lüshi chunqiu* I use the edition of Chen Qiyou (Shanghai, 1984), but I adopt the chapter subdivisions in Knoblock and Riegel (Stanford, 2000) and for *Xunzi* I adopt the chapter subdivisions in Knoblock (Stanford, 1988–94).

Greek and Latin authors are similarly cited according to the standard editions, for instance the Presocratic philosophers according to the edition of H. Diels, revised by W. Kranz, *Die Fragmente der Vorsokratiker*, 6th edn. (Berlin, 1952) and the Hellenistic philosophers according to the collection of that name by A. A. Long and D. N. Sedley (Cambridge, 1987).

All modern works are cited by author's name and year of publication. Full details are to be found in the Bibliography that follows.

BIBLIOGRAPHY

AHN, W.-K., KALISH, C., GELMAN, S. A., MEDIN, D. L., LUHMANN, C., ATRAN, S., COLEY, J. D., and SHAFTO, P. (2001), 'Why essences are essential in the psychology of concepts', *Cognition* 82: 59–69.

ÅRHEM, K. (1993), 'Ecosofía Makuna', in F. Correa (ed.), *La selva humanizada: ecología alternativa en el trópico húmedo colombiano* (Bogota), 105–22.

—— (1996), 'The cosmic food web: Human-nature relatedness in the Northwest Amazon', in Descola and Pálsson (1996), 185–204.

ASTUTI, R. (2001), 'Are we all natural dualists? A cognitive developmental approach', *Journal of the Royal Anthropological Institute*, 7: 429–47.

ATRAN, S. (1990), *Cognitive Foundations of Natural History: Towards an Anthropology of Science* (Cambridge).

—— (1994), 'Core domains versus scientific theories: Evidence from systematics and Itza-Maya folkbiology', in Hirschfeld and Gelman (1994), 316–40.

—— (1995), 'Causal Constraints on Categories and Categorical Constraints on Biological Reasoning across Cultures', in Sperber, Premack, and Premack (1995), 205–33.

—— (1998), 'Folk biology and the anthropology of science: Cognitive universals and cultural particulars', *Behavioral and Brain Sciences*, 21: 547–609.

—— (1999), 'Itzaj Maya Folkbiological Taxonomy: Cognitive Universals and Cultural Particulars', in Medin and Atran (1999), 119–203.

—— (2001a), 'The Case for Modularity: Sin or Salvation', *Evolution and Cognition* 7: 46–55.

—— (2001b), 'A Cheater-Detection Module? Dubious Interpretations of the Wason Selection Task and Logic', *Evolution and Cognition* 7: 187–93.

—— MEDIN, D., and ROSS, N. (2004), 'Evolution and devolution of knowledge: A tale of two biologies', *Journal of the Royal Anthropological Institute* 10: 395–420.

—— —— LYNCH, E., VAPNARSKY, V., UCAN EK', E., and SOUSA, P. (2001), 'Folkbiology doesn't come from Folkpsychology: Evidence from Yukatek Maya in Cross-Cultural Perspective', *Journal of Cognition and Culture* 1: 3–42.

BAILLARGEON, R., KOTOVSKY, L., and NEEDHAM, A. (1995), 'The acquisition of physical knowledge in infancy', in Sperber, Premack, and Premack (1995), 79–116.

BAKER, R. R. (1989), *Human Navigation and Magnetoreception* (Manchester).

BARKOW, J. H., COSMIDES, L., and TOOBY, J. (eds.) (1992) The Adapted Mind: Evolutionary Psychology and the Generation of Culture (Oxford).

BARON-COHEN, S. (2003), The Essential Difference: Men, Women and the Extreme Male Brain (London).

BATESON, PATRICK (1990), 'Animal communication', in D. H. Mellor (ed.), Ways of Communicating (Cambridge), 35–55.

BAYLOR, D. (1995), 'Colour Mechanisms of the Eye', in Lamb and Bourriau (1995), 103–26.

BEATTY, A. (2005), 'Emotions in the field: What are we talking about?', Journal of the Royal Anthropological Institute NS 11: 17–37.

BEIDELMAN, T. O. (1973), 'Kaguru symbolic classification', in Needham (1973), 128–66.

BERLIN, B., and KAY, P. (1969), Basic Color Terms: Their Universality and Evolution (Berkeley).

——— BREEDLOVE, D. E., and RAVEN, P. H. (1973), 'General principles of classification and nomenclature in folk biology', American Anthropologist, 75: 214–42.

BLOCH, M., SOLOMON, G. E. A., and CAREY, S. (2001), 'Zafimaniry: An understanding of what is passed on from parents to children: A cross-cultural investigation', Journal of Cognition and Culture 1: 43–68.

BOAS, F. (1911/1938), The Mind of Primitive Man, rev. edn. (originally 1911) (New York).

BOESCH, C. (1996), 'The emergence of cultures among wild chimpanzees', in Runciman, Maynard Smith, and Dunbar (1996), 251–68.

BOND, A. B. (1989), 'Toward a resolution of the paradox of aggressive displays', Ethology 81: 29–46 and 235–49.

BOWERMAN, M., and LEVINSON, S. C. (eds.) (2001), Language Acquisition and Conceptual Development (Cambridge).

BOYD, R., and RICHERSON, P. J. (1996), 'Why culture is common, but cultural evolution is rare', in Runciman, Maynard Smith, and Dunbar (1996), 77–93.

——— ——— (2005), The Origin and Evolution of Cultures (Oxford).

BOYER, P. (ed.) (1993), Cognitive Aspects of Religious Symbolism (Cambridge).

——— (1994), The Naturalness of Religious Ideas: A Cognitive Theory of Religion (Berkeley).

BRASHIER, K. E. (1996), 'Han thanatology and the division of "souls"', Early China 21: 125–58.

BROCA, P. (1861), 'Nouvelle observation d'aphémie produite par une lésion de la troisième circonvolution frontale', Bulletins de la Société Anatomique de Paris, 2nd ser., 6: 398–407.

BROWN, P., and LEVINSON, S. C. (2000), 'Frames of spatial reference and their acquisition in Tenejapan Tzeltal', in L. P. Nucci, G. B. Saxe, and E. Turiel (eds.), *Culture, Thought, and Development* (Mahwah, NJ), 167–97.

BURNYEAT, M. F. (1994), 'Enthymeme: Aristotle on the logic of persuasion', in D. J. Furley and A. Nehamas (eds.), *Aristotle's Rhetoric: Philosophical Essays* (Princeton), 3–55.

CAMPOS, J. J., and BARRETT, K. C. (1984), 'Toward a new understanding of emotions and their development', in Izard, Kagan, and Zajonc (1984*b*), 229–63.

CAREY, S. (1985), *Conceptual Change in Childhood* (Cambridge, Mass.)

—— (1995), 'On the Origin of Causal Understanding', in Sperber, Premack, and Premack (1995), 268–302.

—— and SPELKE, E. S. (1994), 'Domain-specific knowledge and conceptual change', in Hirschfeld and Gelman (1994), 169–200.

CARRUTHERS, P., and CHAMBERLAIN, A. (2000), *Evolution and the Human Mind* (Cambridge).

CHANGEUX, J.-P. (1985), *Neuronal Man* (trans. L. Garey of *L'Homme neuronal* (Paris 1983)) (New York).

—— and RICŒUR, P. (2000), *What Makes Us Think* (trans. M. B. DeBevoise of *Ce qui nous fait penser: la nature et la règle* (Paris 1998)) (Princeton).

CHEVALIER-SKOLNIKOFF, S. (1982), 'A cognitive analysis of facial behaviour in Old World monkeys, apes and human beings', in C. T. Snowdon, C. H. Brown, M. R. Petersen (eds.) *Primate Communication* (Cambridge), 303–68.

CHOMSKY, N. (1965), *Aspects of the Theory of Syntax* (Cambridge, Mass.).

—— (1968), *Language and Mind* (New York).

CLARK, H. H. (1973), 'Space, time, semantics, and the child', in Moore (1973), 27–63.

COLLETT, T. S., and ZEIL, J. (1998), 'Places and landmarks: An arthropod perspective', in Healy (1998), 18–53.

CONKLIN, H. C. (1955), 'Hanunoo color terms', *Southwestern Journal of Anthropology*, 11: 339–44.

COOPER, R. (2002), 'Disease', *Studies in History and Philosophy of Biological and Biomedical Sciences*, 33: 263–82.

COSMIDES, L., and TOOBY, J. (1994), 'Origins of domain specificity. The evolution of functional organization', in Hirschfeld and Gelman (1994), 85–116.

CROMBIE, A. C. (1994), *Styles of Scientific Thinking in the European Tradition*, 3 vols. (London).

CULLEN, C. (1996), *Astronomy and Mathematics in Ancient China: The Zhou bi suan jing* (Cambridge).

DAHL, H. (1979), 'The appetite hypothesis of emotions: A new psychoanalytic model of motivation', in C. E. Izard (ed.), *Emotions in Personality and Psychopathology* (New York), 201–25.

DAMASIO, A. R. (1994), *Descartes' Error: Emotion, Reason and the Human Brain* (New York).

—— (2000), *The Feeling of What Happens* (London).

DARWIN, C. (1872), *The Expression of Emotions in Man and Animals* (London).

DAVIDSON, D. (2001), *Essays on Actions and Events*, 2nd edn. (Oxford).

DAWKINS, R. (2004), *The Ancestor's Tale: A Pilgrimage to the Dawn of Life* (London).

DELPLA, I. (2001), *Quine, Davidson. Le principe de charité* (Paris).

DENNETT, D. (1995), *Darwin's Dangerous Idea* (London).

DERRYBERRY, D., and ROTHBART, M. K. (1984), 'Emotion, attention, and temperament', in Izard, Kagan, and Zajonc (1984*b*), 132–66.

DESCOLA, P. (1996), *The Spears of Twilight* (trans. J. Lloyd of *Les Lances du crépuscule* (Paris, 1993)) (London).

—— (2005), *Par-delà nature et culture* (Paris).

—— and PÁLSSON, G. (eds.) (1996), *Nature and Society: Anthropological Perspectives* (London).

DIENER, E., and SUH, E. M. (2000*a*), 'Measuring subjective well-being to compare the quality of life of cultures', in Diener and Suh (2000*b*), 3–12.

—— —— (eds.) (2000*b*), *Culture and Subjective Well-being* (Cambridge, Mass.).

DIENSTBIER, R. A. (1984), 'The role of emotion in moral socialization', in Izard, Kagan, and Zajonc (1984*b*), 484–514.

DIHLE, A. (1977), *Euripides' Medea* (Sitzungsberichte der Heidelberger Akademie der Wissenschaften, philosophisch-historische Klasse, Jahrgang 1977: 5, Heidelberg).

DODDS, E. R. (1951), *The Greeks and the Irrational* (Berkeley).

DORAIS, J.-L. (1996), *La Parole Inuit: Langue, culture et société dans l'arctique nord-américain* (Paris).

DUPRÉ, J. (1993), *The Disorder of Things* (Cambridge, Mass.).

—— (2001), 'In Defence of Classification', *Studies in History and Philosophy of Biological and Biomedical Sciences*, 32: 203–19.

EKMAN, P. (1980), *The Face of Man: Expressions of Universal Emotions in a New Guinea Village* (San Francisco).

—— (ed.) (1982), *Emotion in the Human Face*, 2nd edn. (Cambridge).

—— and DAVIDSON, R. J. (eds.) (1994), *The Nature of Emotion: Fundamental Questions* (Oxford).

ELLEN, R. F. (1993), *The Cultural Relations of Classification* (Cambridge).

—— (1996), 'The cognitive geometry of nature: A contextual approach', in Descola and Pálsson (1996), 103–23.

ELSTER, J. (1983), *Sour Grapes* (Cambridge).

EVANS, E. P. (1906), *Criminal Prosecutions and Capital Punishment of Animals* (London).

EVANS, J. St.-B. T. (1982), *The Psychology of Deductive Reasoning* (London).

―― (1989). *Bias in Human Reasoning* (Hove).

FERNANDEZ, J. W. (1982), *Bwiti: An Ethnography of the Religious Imagination in Africa* (Princeton).

FERRARI, G. R. F. (1987), *Listening to the Cicadas* (Cambridge).

FESTINGER, L. (1964), *Conflict, Decision and Dissonance* (London).

FEYERABEND, P. K. (1975), *Against Method* (London).

FIDDICK, L., COSMIDES, L., and TOOBY, J. (2000), 'No interpretation without representation: The role of domain-specific representations and inferences in the Wason selection task', *Cognition* 77: 1–79.

FISCHHOFF, B. (1975), 'Hindsight ≠ Foresight. The Effect of Outcome Knowledge on Judgment under Uncertainty', *Journal of Experimental Psychology: Human Perception and Performance* 1: 288–99.

FLEMMING, R. (2000), *Medicine and the Making of Roman Women* (Oxford).

FODOR, J. (1983), *The Modularity of Mind* (Cambridge, Mass.).

FOUCAULT, M. (1967), *Madness and Civilization* (trans. R. Howard of *Histoire de la folie* (Paris, 1961)), (London).

―― (1972), *The Archaeology of Knowledge* (trans. A. M. Sheridan Smith of *L'Archéologie du savoir* (Paris, 1969)) (London).

FRAZER, J. G. (1890), *The Golden Bough* (London).

FRIDLUND, A. J. (1997), 'The new ethology of human facial expressions', in J. A. Russell and J. M. Fernández-Dols (eds.), *The Psychology of Facial Expression* (Cambridge), 103–29.

FRISCHER, B. (1982), *The Sculpted Word* (Berkeley).

GALLISTEL, C. R. (1990), *The Organization of Learning* (Cambridge, Mass.).

GELLNER, E. (1974), *Legitimation of Belief* (Cambridge).

GELMAN, S. A. (2003), *The Essential Child: Origins of Essentialism in Everyday Thought* (Oxford).

―― and COLEY, J. D. (1990), 'The importance of knowing a dodo is a bird: Categories and inferences in two-year-old children', *Developmental Psychology* 26: 796–804.

―― ―― and GOTTFRIED, G. M. (1994), 'Essentialist beliefs in children: The acquisition of concepts and theories', in Hirschfeld and Gelman (1994), 341–65.

GHISELIN, M. T. (1997), *Metaphysics and the Origin of Species* (Albany, NY).

GIL-WHITE, F. J. (2001), 'Are ethnic groups biological "species" to the human brain?', *Current Anthropology* 42: 515–36.

GOODMAN, N. (1978), *Ways of Worldmaking* (Hassocks).

GOODY, J. (1977), *The Domestication of the Savage Mind* (Cambridge).

GRAHAM, A. C. (1989), *Disputers of the Tao* (La Salle, Ill.).

GREGORY, R. L. (1970), *The Intelligent Eye* (London).

GREIMAS, J., and RASTIER, E. (1968), 'The interaction of semiotic constraints', *Game, Play, Literature,* Yale French Studies 41 (New Haven).

GRIFFITHS, P. E. (1997), *What Emotions Really Are* (Chicago).

GRMEK, M. (1989) *Diseases in the Ancient Greek World* (trans. M. and L. Muellner of *Les Maladies à l'aube de la civilisation occidentale* (Paris 1983)) (Baltimore).

HACKING, I. (1991), 'The making and molding of child abuse', *Critical Inquiry* 17: 235–58.

—— (1992a), 'Multiple personality disorder and its hosts', *History of the Human Sciences,* 5/2: 3–31.

—— (1992b), ' "Style" for historians and philosophers', *Studies in History and Philosophy of Science,* 23: 1–20.

—— (1995), 'The Looping Effects of Human Kinds', in Sperber, Premack, and Premack (1995), 351–83.

—— (2005), 'Why race still matters', *Daedalus,* Winter 2005: 102–16.

HALLIDAY, T. R., and SLATER, P. J. B. (eds.) (1983), *Animal Behaviour,* ii. *Communication* (Oxford).

HARBSMEIER, C. (1998), *Science and Civilisation in China,* vii/1. *Language and Logic* (Cambridge).

HARDIN, C. L., and MAFFI, L. (eds.) (1997), *Color Categories in Thought and Language* (Cambridge).

HARLOW, J. M. (1993), 'Recovery from the passage of an iron bar through the head' (originally read before the Massachusetts Medical Society 3 June 1868) (introduced by Edgar Miller), *History of Psychiatry* 4: 271–81.

HARPER, D. (1998), *Early Chinese Medical Literature: The Mawangdui Medical Manuscripts* (London).

—— (1999), 'Physicians and diviners: The relation of divination to the medicine of the *Huangdi neijing* (Inner canon of the Yellow Thearch)', *Extrême-Orient Extrême-Occident,* 21: 91–110.

HARRÉ, R. (ed.) (1986), *The Social Construction of Emotion* (Oxford).

HATANO, G., and INAGAKI, K. (1994), 'Young children's naive theory of biology', *Cognition* 50: 171–88.

—— —— (1999), 'A developmental perspective on informal biology', in Medin and Atran (1999), 321–54.

—— SIEGLER, R. S., RICHARDS, D. D., INAGAKI, K., STAVY, R., and WAX, N. (1993), 'The development of biological knowledge: A multi-national study', *Cognitive Development* 8: 47–62.

HEALY, S. (ed.) (1998), *Spatial Representation in Animals* (Oxford).

HEELAS, P., and LOCK, A. (eds.) (1981), *Indigenous Psychologies: The Anthropology of the Self* (London).

HEINE, B. (1997), *Cognitive Foundations of Grammar* (Oxford).

Hess, W. R. (1964), *The Biology of Mind* (trans. G. von Bonin of *Psychologie in biologischer Sicht* (Stuttgart 1962)) (Chicago).

Hinde, R. A. (1970), *Animal Behaviour*, 2nd edn. (New York).

—— (ed.) (1972), *Non-Verbal Communication* (Cambridge).

—— (1981), 'Animal signals: Ethological and games-theory approaches are not incompatible', *Animal Behaviour* 29: 535–42.

Hirschfeld, L. A., and Gelman, S. A. (eds.) (1994), *Mapping the Mind: Domain Specificity in Cognition and Culture* (Cambridge).

Hobbs, A. (2000) *Plato and the Hero: Courage, Manliness and the Impersonal Good* (Cambridge).

Howell, S. (1981), 'Rules not Words', in Heelas and Lock (1981), 133–43.

Hsu, E. (2002), *The Telling Touch* (Habilitationschrift, Sinology, University of Heidelberg).

Hu, Shiu-Ying (2005), *Food Plants of China* (Hong Kong).

Hudson, L. (1966), *Contrary Imaginations* (London).

Hughes, H. C. (1999), *Sensory Exotica: A World Beyond Human Experience* (Cambridge, Mass.).

Hull, D. L. (1997), 'The ideal species concept—and why we can't get it', in M. F. Claridge, H. A. Dawah, and M. R. Wilson (eds.) *Species: The Units of Biodiversity* (London), 357–80.

Hulme, T., and Matsuzawa, T. (2002), 'Ant-dipping among the chimpanzees of Bossou, Guinea, and some comparisons with other sites', *American Journal of Primatology* 58: 133–48.

Ingold, T. (1990), 'An anthropologist looks at biology', *Man* ns 25: 208–29.

—— (2000), *The Perception of the Environment* (London).

—— (2001), 'Commentary on Gil-White', *Current Anthropology* 42: 541–2.

Izard, C. E. (1977), *Human Emotions* (New York).

—— Kagan, J., and Zajonc, R. B. (1984*a*), 'Introduction', in Izard, Kagan, and Zajonc (1984*b*), 1–14.

—— —— —— (eds.) (1984*b*), *Emotions, Cognition and Behavior* (Cambridge).

Jardine, N., and Sibson, R. (1971), *Mathematical Taxonomy* (London).

Johnson-Laird, P. N., and Byrne, R. M. J. (1991), *Deduction* (Hove).

—— Legrenzi, P., and Legrenzi, M. S. (1972), 'Reasoning and a sense of reality', *The British Journal of Psychology* 63: 395–400.

Jordan, G., and Mollon, J. D. (1993), 'A study of women heterozygous for colour deficiencies', *Vision Research* 33/11: 1495–508.

Kagan, J. (1984), 'The idea of emotion in human development', in Izard, Kagan, and Zajonc (1984*b*), 38–72.

Karmiloff-Smith, A. (1992), *Beyond Modularity* (Cambridge, Mass.).

Kay, P., and Kempton, W. (1984), 'What is the Sapir-Whorf Hypothesis?', *American Anthropologist* 86: 65–79.

KAY, P., and MCDANIEL, C. K. (1978), 'The linguistic significance of the meanings of basic color terms', *Language* 54: 610–46.

KEIL, F. C. (1989), *Concepts, Kinds and Cognitive Development* (Cambridge, Mass.).

—— (1994), 'The birth and nurturance of concepts by domains: The origins of concepts of living things', in Hirschfeld and Gelman (1994), 234–54.

—— (1995), 'The growth of causal understandings of natural kinds', in Sperber, Premack, and Premack (1995), 234–62.

KITAYAMA, S., and MARKUS, H. R. (2000), 'The pursuit of happiness and the realization of sympathy: Cultural patterns of self, social relations, and well-being', in Diener and Suh (2000b), 113–61.

KLEINMAN, A., and GOOD, B. (eds.) (1985), *Culture and Depression: Studies in the Anthropology and Cross-Cultural Psychiatry of Affect and Disorder* (Berkeley).

KNOBLOCK, J. (1988–94), *Xunzi: A Translation and Study of the Complete Works*, 3 vols. (Stanford).

—— and RIEGEL, J. (2000), *The Annals of Lü Buwei* (Stanford).

KOLB, B., and WHISHAW, J. (2003), *Fundamentals of Human Neuropsychology*, 5th edn. (New York).

KONSTAN, D. (2006), *The Emotions of the Ancient Greeks* (Toronto).

KRIPKE, S. A. (1980), *Naming and Necessity*, rev. edn. (Oxford).

LAMB, T., and BOURRIAU, J. (eds.) (1995), *Colour: Art and Science* (Cambridge).

LANG, P. J. (1984), 'Cognition in emotion: Concept and action', in Izard, Kagan, and Zajonc (1984b), 192–226.

LEDOUX, J. E. (1996), *The Emotional Brain* (New York).

LESLIE, A. (1995), 'A Theory of Agency', in Sperber, Premack, and Premack (1995), 121–41.

LEVINSON, S. C. (2003), *Space in Language and Cognition* (Cambridge).

—— KITA, S., HAUN, D. B. M., and RASCH, B. H. (2002), 'Returning the tables: Language affects spatial reasoning', *Cognition* 84: 155–88.

LÉVI-STRAUSS, C. (1955/1973), *The World on the Wane* (trans J. and D. Weightman of *Tristes Tropiques* (Paris, 1955)) (London).

—— (1958/1968), *Structural Anthropology* (trans. C. Jacobson and B. G. Schoepf of *Anthropologie structurale* (Paris, 1958)) (London).

—— (1962/1969), *Totemism* (trans. R. Needham of *Le Totémisme aujourd'hui* (Paris, 1962)) (Harmondsworth).

—— (1964/1969), *The Raw and the Cooked* (trans. J. and D. Weightman of *Le cru et le cuit* (Paris, 1964)) (London).

LÉVY-BRUHL, L. (1923), *Primitive Mentality* (trans. L. A. Clare of *La Mentalité primitive* (Paris, 1922)) (London).

LEWIS, D. (1994), *We, the Navigators*, 2nd edn. (Honolulu).

LEWIS, G. (1975), *Knowledge of Illness in a Sepik Society* (London).

Li, P., and Gleitman, L. (2002), 'Turning the Tables: Language and Spatial Reasoning', *Cognition* 83: 265–94.

Lindsey, D. T., and Brown, A. M. (2002), 'Color naming and the phototoxic effects of sunlight on the eye', *Psychological Science* 13: 506–12.

Lloyd, G. E. R. (1966), *Polarity and Analogy* (Cambridge).

―――― (1983), *Science, Folklore and Ideology* (Cambridge).

―――― (1987), *The Revolutions of Wisdom* (Berkeley).

―――― (1990), *Demystifying Mentalities* (Cambridge).

―――― (1991), *Methods and Problems in Greek Science* (Cambridge).

―――― (1996a), *Adversaries and Authorities* (Cambridge).

―――― (1996b), *Aristotelian Explorations* (Cambridge).

―――― (2002), *The Ambitions of Curiosity* (Cambridge).

―――― (2003), *In the Grip of Disease* (Oxford).

―――― (2004), *Ancient Worlds, Modern Reflections* (Oxford).

―――― (2005), *The Delusions of Invulnerability* (London).

―――― and Sivin, N. (2002), *The Way and the Word* (New Haven).

Long, A. A., and Sedley, D. N. (1987), *The Hellenistic Philosophers*, 2 vols. (Cambridge).

Lucy, J. A. (1992), *Language Diversity and Thought* (Cambridge).

―――― (1997), 'The linguistics of "color"', in Hardin and Maffi (1997), 320–46.

―――― and Gaskins, S. (2001), 'Grammatical categories and the development of classification preferences: A comparative approach', in Bowerman and Levinson (2001), 257–83.

Luria, A. R. (1976). *Cognitive Development: Its Cultural and Social Foundations* (Cambridge, Mass.).

Lutz, C. (1988), *Unnatural Emotions: Everyday Sentiments on a Micronesian Atoll and their Challenge to Western Theory* (Chicago).

Lyons, J. (1977), *Semantics*, 2 vols. (Cambridge).

―――― (1995), 'Colour in language', in Lamb and Bourriau (1995), 194–224.

―――― (1999), 'The vocabulary of color with particular reference to Ancient Greek and Classical Latin', in A. Borg (ed.), *The Language of Color in the Mediterranean*, Stockholm Oriental Studies 16 (Stockholm), 38–75.

MacDowell, D. M. (1978), *The Law in Classical Athens* (London).

Maffi, L., and Hardin, C. L. (1997), 'Closing Thoughts', in Hardin and Maffi (1997), 347–72.

Maguire, E. A., Gadian, D. G., Johnsrude, I. S., Good, C. D., Ashburner, J., Frackowiak, R. S. J., and Frith, C. D. (2000), 'Navigation-related structural change in the hippocampi of taxi drivers', *Proceedings of the National Academy of Sciences of the United States of America* 97/8: 4398–403.

Major, J. S. (1993), *Heaven and Earth in Early Han Thought* (Albany, NY).

MALLON, R., and STICH, S. P. (2000), 'The odd couple. The compatibility of social construction and evolutionary psychology', *Philosophy of Science* 67: 133–54.

MALOTKI, E. (1983), *Hopi Time: A Linguistic Analysis of the Temporal Concepts in the Hopi Language* (Berlin).

MARCOVITCH, H. (ed.) (2005), *Black's Medical Dictionary*, 41st edn. (London).

MASTERS, J. C., and CARLSON, C. R. (1984), 'Children's and adults' understanding of the causes and consequences of emotional states', in Izard, Kagan, and Zajonc (1984*b*), 438–63.

MAYR, E. (ed.) (1957), *The Species Problem*, American Association for the Advancement of Science Publications 50 (Washington, DC).

MEDIN, D. L., and ATRAN, S. (eds.) (1999), *Folkbiology* (Cambridge, Mass.).

——— and ORTONY, A. (1989), 'Psychological Essentialism', in S. Vosniadou and A. Ortony (eds.), *Similarity and Analogical Reasoning* (Cambridge), 179–95.

MIDDLETON, J. (1973), 'Some Categories of Dual Classification Among the Lugbara of Uganda', in Needham (1973), 369–90.

MILLER, G. A., and JOHNSON-LAIRD, P. N. (1976), *Language and Perception* (Cambridge).

MOLLON, J. (1995), 'Seeing Colour', in Lamb and Bourriau (1995), 127–50.

MOMMSEN, T., KRUEGER, P., and WATSON, A. (1985), *The Digest of Justinian*, 4 vols. (Philadelphia).

MOORE, B., UNDERWOOD, B., and ROSENHAN, D. L. (1984), 'Emotion, self, and others', in Izard, Kagan, and Zajonc (1984*b*), 464–83.

MOORE, T. E. (ed.) (1973), *Cognitive Development and the Acquisition of Language* (New York).

NEEDHAM, R. (ed.) (1973), *Right and Left: Essays on Dual Symbolic Classification* (Chicago).

NISBETT, R. E. (2003), *The Geography of Thought: How Asians and Westerners Think Differently . . . and Why* (New York).

OLDS, J., and MILNER, P. (1954), 'Positive reinforcement produced by electrical stimulation of septal area and other regions of rat brain', *Journal of Comparative and Physiological Psychology* 47: 419–27.

ORTNER, S. (2003), 'East Brain, West Brain', *New York Times Book Review*, April 2003, Sect. 7: 17.

ORTONY, A., CLORE, G. L., and COLLINS, A. (1988), *The Cognitive Structure of Emotions* (Cambridge).

PADEL, R. (1992), *In and Out of the Mind* (Princeton).

——— (1995), *Whom Gods Destroy* (Princeton).

PANKSEPP, J. (1982) 'Toward a general psychobiological theory of emotions', *Behavioral and Brain Sciences* 5: 407–67.

——— (1998), *Affective Neuroscience* (Oxford).

PANKSEPP, J., and PANKSEPP, J. B. (2000), 'The seven sins of evolutionary psychology', *Evolution and Cognition* 6: 108–31.

PECK, A. L. (1937), *Aristotle: Parts of Animals* (Cambridge. Mass.).

PIAGET, J., and INHELDER, B. (1948/1956), *The Child's Conception of Space* (trans. F. J. Langdon and J. L. Lunzer of *La Représentation de l'espace chez l'enfant* (Paris 1948)) (London).

PINKER, S. (1997), *How the Mind Works* (London).

PUTNAM, H. (1975), *Mind, Language and Reality: Philosophical Papers* (Cambridge), ii.

QUINE, W. van O. (1960), *Word and Object* (Cambridge, Mass.).

RAVEN, J. E. (2000), *Plants and Plant Lore in Ancient Greece* (orig. publ. *Annales Musei Goulandris* (1990) 8: 129–80) (Oxford).

ROSALDO, M. Z. (1980), *Knowledge and Passion: Ilongot Notions of Self and Social Life* (Cambridge).

—— (1984), 'Toward an Anthropology of Self and Feeling', in Shweder and LeVine (1984), 137–57.

ROSS, N. (2002), 'Cognitive aspects of intergenerational change: Mental models, cultural change, and environmental behavior among the Lacandon Maya of Southern Mexico', *Human Organization* 61: 125–38.

—— MEDIN, D. L., COLEY, J. D., and ATRAN, S. (2003), 'Cultural and experiential differences in the development of folkbiological induction', *Cognitive Development* 18: 25–47.

RUNCIMAN, W. G., MAYNARD SMITH, J., and DUNBAR, R. I. M. (eds.) (1996), 'Evolution of social behaviour patterns in primates and man', *Proceedings of the British Academy* 88.

RYLE, G. (1949), *The Concept of Mind* (London).

—— (1954), *Dilemmas* (Cambridge).

SAHLINS, M. (1976), 'Colors and cultures', *Semiotica* 16/1: 1–22.

SAPIR, E. (1949), *Selected Writings of Edward Sapir in Language, Culture, and Personality* (Berkeley).

SCHÖNE, H. (1984), *Spatial Orientation* (trans. C. Strausfeld of *Orientierung im Raum* (Stuttgart 1980)) (Princeton).

SCHULZ, F. (1951), *Classical Roman Law* (Oxford).

SCHWARTZ, R. M., and TRABASSO, T. (1984), 'Children's understanding of emotions', in Izard, Kagan, and Zajonc (1984*b*), 409–37.

SHWEDER, R. A. (1984), 'Anthropology's romantic rebellion against the enlightenment, or there's more to thinking than reason and evidence', in Shweder and LeVine (1984), 27–66.

—— (1985), 'Menstrual pollution, soul loss, and the comparative study of emotions', in Kleinman and Good (1985), 182–215.

—— and LeVINE, R. A. (eds.) (1984), *Culture Theory: Essays on Mind, Self, and Emotion* (Cambridge).

SIEGEL, J. (2005), *The Idea of the Self: Thought and Experience in Western Europe since the Seventeenth Century* (Cambridge).

SIMPSON, A. G. B., and ROGER, A. J. (2004), 'The real "kingdoms" of eukaryotes', *Current Biology* 14: 693–6.

SIVIN, N. (1987), *Traditional Medicine in Contemporary China* (Ann Arbor).

SKINNER, B. F. (1950), 'Are theories of learning necessary?', *Psychological Review* 57: 193–216.

SNELL, B. (1948/1953), *The Discovery of the Mind* (trans. T. G. Rosenmeyer of *Die Entdeckung des Geistes*, 2nd edn. (Hamburg, 1948)) (Oxford).

SORABJI, R. (2000), *Emotion and Peace of Mind* (Oxford).

SPERBER, D. (1975), *Rethinking Symbolism*, trans. A. Morton (Cambridge).

—— (1994), 'The modularity of thought and the epidemiology of representations', in Hirschfeld and Gelman (1994), 39–67.

—— (1996), *Explaining Culture* (Oxford).

—— CARA, F., and GIROTTO, V. (1995), 'Relevance theory explains the selection task', *Cognition* 57: 31–95.

—— PREMACK, D., and PREMACK, A. J. (eds.) (1995), *Causal Cognition: A Multidisciplinary Debate* (Oxford).

SPIRO, M. E. (1984), 'Some reflections on cultural determinism and relativism with special reference to emotion and reason', in Shweder and LeVine (1984), 323–46.

STERELNY, K. (2003), *Thought in a Hostile World* (Oxford).

STRATHERN, M. (1980), 'No nature, no culture: the Hagen case', in C. MacCormack and M. Strathern (eds.), *Nature, Culture and Gender* (Cambridge), 174–222.

STREVENS, M. (2001), 'Only causation matters: Reply to Ahn *et al*', *Cognition* 82: 71–6.

SVOROU, S. (1994), *The Grammar of Space* (Amsterdam).

TAMBIAH, S. J. (1990), *Magic, Science, Religion and the Scope of Rationality* (Cambridge).

TOMASELLO, M. (1999),*The Cultural Origins of Human Cognition* (Cambridge, Mass.).

TOOBY, J., and COSMIDES, L. (1989), 'Evolutionary Psychology and the Generation of Culture: Part I, Theoretical Considerations', *Ethology and Sociobiology* 10: 29–49.

—— (1990), 'The past explains the present: Emotional adaptations and the structure of ancestral environments', *Ethology and Sociobiology* 11: 375–424.

—— (1996), 'Friendship and the banker's paradox: Other pathways to the evolution of adaptations for altruism', in Runciman, Maynard Smith, and Dunbar (1996), 119–43.

TRAVERSO, E. (2003), *The Origins of Nazi Violence* (trans. J. Lloyd of *La Violence nazie* (Paris, 2002)) (New York).

TVERSKY, A., and KAHNEMAN, D. (1974), 'Judgement under uncertainty: Heuristics and biases', *Science* NS 185: 1124–31.

TYLOR, E. B. (1871), *Primitive Culture*, 2 vols. (London).

VERNANT, J.-P. (1983), *Myth and Thought among the Greeks* (trans. J. Lloyd of *Mythe et pensée chez les grecs* (2nd edn., Paris 1965)) (London).

—— (1989), *L'Individu, la mort, l'amour* (Paris).

VIVEIROS DE CASTRO, E. (1998), 'Cosmological Deixis and Amerindian Perspectivism', *Journal of the Royal Anthropological Institute*, NS 4: 469–88.

VYGOTSKY, L. S. (1962), *Thought and Language* (Cambridge: Mass.).

WAKEFIELD, J. C. (1992), 'Disorder as harmful dysfunction: A conceptual critique of *DSM-III-R*'s definition of mental disorder', *Psychological Review* 99: 232–47.

WALKER, G. (in preparation), 'The evidence for eukaryote relationships'.

—— and PATTERSON, D. J. (in preparation), *The Eukaryotes*.

WALTERS, S. M. (1961), 'The shaping of angiosperm taxonomy', *The New Phytologist* 60: 74–84.

—— (1986), 'The Name of the Rose: A review of ideas on the European bias in angiosperm classification', *The New Phytologist* 104: 527–46.

WARDY, R. B. B. (2000), *Aristotle in China: Language, Categories and Translation* (Cambridge).

WASON, P. C. (1966), 'Reasoning', in B. M. Foss (ed.), *New Horizons in Psychology* (Harmondsworth), 135–51.

—— (1968), 'Reasoning about a rule', *Quarterly Journal of Experimental Psychology* 20: 273–81.

—— and JOHNSON-LAIRD, P. N. (1972), *Psychology of Reasoning: Structure and Content* (London).

WATERMAN, T. H. (1989), *Animal Navigation* (New York).

WATSON, J. B. (1931), *Behaviorism*, rev. edn. (Chicago).

WHORF, B. L. (1967) *Language, Thought and Reality*, ed. J. Carroll (1st pub. 1956), repr. (Cambridge, Mass.).

WIERZBICKA, A. (1992), *Semantics, Culture, and Cognition* (Oxford).

—— (1999), *Emotions across Languages and Cultures* (Cambridge).

WILEY, R. H. (1983), 'The evolution of communication: information and manipulation', in Halliday and Slater (1983), 156–89.

WILLIAMS, BERNARD (1993), *Shame and Necessity* (Berkeley).

ZANKER, P. (1988) *The Power of Images in the Age of Augustus* (trans. A. Shapiro of *Augustus und die Macht der Bilder* (Munich 1987)) (Ann Arbor).

INDEX

.